On Repeat

# On Repeat

HOW MUSIC PLAYS THE MIND

ELIZABETH HELLMUTH MARGULIS

OXFORD
UNIVERSITY PRESS

# OXFORD

UNIVERSITY PRESS

Oxford University Press is a department of the University of Oxford.
It furthers the University's objective of excellence in research, scholarship,
and education by publishing worldwide.

Oxford   New York
Auckland   Cape Town   Dar es Salaam   Hong Kong   Karachi
Kuala Lumpur   Madrid   Melbourne   Mexico City   Nairobi
New Delhi   Shanghai   Taipei   Toronto

With offices in
Argentina   Austria   Brazil   Chile   Czech Republic   France   Greece
Guatemala   Hungary   Italy   Japan   Poland   Portugal   Singapore
South Korea   Switzerland   Thailand   Turkey   Ukraine   Vietnam

Oxford is a registered trademark of Oxford University Press in
the UK and certain other countries.

Published in the United States of America by
Oxford University Press
198 Madison Avenue, New York, NY 10016

Library of Congress Cataloging in Publication Data

Margulis, Elizabeth Hellmuth.
On repeat : how music plays the mind / Elizabeth Hellmuth Margulis.
pages ; cm
Includes bibliographical references and index.
ISBN 978–0–19–999082–5 (hardback : alk. paper)   1. Repetition in music.
2. Music—Psychological aspects.   3. Musical perception.   4. Cognition.   I. Title.
ML3877.M37 2013
781'.11—dc23
2013025089

9  8  7  6
Printed in the United States of America
on acid-free paper

*For Martin, Alexander, and Nikolai*

*The ear tends to be lazy, craves the familiar*
*and is shocked by the unexpected; the eye,*
*on the other hand, tends to be impatient,*
*craves the novel and is bored by repetition.*
—W. H. Auden

# Contents

*Acknowledgments* ix

1. The Puzzle of Musical Repetition 1

2. From Acoustic to Perceived Repetition 26

3. Attention, Temporality, and Music that Repeats Itself 55

4. Earworms, Technology, and the Verbatim 75

5. Relistenings 95

6. In Performance 117

7. Overt Participation, Implied Participation 140

8. Repetition, Music, and Mind 159

*References* 181
*Index* 197

# Acknowledgments

There are so many people without whose input, example, insight, and support this book would not exist that it seems almost disingenuous to put only one name on the cover.

I would like to start by thanking the University of Arkansas, my academic home for the better part of a decade. I have benefitted from a Summer Research Stipend, and from the opportunity to teach interdisciplinary Honors Colloquia that bring me into regular contact with students and faculty from departments across campus. The Music and Psychology Departments, in particular, have been creative about finding ways to support work that crosses disciplinary boundaries. My department chair, Ronda Mains, has been unfailingly supportive as well as personally inspirational, and Charles Adams, Robin Roberts, Don Pederson, and Jeannine Durdik at the University of Arkansas, as well as past deans Donald Bobbitt and William Schwab have all contributed to establishing a thriving environment for interdisciplinary work on campus. Between 2011 and 2012, Fulbright College made it possible for me to spend a year in residence at Wolfson College and the Centre for Music and Science at the University of Cambridge, giving me a full twelve months in a vibrant environment where I was able to write the majority of this book.

Ian Cross and Sarah Hawkins were consummate hosts at the University of Cambridge, and I learned much at the Centre for Music and Science community, especially from Andrew Goldman, Sarah Knight, Zora Schärer, Jenny Judge, Barry Ross, Jiaxi Liu, Guy Hayward, and Charlie Williams. Monique Ingalls made invaluable contributions with references to ethnomusicological case studies and perspectives, and during my time in Cambridge, Juniper Hill, Amanda Vincent, Alison Pollet, and Lawrence King all provided sage advice about the book-writing process.

I also gained critical new perspectives during my time as a fellow at the NEH Summer Institute on Ethnomusicology and Global Culture at Wesleyan

University in Connecticut during the summer of 2011. Thank you to the orga-
nizers and to all the participants for indulging my monomaniacal interest in
repetition, and for engaging with foundational questions about disciplinary
perspective.

The Society for Music Theory provided a generous Subvention Grant that
offset expenses relating to the preparation of the figures and the index. I am
grateful to SMT for this support. Thank you also to Haley Beverburg Reale for
making the musical examples look great.

The Centre for Interdisciplinary Research in Music, Media, and Technology
(CIRMMT) at McGill University in Montreal, Canada, provided an important
initial impetus for this book by inviting me to present a Distinguished Lecture
on the Science and Technology of Music in February of 2009. I took that opportunity to step back from my work and look at a topic that seemed to be lurking,
neglected, underneath all of it: music's repetitiveness. That talk represented the
first step on the path that has led to this book. I would like to thank Stephen
McAdams for the invitation, and all the faculty and students who participated
in the follow-up Seminar on Repetition the next day, especially Peter Schubert,
William Caplin, René Rusch, and Christoph Neidhöfer.

Since 2009, I have given talks on subjects related to this book in the UK at
University of Cambridge, University of Sheffield, University of Southampton,
Anglia Ruskin University, and at the Music, Mind, and Brain Program at
Goldsmith's–University of London, and in the US at New York University, the
University of Texas at Austin, the Symposium on Research in Music Theory at
Indiana University, Bloomington, the University of Chicago, Michigan State
University, Northwestern University, and the Eastman/University of Rochester/
Cornell/Buffalo Music Cognition Symposium, as well as conference papers
on related subjects at the Annual Meeting of the Society for Music Theory in
Minneapolis, the International Conference on Music Perception and Cognition
in Seattle, and the Biennial Meeting of the Society for Music Perception and
Cognition in Rochester. I received valuable feedback at each of these events, and
would like to thank everyone involved in organizing these talks, as well as the
participants who offered insightful comments and questions.

Many colleagues contributed to this work in far-reaching ways; their voices
and perspectives have shaped the thinking reflected throughout this book. I'd
like to particularly thank Richard Ashley, Douglas Behrend, Steven Brown, Karen
Chan, Eric Clarke, Johanna Devaney, Joseph Dubiel, Zohar Eitan, Morwaread
Farbood, Marlon Feld, Alf Gabrielsson, Luis-Manuel Garcia, Kirill Gerstein,
Robert Gjerdingen, Werner Goebl, Jessica Grahn, Marion Guck, Robert Hatten,
Anne Harrison, Henkjan Honing, Mark Katz, Carol Krumhansl, Edward Large,
Steve Larson, Fred Lerdahl, William Levine, Steven Livingstone, Justin London,
Jack Lyons, Gary Marcus, Elizabeth Marvin, Danuta Mirka, Daniel Müllensiefen,

Eugene Narmour, Adam Ockleford, Arewa Olufunmilayo, Ève Poudrier, Peter Rentfrow, Bruno Repp, Steven Rings, John Roeder, Alexander Rozin, Glenn Schellenberg, Benjamin Steege, David Temperley, Michael Tenzer, Renee Timmers, Ian Quinn, Leigh VanHandel, Anja Volk, Patrick Wong, and Lawrence Zbikowski. A special thanks goes to David Huron, whose observations years ago about the puzzle of musical repetition lodged the initial gnawing curiosity about this topic in the back of my mind. His insight and support have been essential to the development of these ideas.

Titling this book turned out to be an odyssey of epic proportions. I'd like to thank everyone who contributed ideas, criticisms, and suggestions, especially Geoff Brock, Padma Viswanathan, Bret Schulte, Stephanie Schulte, Tyler Nix, Martin Miller, Amy Herzberg, and Bob Ford.

Thanks to the students at the University of Arkansas for discussing and influencing many of the ideas in this book in their earliest stages.

A heartfelt thank you also goes to the editorial team at Oxford University Press, who have made this process a pleasure. Those of us who work in music have been spoiled by having someone as visionary, incisive, and supportive as Suzanne Ryan publishing our scholarship. Every discipline should be so lucky! I am truly grateful to her, Adam Cohen, Samara Stob, and everyone who helped make this book a reality.

Thank you to my parents, my sister, my brother and the incredible community of friends in Fayetteville, Cambridge, and farther flung, without whose description-defying support and friendship over the past few years I would never have gotten to page one.

Finally, I'd like to thank my family, who humored me in the notion that moving us all to England for a year would be no big deal. Thanks to my children for loving their school and their adventures in Cambridge and then turning right around and loving their school and their adventures in Arkansas. Thanks to my husband, then fiancé, for crisscrossing the Atlantic all year like it was an Ozark creek, and for spending an unthinkable number of evenings at the dining room table editing these pages. He also brought me snacks. It is my incredible good fortune—their support and love—that has put me in the position to write this book.

On Repeat

# 1

# The Puzzle of Musical Repetition

Music can never have enough of saying over again what has already been said,
not once or twice, but dozens of times; hardly does a section, which consists
largely of repetition, come to an end, before the whole story is happily told
all over again.
—Zuckerkandl, *1956*

Music's repetitiveness is at once entirely ordinary and entirely mysterious. The radio is full of songs whose choruses repeat again and again, and these repetitive songs often get downloaded and replayed over and over while a listener drives or runs or makes dinner. Musical repetitiveness is so common as to seem almost invisible. But when something draws your attention to it, this repetitiveness comes to seem quite strange. Try replacing the word "music" in the quotation at the start of this chapter with the word "Freddy." Freddy can never have enough of saying over again what he's already said dozens of times. Once he's finished telling one repetitive story, Freddy goes back to the start and tells the whole thing again.

Would you want to spend time with Freddy?

Yet this is precisely what our favorite music is like, and we go back again and again to rehear its stories. It's hard to understand why this fundamental puzzle has not been investigated with more fervor. The topic's general neglect is tied in with the history of music scholarship, and particularly with the history of the relationship between music and science. Music is a fundamentally human capacity, present in all known cultures, and important to intellectual, emotional, and social experience. Among domains of human communication, perhaps only language rises to a similar level of pervasiveness and occupies a similar position of centrality in everyday notions of what it means to be human. But until recently, cognitive science looked primarily to language as a window into the human mind. It is only in the last thirty years or so, and especially in the last decade, that the comparative case of music has received substantial attention.

The reasons for this surprising delay are manifold. In Western culture, music is often viewed to be the exclusive purview of the specialist, and there is typically a clear distinction between performers, who produce the music, and listeners, who receive it. People competent in a language, on the other hand, both speak (produce the language) and understand (receive it). Production competence in language—the ability to speak—is typically achieved without special training, whereas production competence in music—the ability to sing or perform on an instrument—often requires years of formal lessons. Most people acquire production competence in language, but only a subset acquires production competence in music. This imbalance has led people to conceptualize music as a secondary ability; yet the imbalance only arises if production (performance/speech) is taken as the comparative measure, and only if culturally specific notions of what constitutes expertise are brought to bear.

Only some people develop the level of proficiency with music that will allow them to perform at Carnegie Hall, but, similarly, only some people develop the level of proficiency with language that will allow them to win the Man Booker Prize. Yet reflexive cultural notions equate musical competence more with this rare variety of performance expertise than with ordinary abilities. In a study of music students in Britain, Pitts (2005) found that even highly proficient student instrumentalists were loathe to describe themselves as "musicians," preferring to reserve the term for more accomplished professionals. If people were this shy about language, they'd reserve the term "speaker" for professional orators. Although production competence is more widespread for language than for music, the difference is exaggerated by the two domains' unequal criteria for competence. Moreover, were it not for cultural factors emphasizing the development of other skills, it is possible production competence in music would be more widespread. Children, for example, are almost universally capable not only of singing back tunes that have been sung to them, but also of vocally improvising simple new tunes. Receptive competence, on the other hand, is widespread for music and for language. Just as most people can understand, identify errors in, and answer questions about speech in their native language, most people can tap along to, identify errors in, and be moved (sometimes deeply moved) by music in the style with which they're most familiar (whether classical, rock, or something else).

The idea that music is ineffable or resistant to articulation (see Jankélévitch, 1961/2003; Abbate, 2004; Gallope & Kane, 2012) is another cultural attitude that has contributed to the relative historical neglect of music by cognitive scientists. For one thing, music is ephemeral, sounding and then disappearing, and its meaning cannot be summarized or handily captured. For another, it is subjective, with experience and response changing from listener to listener. Language could be viewed as similarly ephemeral, resistant to summary, and subjective, but its capture, via writing, is more widely understood than musical notation. In many cases as well, people are able to provide a brief account of the gist of a passage of spoken text, but lack this capacity to summarize a passage of performed music. Although the interpretation of the typical spoken utterance certainly admits of subjectivity, basic aspects of comprehension can be tested with simple questions: "According to the passage, did Mary, in fact, catch the ball?" People are accustomed to reading books and talking about them, but much less accustomed to talking about the music they hear. It is common to participate in book groups where people sustain elaborate discussions about read material, but when groups leave a concert, the most nuanced comments often involve an enthusiastic "awesome!" or a skeptical shrug. As David Huron (2007) has noted, two audience members at a classical concert, one having a revelatory experience and one thinking about what to make for dinner, look exactly the same—mute, hands in lap, staring toward the stage. Since behavioral methodologies in cognitive science rely on eliciting and measuring responses to stimuli, language— where responses are more overt and easier to tally—has seemed more tractable.

Work in evolutionary psychology has sometimes suggested that while language is fundamental to human identity, and a clear product of natural selection, music represents a kind of "auditory cheesecake" (in Steven Pinker's infamous 1997 assessment) that exploits pleasure circuitry that evolved for other purposes. The tendency to privilege language over music was especially dominant in early cognitive science, which emphasized "cognitive" skills—those related to logic and reasoning—over more holistic, emotion-related, and social abilities. A shift in these priorities has coincided with the publication, over the last ten years, of a number of theories that argue for natural selection as a direct determiner of the capacity for music (Cross, 1999, 2003, 2008, 2009, 2012; Miller, 2000; Mithen, 2006). Since this area involves much speculation and little opportunity for experimental verification, the theories in vogue at a particular moment can reveal much about cultural attitudes to the subject under inquiry.

In addition to these factors, which have been well documented elsewhere, I suspect that still another cultural reflex has contributed to the long reign of language as the form of communication at the center of cognitive science: the ubiquity of repetition in music, and the tendency to view repetition as regressive, childlike, and embarrassing. In a passionate plea within the pages of a late nineteenth-century edition of the *Proceedings of the Royal Music Association*, composer and writer Ferdinand Praeger (pointedly described by Wagner as "an unusually good-natured man, though one too excitable for his standard of culture") argues against the practice of part repetition in performance. Part repetition entails repeating individual parts within a musical form—the exposition or the development and recapitulation in a sonata, for example—when performing for an audience. This practice has declined over time—recording technology now ensures many listeners arrive at performances already familiar with the piece—but it was still quite common in Praeger's day. His "excitable" take on the subject was presented to an assembly of musical thinkers and performers who had gathered for this debate:

> Would ever a poet think of repeating half of his poem; a dramatist a whole act; a novelist a whole chapter? Such a proposition would be at once rejected as childish. Why should it be otherwise with music?... Since any whole part-repetition in poetry would be rejected as childish, or as the emanation of a disordered brain, why should it be otherwise with music? (Praeger, 1882-1883)

"The emanation of a disordered brain"—for Praeger, repetitiveness links music with nonsense and even insanity; its abolition is critical if music is to be received as serious and important. But this enterprise, of course, is entirely quixotic; even if Praeger had succeeded in purging nineteenth-century music of the practice of part repetition, he would have been left with an art that persisted in repetitiveness along myriad other dimensions, at the level of the theme, and the section, and otherwise. Better to embrace the situation and ask, Why is it that we accept, even enjoy, degrees of repetition in music that would be repugnant in almost any other domain?

Other communicative spheres do not entirely lack repetition—consider conversations where one individual's contribution consists entirely of utterances of "uh-huh," or stand-up comedy acts based on the repetition of a catchphrase (think "We are two wild and crazy guys!" in Saturday Night Live sketches from the late '70s). But music is the canonical domain of repetition, and when we reinterpret another domain to emphasize its repetitiveness, we are, in fact, examining a quasi-musical aspect of that domain. Repetition in music is of two sorts: not only is there often a large amount of repetition within particular pieces, as Zuckerkandl observes, but we also tend voluntarily to reexpose ourselves to familiar pieces, again and again and again.

There's a stubborn repeatability to music at every turn that philosophers, ethnomusicologists, cultural historians, semioticians, theorists, and composers have banged their heads against for ages—in most cases, banged their heads against and then abandoned the pursuit. But it is only recently that cognitive scientists have begun to turn their attention to this phenomenon. It is the claim of this book that this particular brand of head-banging—cognitive science against musical repetition, in conjunction with a certain tenacious commitment to making repetition a center of inquiry rather than a peripheral issue—might be especially productive.

Biologist W. Tecumseh Fitch calls repetition a "design feature" of music (2006); not only is music found in all known human cultures, but also musical *repetition*. Repetition is not an arbitrary characteristic that has arisen in a particular style of music; rather, it is a fundamental characteristic of what we experience as music. Particular styles (e.g., modernist and expressively avant-garde approaches) can seek expressly to avoid repetition. Consider aleatoric musics, for example, which incorporate chance into their composition. John Cage's *Imaginary Landscape No. 4,* a symphony for 12 radios, involves portable devices tuned to whatever stations are findable at the moment, resulting in a unique constellation of sounds that changes entirely on re-performance. But pieces in this tradition consciously set themselves against a standard practice and generally require the cultivation of special attitudes and ideas to appreciate. Both the prevalence and the extent of repetition in music around the world argue for a special biological role. Although a behavior's universality does not necessarily signify innateness (see the discussion in McDermott and Hauser, 2005), it does suggest that something interesting is afoot.

As a composer explicitly concerned with generating a sense of structure in music but resistant to traditional ways of doing so, Arnold Schoenberg admitted, "Intelligibility in music seems to be impossible without repetition" (1967). So prevalent is the practice of repetition, that notation possesses not one but many symbols for it. Peter Kivy (1993) surveys the different symbols that, one way or another, instruct performers to repeat, from the tremolo to simile marks to the repeat sign and da capo. The technique of repetition permeates musical practice to such a degree and in so many different ways that it is rarely considered as a single thing; the range of symbols used to notate it masks the fundamental connection among diverse types of repetition.

Not only is repetition a feature of the music of all known cultures, it is also rather irresistible. Making up a little melody and repeating it is fun. The applet Tone Matrix (http://tonematrix.audiotool.com/) exploited this fact so successfully that it became an Internet phenomenon. Users could click any of the squares in a 16x16 grid, randomly drawing their mouse across the board, or drawing pictures or writing their name, and end up creating something that sounded convincingly musical. The ease of producing likable results had to do with the isochronous metric grid represented by the x axis, and the pitch-forgiving pentatonic scale along the y-axis, but it also had essentially to do with the loop: the 16-beat segments repeat until the user clicks more squares or presses stop. Almost anything producible on the matrix sounds credibly musical after a few loops; this applet makes apparent the degree to which repetition can serve to musicalize. Making up tunes and repeating them when children are around might be hazardous to your ability to spend the afternoon doing anything else; children have a special passion for repetition that extends well beyond the musical. Conversely, making up tunes and repeating them around adults might be hazardous to your ability to retain friends; repeated tunes are likely to burrow in where they aren't wanted in the form of earworms—those ditties that seem to get irrevocably stuck in your head (Bennett, 2002).

Repetition is an important component of music's shareability, of its social and biological role in the creation of interpersonal cohesion. At many nursery schools, songs feature in the everyday routine—everybody sings, for example, a particular cleanup song at the appropriate transition time every day. Or imagine a responsorial psalm in a church, the leader teaching the congregation a new responsorial, and them repeating it after each verse, en masse. Imagine a group of children playing *Ring Around the Rosie*, or adults singing *Auld Lang Syne* at midnight on New Year's Day. Repeatability is how songs become the property of a group or a community instead of an individual, how they come to belong to a tradition rather than to a moment.

While many theorists, most recently Gjerdingen (2007), have demonstrated that music is compiled of numerous stock patterns, riffs, and schemata, language also partakes of these structures to a certain extent. Tannen (2007) claims that much more speech than we normally acknowledge is comprised of formulaic expressions—memorized sequences of words, such as those you find in idioms and proverbs. These are often the first things adults immersing themselves in a new language learn—stock phrases such as "how are you?" Van Lancker-Sidtis and Rallon (2004) analyzed the instances of formulaic expressions in a screenplay and found them to make up a full 25 percent of the text. Pawley and Snyder (1983) found that formulaic expressions are processed more quickly than similar-length sequences generated creatively, and Conklin and Schmitt (2008) showed that they were also read more quickly.

Richman (2001) postulates precisely this kind of formulaic repetition as the shared origin of music and language. "In the beginning, speech and music making were one and the same: they were collective, real-time repetitions of formulaic sequences" (p. 300). He points to nonsense formulas, like eenymeenymineymo, as an example of this kind of communication—vocalizations whose component parts lack individual meaning, and which acquire meaning as a whole through their social function. Music psychology has been busy looking at the ways in which music might be similar to language, but Richman, Tannen, and others might be understood to be asking the inverse question, when is language processed musically? This question has been examined in terms of beat structure and intonation, but it might also be considered in terms of repetition structure: highly repetitive forms of language, such as chants and nursery rhymes, veer away from the typical syntactic and semantic modes of understanding speech, and toward modes of comprehension that are more characteristically musical—emotive, social, and holistic.

# Repetition, Prediction, Participation

Music takes place in time, but repetition beguilingly makes it knowable in the way of something outside of time. It enables us to "look" at a passage as a whole, even while it's progressing moment by moment. But this changed perspective brought by repetition doesn't feel like holding a score and looking at a passage's notation as it progresses. Rather, it feels like a different way of inhabiting a passage—a different kind of orientation. Work in my lab traced this shift in attention across repeated exposures (Margulis, 2012). Listeners heard short excerpts from commercially available recordings of classical music by composers ranging from Rameau to Strauss. The excerpt order was randomized, but blocked so that they heard all four repetitions of each individual excerpt successively. The participants' task was simple: they pressed a button as soon as they detected something repeating within the excerpt. At the start of the experiment, each participant received training and practice on this task, and was explicitly shown, using examples, that the repeating entity could be short (a two-note gesture), or long (a sixteen-bar phrase). They were asked to respond as quickly and accurately as possible. After each excerpt, they also provided free text descriptions of each repetition they'd reported. These descriptions were collected as a means of disambiguating responses in cases where the click was interpretable as referring to more than one repetition.

The repeating units in each excerpt (defined as passages with the identical pitches and rhythms) were identified, timed, and tabulated. Listeners' identifications of repeating units, made by pressing buttons while listening, were then tallied against these actual repeating units. Figure 1.1 shows exposures (from first to fourth) along the x-axis, and probability of correct response along the y-axis. The probability of correct response captures the likelihood that, given an actual repeating unit, the listener would identify it as a repetition. One excerpt, from a Rameau piece for keyboard, featured mostly very short repeating units, and another, from the Strauss opera *Der Rosenkavalier*, featured mostly long repeating units. (Length of repeating unit—LRU—refers to the length in seconds of the entity heard to be repeating). When participants' success at repetition detection for each of these excerpts is tracked across exposures, it becomes apparent that with each rehearing, they got better at identifying repetitions in the Strauss, but worse at identifying repetitions in the Rameau.

To determine whether this pattern was due to the different average length of the repeating units (short in the Rameau, long in the Strauss) in the two pieces, or whether it was attributable to one of the many other differences between these two works, data from all the pieces were collapsed together, regardless of composer. Task performance across exposures was tracked for short, medium,

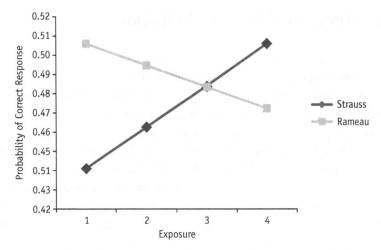

*Figure 1.1* Probability of correct response by exposure for repetitions in the Strauss (the excerpt with the longest mean length of repeating unit) and Rameau (the excerpt with the shortest mean length of repeating unit). Reprinted with permission from Margulis, 2012.

and long repeating units, and the same pattern emerged (see Figure 1.2)—people were more likely to detect the repetition of a short unit on the first hearing, but more likely to detect the repetition of a long unit after multiple exposures.

Perhaps something about the kinds of changes that tend to take place between repeated instances of a short or long pattern accounted for the results. To eliminate this explanation, we looked at cases where the repetition happens

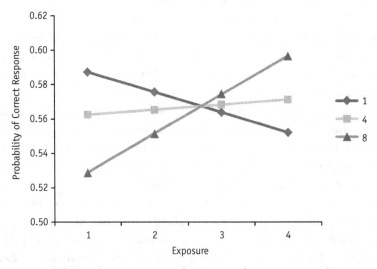

*Figure 1.2* Probability of correct response by exposure for repetitions with repeating unit lengths of 1, 4, and 8 s. Reprinted with permission from Margulis, 2012.

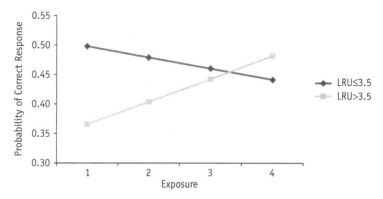

*Figure 1.3* Probability of correct response by exposure for immediate repetitions when the repeating unit length was ≤ 3.5 s, and when it was > 3.5 s. Reprinted with permission from Margulis, 2012.

immediately, with no confounding intermediary material: cases where a passage is played, and then immediately played again. Since there were fewer cases in this category, occurrences were collapsed into two groups instead of three— short and long. Even in this case, the trend held, as shown in Figure 1.3. People detected more short repetitions when they were first encountering a piece, and detected more long repetitions after several exposures.

Together, these data suggest that repeated exposures trigger an attentional shift from more local to more global levels of musical organization. Repetition, thus, can be understood to affect a listener's orientation toward the music; the horizon of involvement widens with additional exposures, so that the music doesn't seem to be coming at the listener in small bits, but rather laying out broader spans for consideration.

Our experience of expectation, as Leonard Meyer (1956) has observed, is often a "felt" rather than a thought phenomenon. We hear the dominant leaning into the tonic—leading forward into it—and share this sense of directedness in time. To some extent always, but especially when the music is familiar—when it has been repeated—each moment seems not like a bead strung along a necklace, resting next to dozens of other beads, but more like a drink just when it starts to be poured—the cascade of liquid is so much a part of the gesture as to seem to be contained within it. Repetition makes it possible for us to experience a sense of expanded present characterized not by the explicit knowledge that *x* will occur at time point *y*, but rather by a heightened sense of orientation and involvement.

Music theory has examined temporal orientation through the lens of phenomenology, most famously in David Lewin's 1986 paper *Music Theory, Phenomenology, and Modes of Perception*. But the experience of listening to music was understood much earlier to be illustrative of general principles of time perception. Edmund Husserl, for instance, used the example of listening to a musical tone to illustrate that every event both leans into the future, conditioning expectations (however implicit) about what might come next, and trails from the past, carrying residue of the events and expectations that preceded it. Lewin constructs a formal model of musical events and their associated percepts, drawing special attention to the way that these percepts function recursively, calling on one another in increasingly complex ways as time progresses. He devises a symbology for discussing these percepts, specifying for each both the triggering event and the context being allowed to influence it. Thus, for example, in an analysis of Schubert's *Morgengruss*, he lists a percept of mm. 12-13 considered within the most local context, mm. 12-13, and another percept of mm. 12-13 considered within the larger context of mm. 9-13, and yet another percept of mm. 12-13 considered within the context of mm. 12-13 plus the expected mm. 14. Using this terminology, repeated exposures to a piece might be understood to shift the dominant contextual influences to wider spans, subtly recasting the listening experience to a different set of perceptions of the same events.

There are clear biological rationales for experiencing pleasure when predictions are fulfilled, as David Huron explores in his 2006 book *Sweet Anticipation*. Such pleasure can be understood to reward successful prediction, and encourage more of it in the future. Familiar music can have a transportive quality, part of which may relate to the special way that surrounding events and sensations can seem to glom onto musical experiences, such that when we rehear familiar repertoire, vivid episodic memories arise. We all have examples of a commercial jingle or radio song summoning forth a forgotten moment from childhood, as suddenly and distinctly as if no time had passed at all. Indeed, Andrea Halpern has shown that auditory imagery possesses particular robustness (see Zatorre and Halpern, 2005, for a review). And Warker and Halpern (2005) have shown, using a musical stem completion task, that people have implicit memories for what notes will come next in melodies to which they were recently exposed, even when they lack the ability to explicitly produce (i.e., sing) these notes. Repetition, in other words, binds the notes in a piece of music closely together, such that hearing only a few of them is sufficient for the rest to mentally unfold, along with, sometimes, a set of associated autobiographical memories (see Janata, 2009).

Consider a common earworm. If I play you just the bit of The Muppets song that goes "Mahna-mahna," I wager that it is all but inevitable that you will subsequently have the auditory image that goes "Doo doo dee doo doo." Yet if I show you a portion of a famous image, such as Rosie the Riveter, you may know what the missing part looks like, but it doesn't occupy your imagination with vividness and irrevocability the way the missing music did. For one thing, you could probably imagine the missing part of the image, and then voluntarily put it aside, but you couldn't imagine the rest of the music and put it aside; the music had to play to a resting point in your head, however long that took. And worse, after it stopped, there's a chance it might have started replaying. It is my intuition that one reason for this stickiness is our inability to conjure up one musical moment and leave it; if our brain flits over any part of the music, we are captured by it, and must play it forth to a point of rest. So we constantly have a sense of being gripped, even unwillingly, by the tune. And note that an earworm is usually a tune—something with a trajectory in time—not a timbre or a special harmony. In the very way we remember music, there's some need for it to play itself out, again and again. Every time we recollect a musical performance, it's to a certain extent a replay. This link between memory and repetition pulls us into repeated music and invites us to inhabit it.

Turino (2008) goes so far as to distinguish two entirely different types of musical practice—presentational, where there is a clear distinction between the music-producing performers and the music-receiving audience, and participatory, where no such distinction exists, and everyone is expected to join in and contribute to making and enjoying the music. In Turino's construct, a classical concert is a canonical example of presentational music, and bluegrass jams or campfire songfests are canonical examples of participatory music. Turino identifies the kind and extent of repetition as a feature distinguishing participatory from presentational music, with "an emphasis on the heightened repetition of musical material—at the level of motives, phrases, sections, and the entire form—which is then repeated over and over again for a relatively long time" disproportionately concentrated in participatory musics (p. 38). Although repetition plainly invites participation in the way Turino describes, enabling newcomers to catch on and join in quickly, I'm not convinced that presentational music has so clearly shed this characteristic. "The use of stock forms, formulas, and a good deal of motivic repetition" (p. 40), although introduced to exemplify music that is essentially participatory, might just as easily be observed to describe much classical, presentational music as well (cf. Caplin, 1998; Gjerdingen, 2007). What I would like to propose is that the notions of participatory and presentational are imaginary poles, with substantial residue of the participatory clinging to much music that appears to be strictly presentational. When elements of the participatory, such as repetition, occur in presentational styles, they don't ordinarily trigger overt participation, but they do elicit a kind of imagined, virtual participation that can serve to powerfully involve an audience.

Repetition links disparate intellectual approaches to music as well. Ethnomusicologist Charles Keil (1987) articulates a reading of music that places itself in direct opposition to music-theoretical approaches:

> The syntactic or structural aspect of all music (Meyer 1956), but especially in thought-composed Western and other civilized musics, can create tensions, set up melodic/harmonic relationships that defer

resolutions and gratifications and thereby involve the listener in the music. But isn't this involvement more analytic, sequential, conscious, rather than "participatory"...? Even in these civilized musical systems, syntax does not invite the listener to participate in the phenomena with the same powers that process and texture have. It is really only in relatively recent historical periods of Western music that syntax and a peculiarly rationalist approach to it (Weber et al. 1958) have managed to squeeze the mysteries of musical participation to the furthest corners of our awareness (Keil, 1987, 275).

Yet repetition plays an important role in both musical syntax and the kind of processes highlighted by Keil. This book will argue that investigations of musical syntax and investigations of musical processes examine different sides of the same musical experience, with repetition serving as a clear point of intersection between the two. Repetition can at once erect perceived syntactic structures and invite a kind of participatory, shared subjectivity. These twin functions underscore that part of music's distinct phenomenology consists of its merging of the objective and subjective stance.

Auditory imagery can be stunningly vivid and robust (Halpern, 1988; Halpern & Zatorre, 1999; Kraemer, Macrae, Green & Kelley, 2005; King, 2006). Kraemer et al. (2005) found enhanced activity in the primary auditory cortex and in auditory association areas when silent gaps were inserted into familiar songs such as *Satisfaction* by the Rolling Stones, in comparison to when the same gaps were inserted into unfamiliar songs—a neuroimagistic trace of the way familiar songs can continue to play through listeners' minds even after the sound has been paused. We know what it's like to "think a phrase," to be mentally gripped by imagined music. When we know what's coming in a musical excerpt, the listening becomes a motion, an enactment, it "moves" us. We are constantly in the future as we listen, such that we can seem to embody it—a topic to be explored in Eric Clarke's forthcoming book on music and subjectivity. My claim is that part of what makes us feel that we're a musical subject rather than a musical object is that we are endlessly listening ahead, such that the sounds seem almost to execute our volition, after the fact. This sense of superexpressive voice (see Juslin, 2001) can be pleasurable in and of itself. It is the pleasure of expansion, of movement beyond limits, of increased power—all characteristic of strong experiences of music as chronicled by existing experimental work (Gabrielsson, 2011). Repetition, I would argue, encourages embodiment. And this embodiment contributes to musical pleasure.

Some modicum of empirical support for this notion comes from neuroimaging work by Petr Janata showing that when people listen to familiar music, in comparison to when they listen to unfamiliar music, there is widespread activation "within structures that underlie sequencing and motor planning" (2009, p. 10). This is consistent with the notion that an embodied kind of forward listening characterizes the experience of rehearing music. Relatedly, I would argue, Pereira et al. (2011) showed that emotion-related limbic and paralimbic regions, as well as reward circuitry, were more active when listening to familiar rather than unfamiliar music—regardless of whether or not it was liked. This finding is consistent with the idea that familiarity makes it possible for us to experience a sense of inhabiting external sound, an experience which is itself pleasant, even if we dislike the music that triggers it. Research on subvocalization, the kind of silent, internal speech that can accompany reading or various kinds of thought, demonstrates that it sometimes consists of auditory imagery (a percept of internal sounds), and sometimes consists of kinesthetic imagery (a percept of internal mouth movements) (Smith, Wilson & Reisberg, 1995). Music is cross-modally linked with sensations and perceptions of motion (Todd, 1995; Zatorre, Chen & Penhune, 2007).

## Nuance and the Aesthetic Mode of Attending

Allow me to erect a straw man for a moment, because this one plagues us even though we know he's flimsy: the notion that music is communicative, in the sense that it conveys information. Repetition is one of the things that show us that this cannot be music's primary function. Once you read Stephen Covey's *Seven Habits of Highly Effective People*, you don't need to keep revisiting the text. In fact, it may be that reading a five-page summary of the book would suffice. The book conveys information, and once the information has been transmitted, there's little residual value within the text, little impetus to reread or repeat the experience. But imagine hearing Beethoven's Fifth Symphony once, and being done. Or hearing a five-minute summary. Neither of these would suffice in the way that they might for the book. Part of this difference is an issue of grain—just as the image in Figure 1.6 seems to reward lots of staring and seeking and blob scrutinizing before a viewer recognizes the emergent image of a Dalmatian, but becomes arguably less interesting and more discardable once that's been identified, it depends on the *kind* of information we're seeking. Do we want simply to identify an object? Or are we approaching the illustration *aesthetically* (a mode of appreciation self-help books do not generally recognize or reward)? Part of the aesthetic orientation is a perceptual openness, a willingness to notice and believe in connections and meanings that may not be instantly apparent. If we trusted these blobs to convey ever-richer associations and patterns to us the longer we looked, we might want to revisit this drawing ad infinitum. Knox (1994) observes that repetition in spoken discourse

> prompts the hearer to seek implicit meaning in utterances, by indicating that the speaker aims at a meaning different than that conveyed by uttering an expression only once. Thus, when ideas are complex or words are insufficient, speakers may repeat their utterances in order to engage their hearers in interpretive efforts to make more of what is said (p. 197).

Think of some cinematic lug telling his henchman: "Take him outside!" When the henchman answers, "OK, boss," looking confused as to why fresh air would be an appropriate punishment for their captive, the lug might repeat "Take him *outside*!," the repetition communicating that the utterance implies more punishment than its surface might indicate.

Music's function is obviously not to convey information, and its repetitive nature seems to be bound up with this other function—a function that might best be described as aesthetic. But there seems to be something more going on than this term can capture. We revisit favorite paintings, but not with the degree of obsession we revisit musical works (or there would be a painting iPod). Films we rewatch, but again not to the same degree, and not with mounting passion. Poetry is perhaps the best comparative case—it can take a comparable or even smaller amount of time to read a poem as to hear a piece, and poetry unfolds sequentially and dynamically in time (word after word after word), just like music (note after note after note). Poems are reread, and re-enjoyed, but lack both the internal repetition characteristic of music, and the capacity to generate earworms (you don't get stuck in the shower reciting "shall I compare thee to a summer's day?," although if it were set to a pop tune you might). The rereading of poetry is also often the restudying of that poetry, with new "information" being extracted, and whereas the extraction of information *can* be a goal for musical rehearings, this was not the mechanism or goal at play when "Poker Face" was blasted everywhere during the summer of 2009.

Rereading (or rehearing, to take a closer example) familiar poetry is, I would argue, a less consuming experience than rehearing familiar music. Even if you love Robert Frost, you don't hear "Two roads diverged" and think "yes!" the way you might when you hear the opening notes of a favorite song. You could duck out of the poem fairly easily, whereas a snippet of familiar music triggers a cascade of "that song" that takes over and won't let you go. Interestingly, it's much harder to memorize a poem than a song. At first glance, this would seem to make repetition more desirable for poems than for music, where we are able to know "how it goes" much quicker. That the reverse is true suggests that the pleasure we derive from musical repetitions might stem less from increasing knowledge about the piece than from a growing sense of inhabiting the music: a transportive, even transcendent kind of experience. Indeed, recent theoretical work by Carolyn Abbate has questioned the centrality of "knowing" within musical experience (2004), emphasizing instead its momentary lived and sensed aspects. Similarly, my paper *When Program Notes Don't Help* (2010) presents some empirical support for the notion that people enjoy music more when they aren't given explicit information about it. Participants in this study reported increased enjoyment of excerpts from Beethoven String Quartets when the excerpts were presented without any annotations, in comparison to the same excerpts when preceded by verbal descriptions of their dramatic or structural content. Having more explicit "knowledge" about the piece, in other words, not only didn't help enjoyment, it reduced it. It seems that the increased pleasure repetition can afford stems not from enhanced knowledge, but rather from something more implicit, a changed sort of orientation toward the work.

## Repetition and the Music-Language Divide

Repetition is both more prevalent in music than language, and better received. People might like repetition in music that they wouldn't in language, but might also tend to disavow this affection, finding it somehow embarrassing. In a 2012 study, I asked participants without special musical training—everyday music listeners—to listen to excerpts from challenging contemporary art music (atonal pieces by Luciano Berio and Elliott Carter) and rate on a 7-point scale how much they'd enjoyed each excerpt, how interesting they'd found it, and how likely they thought the excerpt was to have been composed by a human artist rather than randomly generated by a computer (Margulis, 2013). Unbeknownst to the participants, mixed in with the original excerpts were adaptations of them. In these adaptations, segments of music had been extracted and reinserted to add repetitions of some material; repetitions that could occur immediately or after some other music had intervened (see Figure 1.4).

Listeners rated the immediate and delayed repetition versions as reliably more enjoyable, more interesting, and more likely to have been composed by a human artist rather than generated randomly by a computer. Even roomfuls of PhD-holding music theorists, when presented these examples at a meeting of the Society for Music Theory (Minneapolis, 2011)—an audience sympathetic to Berio and Carter if ever there were one—confessed to finding the repetitive versions more likable on first pass. This is a stunning finding, particularly as the original versions were crafted by internationally renowned composers and the (preferred) repeated versions were created by brute stimulus manipulation

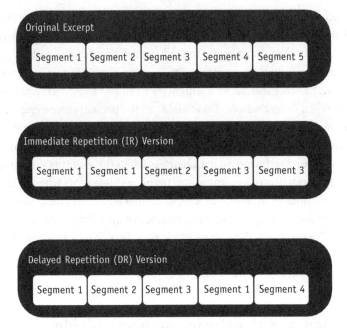

*Figure 1.4* Graphic representations of the three types of stimuli used in Margulis (2013): original excerpts, excerpts with immediate repetitions inserted, and excerpts with delayed repetitions inserted.

without regard to artistic quality. The simple introduction of repetition, independent of musical aims or principles, elevated people's enjoyment, interest, and judgments of artistry. This suggests that repetition is a powerful and often underacknowledged aesthetic operative. And note particularly that introducing the same manipulations into spoken utterances (additional repetition, without regard to linguistic sense) would likely not trigger elevated ratings of enjoyment, interest, or the perceived likelihood of generation by a human speaker rather than a computer—quite the opposite, in fact. Repetition, thus, marks an important divider between the perception of music and language.

Perhaps the most dramatic evidence for the special role of repetition in music comes from Diana Deutsch's speech-to-song illusion (hearable at http://deutsch.ucsd.edu/psychology/pages.php?i=212). In this well-known example (Deutsch, Lapidis, and Henthorn, 2008; Deutsch, Henthorn, and Lapidis, 2011), a sentence of ordinary speech is presented, followed by the excessive and temporally regular repetition of a single clause from the utterance. Finally, the original sentence is played again. For the majority of listeners (approximately 85 percent in most studies), a radical change in perception occurs: although the rest of the sentence sounds normal, the segment that had been repeated has shifted phenomenologically, such that it seems the speaker has suddenly burst

Figure 1.5 The musical sound of the repeated clause from the speech-to-song illusion. Originally published in Deutsch, D. *"Phantom Words and Other Curiosities,"* Philomel Records, 2003, Copyright © Diana Deutsch. Reprinted with permission.

sometimes    behave    so    strangely

into song. In the example featured above, what on first pass sounded like the words "sometimes behave so strangely" (and would continue to sound like such to any person encountering the sentence for the first time), comes to sound like the tune in Figure 1.5. Repetition, in other words, causes ordinary speech to be perceived as music.

A similar phenomenon, first described by Severance and Washburn in 1907, is semantic satiation, where repeated viewings, utterances, or hearings of the same word cause it to seem to degenerate into nonsense. Not just any nonsense, but a nonsense in which the semantics vanish and are replaced by a sort of super-salience of the component parts—letters, phonemes, syllables. In the famous Dalmatian picture (see Figure 1.6), it's as if the sense of the Dalmatian had disappeared (very difficult to do at will), and been replaced by a renewed sensitivity to the characteristics of the blobs. It's interesting that repetition can cause language to dissolve into nonsense on the one hand or music on the other. This is not the first, nor the last time in this volume that the effect of repetition

Figure 1.6 The Dalmation illusion, designed by R. C. James.

will be taken to suggest an affinity between these domains—an affinity, I should add, that I do not view as demeaning to music in the least.

Semantic satiation has sometimes been explained in terms of attention. Bored with repeated encounters with the same signified word, attention shifts to the only other available level—the constituent parts of the word—letters, phonemes, and so on; or, in the case of the speech-to-song illusion, from the sense of the words to the melody—the pitches—within it. What's remarkable in this example is that in shifting this way, we have the sensation that we're approaching the stimulus not in a slightly different manner, but rather as if it were a completely different stimulus altogether—as if speech had magically been transformed into music. Indeed, it could be argued that music is more about the nature of the blobs than about emergent Dalmatians. (There's a long literature devoted to this issue; see, for example, Raffman, 1993.) Nuanced objects are more compelling on repetition—it's not that we extract a Dalmatian and move on, but rather that there's always a richness just out of conscious grasp. There is a sense in which the thing is known, yet constantly rediscovered—never grasped—and this may result in a satisfying pull toward the present moment—perhaps a prerequisite for the loss of self chronicled by Gabrielsson (2011). The more a piece is repeated, the more we think we know it, and the greater the joy of discovery when we are surprised by the blobs. There's a point here where I believe that Paul Silvia's (2006) notion of interest as an emotion becomes relevant: I would submit that interest is an important part of our emotional response to music, and that repetition facilitates the interest response. To my knowledge, the notion of interest as an affective response to music has not been deeply explored. Much has been made of emotional responses to music that entail sadness or happiness or some such feeling, yet often my own involvement with a piece, although deeply engaged, consists not of such feeling-states, but rather of a kind of committed and sustained interest. Repetition can encourage this interest to move away from explicit facts and ideas about a passage toward its actual sounding, making possible a vivid and immediate experience that is intrinsically pleasant.

The fact that repetition can engender such a dramatic perceptual shift from one acoustic domain, language, to another, music, suggests that it's playing an important role in distinguishing these two domains. In a diary entry from 1870, Wagner's wife Cosima quoted him to precisely this effect:

> Repetition! There is the absolute difference between music and poetry; a theme may be repeated because it is a person and not a discourse; on the contrary, in poetry, repetition is absurd, except when it is a refrain or when it has to produce a musical effect (quoted in Deliège, 2007, p. 11).

In setting music and poetry alongside one another, Wagner appeals to an embodied sense of what music is, calling it a "person," and contrasting it with the overtly conceptual content of a "discourse." Given the flurry of recent work comparing the cognition of language and music (see Patel's excellent *Music, Language, and the Brain*, 2008, for a summary), it's intriguing that the role of repetition has been largely neglected.

## Communicative Functions

Although Lydia Goehr (2007) traces the emergence of the Western musical "work-concept" to roughly 200 years ago, ethnomusicologist Bruno Nettl (1983) finds reiterability to be a feature that is universally shared across music cultures. The advent of recording technology has strongly foregrounded this aspect of music, but people have been notating pieces for more than a thousand years, and sharing, transmitting, and replicating standard tunes for far longer than that. Moreover, this practice is not restricted to our species—whales, gibbons, and about half the 900 known species of bird sing. In fact, Suzuki, Buck, and Tyack (2006) report that repetition is a characteristic that leads researchers to characterize an animal vocalization as music: "The term *song* is used in animals, such as songbirds and whales, to describe an acoustic signal that involves a wide variety of sounds repeated in a specific sequence" (p. 1849).

Whale song involves repetition at multiple levels. Humpback whale songs are comprised of complex sequences of twelve or more units, discrete utterances separated by silence. They are constructed hierarchically (Payne & McVay, 1971), with repeated phrases coming together to form themes. In a single song session, the song will be repeated many times with surprising accuracy over a total duration of between seven and thirty minutes (Suzuki, Buck & Tyack, 2006, p. 1849).

These songs develop within particular populations and within particular regions; they gradually change with time and location. It has been suggested that repetition in whale songs functions as a mnemonic device, offering a strategy for coping with the cognitive demands of oral transmission and song evolution (Janik and Slater, 1997; Tyack and Sayigh, 1997; Guinee and Payne, 1988). Suzuki, Buck, and Tyack use information theory to show that entropy in whale songs decreases across the course of a season, as the whales settle in on canonical versions of each song. Moreover, they show that longer songs contain more redundancy. Li and Hombert (2002) report that these especially repetition-laden songs can last over thirty minutes.

> The repetition indicates a gradation of the intensity of the singer's emotional state. The more the repetition, the greater the desire of the male to attract the female and the more it demonstrates the male's physical

fitness. Hence, repetition is not communicatively redundant. It has communicative significance (Li and Hombert, 2002, p. 197).

They note that songbirds repeat themselves with as much gusto as whales, sometimes for hours at a time, each repetition ratcheting up the intensity and advertising more strongly the motivation, strength, and health of the male bird. Searcy, Nowicki, and Peters (1999) report that researchers use the number of songs, as described by combinations of MUPs (minimal units of production), as the unit of analysis for variation in sparrows, and that song types are also meaningful units to the sparrows themselves.

Brown et al. (2004) point to the critical role of vocal learning and mimicry in the human song system. One way in which this manifests itself is in the quasi-musical amount of repetition in infant-directed speech. Informal observation suggests that several factors contribute to this tendency. First, at the stage during which the baby is not talking back, there's not much to push the conversation forward; a low-energy, default way to keep talking is simply to repeat what you just said. This is a pragmatic kind of motivation, which may influence compositional choices in music as well: if you're unsure about what to do next, the least-demanding solution may be simply to repeat the previous material. Second, repetition creates a soothing sort of rhythm—repetition at the sentence level, where I have often noticed it in interactions with babies, in particular creates a slow, calming periodicity. Similarly, repetition in music has been shown to facilitate the emergence of metric hierarchy (Lerdahl and Jackendoff, 1983); meter, in turn, facilitates entrainment, which has clear relevance for parent-infant interactions. Third, repetition aims to teach the infant how to speak an utterance and what it means. A parent will point to a ball and repeat "Ba-all. Ba-all. Ball." This hyper-repetitiveness, the parent hopes, not only shows the infant where the word boundaries lie, but also builds memory of its phonemic content and associations to its semantic referent. Musical repetition might also be profitably conceptualized as a way to teach people how to listen to the piece at hand—to guide them to the proper level of attention (see Margulis, 2012), and to underline the entities considered important. As Lidov (1979) frames it, "Since repetition can be perceived in an unfamiliar style, innovations which lack the support of an established musical language can appeal to repetition to clarify their vocabulary and procedures" (p. 27). This link to musical process makes it instructive to examine repetition's didactic aims in infant-directed speech.

Parents use not only more word repetition, but also more prosodic repetition when they talk to newborns (Fernald and Simon, 1984). This verbal repetition seems to peak in speech directed to children between four and six months old, and declines to the level found in adult-directed speech by age two (Fernald & Morikawa, 1993). Unyk, Trehub, Trainor, and Schellenberg (1992) observe that this repetition, in combination with other distinctive features of infant-direct speech, such as exaggerated prosodic contours, confer a musical quality on this type of speech. When speaking to infants between the ages of four and six months in the context of play, mothers on average repeat every fourth or fifth utterance (Stern et al., 1983). McRoberts, McDonough, and Lakusta (2009) point to the critical window between seven and nine months, when infants are starting to be able to segment familiar words and track probabilities in speech, as a hypothetical peak for a maximum interest in repetitive speech, since "repeated utterances can act as an important scaffold, providing an opportunity to perceptually explore the transient speech signal" (p. 169). Specifically, they may "provide infants with the opportunity to recover additional details from the transient speech signal that they may not be able to access from a single presentation" (p. 180-181). In presenting this hypothesis, McRoberts, McDonough, and Lakusta (2009) assert "repetition in IDS [infant-directed speech] and its role in language and cognitive development is a potentially important but understudied phenomenon" (p. 181). This observation is especially transferrable to music, where repetition plays an even larger role but is similarly understudied. In the study, which systematically varied the amount of verbal repetition in infant-directed speech, the researchers found that six-month olds, but not four-month olds, prefer repetitive speech—potential evidence of a shift around this age from attention to prosodic cues to attention to linguistic structure, since "infants' sensitivity to repeated patterns of speech appears at about the same time that other studies show infants are becoming sensitive to prosodic markers for phrase and clause structure in continuous speech" (p. 191). The authors note that sensitivity to repetition was documented in Fernald and O'Neill (1993), which outlined cross-cultural similarities in peekaboo games, and observed that between the ages of five and seven months old, babies start anticipatory looking in advance of the reappearance of the mother's face.

> The high degree of exactly and partially repeated utterances in IDS during this same period suggests that repetition in speech might play a similar role by allowing infants to anticipate that identical or highly similar sound patterns will be repeated within a short time. This could provide the infant with the opportunity to deploy attentional and perceptual resources to access finer grained structure in the speech signal than would be available from a single presentation (p. 191).

This issue of grain seems particularly relevant to music, since so much expressive power lies in nuance. As musical phrases repeat, listeners gain access to more nuanced, communicative aspects of the sound. It would be interesting to vary the amount of repetition in "infant-directed song" (lullabies, nursery tunes), and assess whether preferences for repetition in music followed the same trajectory, and to determine whether this preference developed at a similar age.

## Repetition's Functions

Three primary roles have been identified for repetitive auditory stimuli, roles in: (1) learning and level-shifting, (2) segmentation, and (3) expectation. This section considers each in turn.

Auditory stimuli are temporally delineated—you can't stop and look at them for as long as you wish. Rather, they're presented and then gone, on their own schedule, and after that you must rely on memory to access them again. But remembering a passage is impractical while listening to music, as the music typically does not stop to allow this kind of rumination (although in my 2007 article *Moved by Nothing*, I discuss instances where composers seem to have inserted a pause expressly to make this possible). Musical repetitions, therefore, can be viewed as a kind of re-presenting, a kind of prosthetic memory, whereby past events are put once more before the ears. As Kivy describes it: "Musical repeats, then, perform an obvious and vital function in that they are the composer's way of allowing us, indeed compelling us to linger; to retrace our steps so that we can fix the fleeting sonic pattern; they allow us to grope so that we can grasp" (p. 356). This groping and grasping facilitates learning, in that details missed on the first hearing can be encoded on the next. Music processing might rely more on fine-grained surface representations than language. In the case of language, once the meaning is abstracted, the particular words and intonation used to convey that meaning can be discarded. When people are asked to recall a story, or even a sentence, they often paraphrase, preserving meaning but substituting new words and expressions. Psychologists have referred to this as a failure of "verbatim memory" (Sachs, 1967; Jarvella, 1971; Gernsbacher, 1985). For example, if asked to recall the sentence, "The grandmother, who lived in a dusty fourth-floor flat she no longer had the energy to vacuum, made her way carefully down the stairs, hand steady on the rail, heels clicking determinedly with each step," participants might say, "A grandmother who lived in a messy fourth floor apartment walked down the stairs with care."

Verbatim memory improves for jokes and insults—statements of "high interactional content," grounded in the context of direct social interaction (Keenan, MacWhinney & Mayhew, 1977). Murphy & Shapiro (1994) advance a pragmatic view of this processing difference: "listeners attend to the level of analysis of text that is most relevant, important, or salient given their current goals;" in other words, the difference is a matter of attentional allocation (p. 87). Assuming this theory's viability for the moment, verbatim memory should be elevated in music as compared to language, because of the surface's importance.

Raffman (1993) suggests that elements of musical nuance are by nature ineffable, and resistant to memory, such that the only way to reencounter them is to rehear them. If the music's emotional power lies in nuance, and nuance can't be vividly recalled, there would be a strong motivation to relisten. Huron (2006) summarizes another perspective, reliant on statistical learning, according to which repetitions always sound new because our schematic expectations have changed since the last hearing, by virtue of whatever we've heard in between. Because the music plays with these new expectations in new ways, it retains affective power. This case strikes me as relatively weaker. If our expectations are derived from the sum of listening experiences across a lifetime, it hardly seems possible that the amount of music encountered between radio replays of a particular song could be sufficient to significantly reorient predictions about it.

The studies on repetition and infant-directed speech also point to the role of repetition in segmentation; an interest in repetition starts to emerge simultaneously with the ability to segregate the speech stream. But as infants become more skilled at segmenting the speech stream, they also become less interested in repetition. This timeline suggests that repetition might be particularly critical at the point when segmentation still represents something of a challenge. Might repetition be more desirable in musical styles where segmentation is a challenge? Might listeners find themselves more favorably disposed to repetition in genres that are unfamiliar? For music in a novel style, repetition is often a listener's first way into what counts as a unit—what should be grouped together and treated as an entity. For example, undergraduates who have not yet developed a good sense of cadence, the standard formulae that mark the ends of phrases, often rely heavily on repetition to identify phrase lengths. Repetition can communicate which temporal span is carrying the piece's principal action—in other words, which temporal level might reward a listener's attention. In an experiment in which the scope of the repeating unit was systematically varied, such that it was sometimes two notes, and sometimes twenty measures, my prediction would be that attention would orient toward a smaller level in the first example, and toward a larger level in the second. This orientation could be assessed by error detection, recognition memory for elements of various sizes, tapping rate, grouping characterizations, or another measure. Some evidence that repetitions guide temporal attending in this manner already exists. When a two-measure repeating unit is followed by one-measure, half-measure, and two-note units in succession, the cumulative effect is of acceleration. The sense of speeding up arises not from any surface change in pace, but rather from repetition having directed attention toward successively smaller units of time.

Starting with Nicolas Ruwet in the early 1970s and continuing through the work of Jean-Jacques Nattiez, semioticians have hypothesized that repetition might serve as a kind of perceptual primitive out of which listeners could construct the sometimes elaborate structures common to traditional music-theoretic accounts. As Lidov (2004) observes, however, the hope of these theorists that high-level structural readings would prove buildable out of direct repetition analysis was not fulfilled. Tracking various kinds of repetition does not on its own produce the broader kinds of insights listeners regularly have in response to music. (Although Ockleford, 2005 does make a compelling case for the power of repetition to define diverse kinds of musical structures.) The more conservative claim made here, that repetition draws attention to particular elements within the musical fabric, should be understood as distinct from the broader claim advanced by early work in semiotics.

Work on infant-directed speech also implies that repetition plays a role in expectation. For example, infants can track regularities in the speech stream and actively predict that a verbatim repetition will occur every four to five seconds. For adult listeners, repetition's function in the establishing, direction, fulfilling, and thwarting of expectations is more complex. Take, for example, the apparently simple question of what repetition might imply. Meyer proposes that repetition triggers an expectation for change, but Narmour explains that repetition triggers an expectation for more repetition. The fact that two such similar theorists (Narmour was Meyer's student) diverge on this fundamental point is revealing. It's simply too reductive to assert that repetition implies either continuation or change. It depends on the type of expectation under consideration (see Margulis, 2007b, and Huron & Margulis, 2010), as well as on the context in which the repetition occurs, and the kind of thing being repeated (for example, a note or a section). Nevertheless, repetition clearly steers expectations in important ways deserving of further study. For example, what are the conditions that cause a listener to expect repetition at a particular point in a piece? How robust are veridical expectations for events within a repeated phrase in various circumstances? How can expressive choices by performers affect these expectations?

Several motivations prompt repetition to be considered as a singular phenomenon, rather than as a special case of more general similarity relations in music. The first is pragmatic: as Sisman (1993) observes, "Repetition is a topic of daunting size" (p. 4). Lidov (1979) notes that although the concept of variation is already laden with human perceptual tendencies, repetition is a more clear-cut case, closer to something directly measurable from the acoustic signal. This characteristic makes it more useful for examining the divergence between acoustic properties and human perceptions of them. The second motivation is grounded in empirical work. While studying semantic satiation induced by spoken recitations of a word, Pilotti et al. (1997) found that only repeated utterances spoken by a single voice triggered the effect. When the stimuli were merely similar (the same word uttered by different speakers), no satiation took place; when they were truly identical (the same word uttered by the same speaker), the result was qualitatively different. Verbatim repetition triggered a special kind of response. Monaghan and Rowson (2008) sought to directly investigate whether repetition of identical stimuli is a special case for learning, or whether it is better conceived as one endpoint of a continuum of similarity. They measured learning success for tone sequences that included different types of patterns, including repetition. Patterns featuring repetition were learned differently and more successfully than other types. These results support "the claim, made in Endress et al. (2007), that identical repetition is a special case for learning." Monaghan goes so far as to claim that repetition's singular effect poses a problem for traditional accounts of statistical learning mechanisms. Repetition seems special, and its prevalence in music makes it the perfect domain in which to explore what precisely this might mean and why precisely it might be.

This chapter offers a few preliminary observations. First, to remember a passage of music requires an uncommonly extended duration of time—the duration it took to play the passage in the first place. Remembering a passage entails mentally replaying it; thus, musical repetitions are quite like musical memories. This resemblance draws us in, and encourages a sort of embodiment of the sound—the music is doing objectively just what we imagined it to, subjectively—that is by its very nature pleasurable. Second, in music, ensuing (future) moments are much more present in the perception of the current moment than in other domains. But this stratified, expanded present can only emerge if the music is familiar—if the future course of the melody is known. Thus, the pleasurable "flow" state described by Csikszentmihalyi (1997) is likeliest to emerge in response to music that has been repeated. Third, essential components of musical expressivity depend on nuance, nonconceptual elements, and aspects resistant to description in words or even to representation in memory. Hearing the piece again is the only way for a listener to reencounter these aspects. Repetition allows for the re-experience of meaningful elements that could not be sufficiently represented in memory, and for the shifting of attention from one level to the other, such that multiple rewarding musical associations can be appreciated.

I want to suggest that repetition is a worthy subject for much more theoretical and empirical attention than it currently receives. I won't say, like Ferdinand Praeger in 1882, that "if the slightest seed has been thrown out to help [this cause], I shall consider this to be one of the happiest days in my life," but I do think we have a lot to learn about diverse and important subjects by making repetition a focus of inquiry. The remainder of this book takes up this task in earnest.

# 2

# From Acoustic to Perceived Repetition

Jose Luis Borges's *Pierre Menard, Author of the Quixote* (1962) is a fictional story written as if it were a review of a book. The (fictional) book it reviews is a word-for-word rewriting of chapters from Cervantes's Don Quixote by the (fictional) contemporary writer Pierre Menard. The reviewer observes, "the text of Cervantes and that of Menard are verbally identical, but the second is almost infinitely richer" (p. 42). Conversely, in *The Library of Babel*, Borges chronicles a library composed of an infinite series of hexagonal rooms lined with books containing every possible permutation of linguistic characters—most amount to gibberish, but everything that has been said or is sayable at all also exists on one of the library's shelves, including the text of the complete works of Shakespeare, the recipe for an excellent turkey burger, and the passages from Don Quixote penned originally by Cervantes, centuries later by Menard, and now by some existential act of arbitrary symbol rearrangement.

Cervantes's, Menard's, and the infinite library's texts replicate one another letter for letter, but Borges's stories underscore the divergent ways in which these identical texts might be experienced. Menard laments the quixoticness(!) of his enterprise—to recreate passages from Don Quixote authentically and naturally, without copying—thus:

> To compose the Quixote at the beginning of the seventeenth century was a reasonable undertaking, necessary and perhaps even unavoidable; at the beginning of the twentieth, it is almost impossible. It is not in vain that three hundred years have gone by, filled with exceedingly complex events. Amongst them, to mention only one, is the Quixote itself (Borges, 1962, p. 41).

And his reviewer rewards the effort:

It is a revelation to compare Menard's Don Quixote with Cervantes'.
The latter, for example, wrote (part one, chapter nine):

> ... truth, whose mother is history, rival of time, depository of
> deeds, witness of the past, exemplar and adviser to the present, and
> the future's counselor.

Written in the seventeenth century, written by the "lay genius"
Cervantes, this enumeration is a mere rhetorical praise of history.
Menard, on the other hand, writes:

> ... truth, whose mother is history, rival of time, depository of
> deeds, witness of the past, exemplar and adviser to the present, and
> the future's counselor.

History, the mother of truth: the idea is astounding. Menard, a contemporary of William James, does not define history as an inquiry into reality but as its origin. Historical truth, for him, is not what has happened;
it is what we judge to have happened. The final phrases—exemplar
and adviser to the present, and the future's counselor —are brazenly
pragmatic.
The contrast in style is also vivid. The archaic style of Menard—quite
foreign, after all—suffers from a certain affectation. Not so that of his
forerunner, who handles with ease the current Spanish of his time
(Borges, 1962, p. 42).

This "revelation" juxtaposes textually identical passages, and identifies the gaping
differences in meaning, resonance, and content effected by a change in context: the
text construed as the work of sixteenth-century writer Miguel de Cervantes, versus
the text construed as the work of contemporary writer Pierre Menard. The textual
repetition serves to expose more clearly the situational, interpretive work that dif-
ferentiates the experience of the two books. The idea that language indigenous to
a certain period can sound archaic or affected when used in another recalls the
multiplicities of meaning that can be generated by musical borrowing. Fugal styles,
for example, native to the Baroque period, came to acquire an intensified quality
of seriousness and the markedly "high" style when used within development sections of nineteenth-century music, as in the excerpt from the development of the
first movement of Brahms's Second Symphony, shown in Figure 2.1. Mirka (forthcoming), in fact, identifies musical topics precisely as distinctive styles imported
into nonnative contexts. Although in their original settings they may have seemed
more transparent and less marked, the use of these topics outside their indigenous
environment permits them to serve as referent-bearing elements of the musical
discourse. Even the most literal forms of repetition, then, are differentiated by the

*Figure 2.1* Brahms, Symphony No. 2, I, mm. 204-209.

associations of the immediately surrounding context—the words or notes that precede or follow it—as well as the relevant compositional, authorial, historical, and intertextual situation of the utterance.

In contemporary popular music, a particular form of borrowing—sampling—is so ubiquitous as to constitute a basic element of the musical material. The entire genre of hip hop music, for example, evolved from the practice of DJs repeating the breaks—the instrumental or percussive interludes—to allow clubbers to continue dancing in between songs; it eventually became common practice to sample one song's break and reuse it as the underlying beat of another. But borrowing is also more prevalent than generally acknowledged in classical music, with Burkholder (1994) noting excessive use of the practice by Handel, and observing that more than one-third of Beethoven's oeuvre consists of some form of reworking of his own previous compositions.

*Figure 2.1 (Continued)*

The Swingle Singers, a largely a cappella group that has remained in existence in some form or other since 1962, covers songs from all genres––including classical—with a cheerful, irreverent quality characteristic of similar work by Bobby McFerrin and the cast of Glee. Welsh singer Jem samples the Swingle Singers' rendition of Bach's Prelude in F Minor, from the second book of the Well-Tempered Clavier, in her single *They*, a song with lyrics that rue the fallibility of conventional wisdom. Within this context, the eighteenth-century structure of the prelude's opening comes to represent precisely this establishment thought, gently mocked in the Swingle Singers' setting, and then underlain with contemporary beats that further communicate the wish, also expressed by the lyrics, to shrug off received patterns of thinking. The topic, in this case, is the kind of classicism and conventionality represented by music of contemporary concert halls, and it is (predictably, perhaps) set against the rebellious and future-oriented implications of music that has its origins in rock and roll. Context draws attention to a single characteristic of the quotation—its representativeness of the established musical canon—where another context might have drawn attention to the cambiata structure of the opening, or to the alternation between stately and frenetic phrases characteristic of the *emfindsamer stil*, or to the motions toward V, or to any other aspect of the excerpt. Context shifts perceptual, cognitive, and emotional orientation such that a passage that recurs verbatim can take on not only wholly different meanings, but also wholly different soundings. Context determines what a passage ultimately *is*, and this on-the-one-hand obvious but on-the-other-hand surprising fact makes repetition a powerful example of the difference between surface content and meaning. There is nothing about the F Minor Prelude that projects conservatism until it is set against a pop song, yet in the Jem track, that is nearly all the tune communicates.

In an article from the *North Carolina Law Review*, Arewa (2006) describes music's fundamental relationality (the dependence of any one element on its context for meaning) as foundational to copyright law. She quotes Agawu's (1991) observation of the most familiar example of such relationality: functional harmony, whereby the tonal context reconfigures the basic perception of individual notes. Only 1 in 10,000 people are estimated to have absolute pitch— the capacity to identify a note independent of context, to recognize a G as a G whether it is articulated in a G or F♯ major context, and whether it is sounded by the vacuum cleaner or within the middle of a Beethoven symphony (for an overview, see Deutsch, 2006 and Levitin & Rogers, 2005). The overwhelming majority of people possess relative pitch, and experience the intervals and relations *between* the notes as essential. For listeners with relative pitch, a G sounds like a stable, resting pitch when they're listening to a passage in G major, but a restless, leading, unfinished one when they're listening to a passage in A♭. The contrasting qualia that arise out of the G's different positions in each tonal context are much more salient than any equivalence based on the G's absolute pitch. Although recent studies have established that this equivalence is represented both in the brainstem (Greenberg et al., 1987) and the cortex (Lauter et al., 1985; Wessinger et al., 1997), people generally lack access to these absolute pitch representations.

It should be stressed that relative pitch affects very basic notions of what constitutes a piece; people can start singing *Happy Birthday* in any key, and everyone else will not only be able to recognize the song, but also join in. Yet in one case, the opening may be sung on F♯s and C♯s, and in another on Gs and Ds— the two renditions may not actually share any actual pitches. It's the intervals between the pitches, not the pitches themselves, that determine the identity of the song. Figure 2.2 shows two renditions of *Happy Birthday* that look very

*Figure 2.2* Two renditions of *Happy Birthday*, made up of entirely different sets of pitches, but instantly recognizable as the same tune.

different on the page, but sound like exactly the same tune. For listeners with relative rather than absolute pitch, the salience of the equivalence between the two tunes' intervals far outstrips the salience of the divergence between their constituent pitches.

Krumhansl (1990) reviews a set of experiments that demonstrated the fundamental context-dependence of pitch perception using the probe-tone methodology. A probe-tone study presents listeners with individual pitches preceded by tonality-establishing contexts, and asks them to rate how well the pitch fits with the preceding context. Without any explicit knowledge of tonal theory, listeners systematically alter their rankings for individual pitches depending on their position within the tonal context. For example, they rate G as a maximally good fit when it follows a G major context, but rate it as a maximally poor fit when it follows an F♯ major context.

The capacity of tonal context to change perceptions of the same pitch represents just one of the many ways in which musical context can serve to make repetition seem like difference. The kind of context that is relevant includes not only other musical events, but also the life history of the listener, the setting within which the listening experience is taking place, the repertoires with which the listener is and is not familiar, and so forth. For some contemporary Israelis, for example, Wagner's music carries ineradicable residue of its appropriation by Hitler and the Nazis, but for others, it is possible to put aside this episode in the music's reception history and engage with it on other terms. This difference underlies the controversy regarding the unofficial ban of Wagner in Israel (see Sheffi, 2000). The same music can mean very different things to different listeners, or to the same listener on different occasions.

But in some ways it is less interesting and better understood how life events can reconfigure listening experiences to the same piece of music, and more interesting and less understood how changes in the objective presentation of a musical object—especially its *musical* presentation—can engender new meanings and percepts. Say, for example, that a particular pop ballad was playing on the sound system at a restaurant when a person chanced upon his wife on a date with his dentist. The song might understandably assume new expressive resonances for that individual. Often referred to as the "they're playing our song" phenomenon, and well-explored in the literature on music and autobiographical memory (see Janata, Tomic & Rakowski, 2007; Schulkind, Hennis & Rubin, 1999), this process is arguably less puzzling than the way that the interpolation of a diminished seventh chord or a new backbeat can elicit markedly changed responses to an otherwise identical sequence of sounds. In Act 2 of Shakespeare's *Much Ado About Nothing*, Benedick articulates the essential mysteriousness of this process when he remarks on the vibration of strings, "Is it not strange that sheeps' guts should hale souls out of men's bodies?" When sounds are tied to emotional life experiences, it is not surprising that they might take on the valence of the associated event, but sound *qua* sound, the vibration of strings in the sense that Benedick observes, has a more enigmatic relationship with affective response.

The process whereby a given element is positioned or understood within a different context can be thought of as recontextualization. Sampling is a ready example—Jem *recontextualizes* the Swingle Singers' performance. But an excerpt need not be quoted in a different piece for recontextualization to occur; in fact, the reiteration of a passage within an individual work is an even clearer example of recontextualization, and the one for which the term was originally coined by Dora Hanninen. Just as Borges's fictional reviewer judged Menard's work to be "almost infinitely richer" than the textually identical Cervantes's, the same could be said of many reprises in familiar repertoire (the end of Gotterdammerung, with the recurrence of the redemption motive; the end of the Goldberg Variations, with the repeat of the aria), where intervening context, or even perhaps the absence of intervening context, conspires to make something that is ostensibly the same sound very different. These are the musical equivalents of the cinematic gambit in *The Usual Suspects*, where the quotation at the beginning of the movie is made to carry a dramatically different resonance when repeated at the end: *The greatest trick the devil ever pulled was to convince the world he didn't exist.* Edward Cone puts so much stock in changing context, that he believes "in general, there is no such thing as true redundancy in music" (1968, p. 46). Yet as Kivy in *The Fine Art of Musical Repetition* protests: still, it repeats. There are important senses in which context reconfigures sound such that no repetition is truly redundant, but there are also senses in which we have to account for the fact that we do experience many reoccurrences as "repetition." It is this double function that Hanninen (2003) terms recontextualization. Repetitions are always repetitive in one sense, and divergent in another.

This fictional account of fluctuating impressions while listening to a telephone—a series of identical, acoustically undifferentiated rings—vividly illustrates the chasm that can emerge between acoustic repetitiveness and perceived transformation. It tells of a family huddled around a table, listening to the repeated peals of a phone call from their absent father.

We stayed at the table for another forty-five minutes, running our fingers around our empty bowls, pressing our thumb tips into the cracker plate and licking the crumbs off, lulled into a trance by the even tempo of the phone's ring, immobilized by the repetition, listening carefully, hoping it would never stop. He was somewhere, at some phone, in a phone booth, or sitting on the edge of a someone else's bed, drunk or sober, and it was loud and hot, or cold, and he was alone, or there were others, but every single ring brought him home, brought him right there before us. The tone of the ringing changed too, from desperate to accusatory to something sad and slow, then it was a heartbeat, then it was eternity—had always rung, would always ring—then it was the piercing bell of an alarm (Torres, 2011 p. 45).

The acoustic repetitions of the telephone's ring mingle with the fears, knowledge, and love of the absent father's family to generate a sense of wild fluctuations in the phenomenology of each superficially identical ring. The experience is not twofold in the sense that the acoustic repetition is recognized even while the subjective impressions change. Rather, the transforming perceptions seem to suffuse the sound itself, such that it actually seems to *be* different. A similar example can be identified in the acoustically undifferentiated clicks of a car's turn signal, which often seem to fall into a binary strong-weak pattern such that every other click sounds accented. Another example can be identified in the famous McGurk effect (McGurk & MacDonald, 1976), in which the syllable "ba" is pronounced over video of the lip movements for "ga"; cross modal interactions ensure that rather than sustaining an impression of incongruity, listeners actually *hear* a third syllable, "da." In all of these cases, the end result is a materially transformed *experience* of sound, rather than a mere cognition or theory *about* a sound.

This distinction between acoustic and perceived phenomena also underpins work in my lab on musical silence (Margulis, 2007a). In those studies, distinguishing between the acoustic phenomenon of silence and its perceptual correlate made it possible to illuminate the way context could reconfigure the same (empty) period such that it was rendered marvelously distinct and musical in experience. For example, context could cause listeners to misremember a pause as having occupied more or less time than it in reality did, or cause them to describe otherwise identical pauses as tense in one case and relaxed in another (depending on whether or not tonal closure had been reached before the silence's onset), or even cause them to fail to recognize that a silence had occurred at all.

This same framework, one that contrasts acoustic with perceived phenomena, can be useful in examining repetition. The "acoustic" part is more problematic in the case of repetition because although two silences of the same length can be acoustically identical in a recording, performers rarely execute two iterations of a passage such that they are fully acoustically equivalent. Unlike in electro-acoustic music, where technology affords literal reproduction, or certain styles where precise replication is highly prized aesthetically (such as the music of the Blackfoot in Montana and Alberta, where recordings made sixty years apart, in 1909 and 1968, were "*virtually identical* down to the very smallest of details" (Witmer, 1993, p. 243), or music for the Shakuhachi, a wind instrument in Japan (Lehmann, 2007), whose close replication from performance to performance Clarke (2005) attributes to the philosophy of Zen Buddhism), in most genres, acoustic identicalness is an abstraction not found in reality. Chapter 6 examines performed repetition more systematically; here it is sufficient to note that this book largely uses notated repetition as an imperfect but pragmatic proxy for acoustic repetition. Passages where pitches, durations, and notated timbral and dynamic levels repeat are treated as acoustic repetitions, although in reality, sub-tle qualities in microtiming, voicing, and dynamics distinguish the so-called rep-etitions from one another. This notation-centric conception of musical identity is well explored historically and philosophically in Lydia Goehr's *The Imaginary Museum of Musical Works* (2007), and is a conception that has seeped even into musical traditions that don't generally rely on notation. People recognize rendi-tions of *Happy Birthday* as such despite all manner of idiosyncrasies in execu-tion—not just idiosyncrasies in pitch, but also idiosyncrasies in tempo, rhythm, and articulation. Lidov describes this place where acoustic realities, subjective perceptions, and cultural norms collide:

> We know that musical repetitions we call identical may actually presup-pose a great deal of culturally determined listening and prior system-atization of materials. For example, in listening to a string quartet we will discount certain vagaries of interpretation as mistakes, if we notice them at all. Nevertheless, when we are dealing with conscious musical experience, repetition is one of the first and most solid elements of that experience, and we are still entitled to recognize repetition as holding a privileged status among formal devices on the basis of its least relative if not absolute concreteness (Lidov, 2004, p. 26).

## The Workings of Context

In a famous essay, Deleuze references Hume to the effect that "repetition changes nothing in the object repeated, but does change something in the mind which contemplates it" (2004, p. 70). Deleuze identifies repetition as a phenomenon particularly well-suited to exposing the elements that the mechanisms of perception bring to an experience over and above the elements that literally exist in the world; the gap between the identicalness of repetition that is "out there" and the kaleidoscopic, shifting percepts of it in subjective experience serve as a striking example of this topic of broad philosophical interest. What Deleuze calls "the imagination"—our perceptual capacities, broadly construed—draws novelty, the "difference" of the essay's title, from repetition, but also imbues repetition with its very repetitiveness, abstracting across time and space to select out this relationship between two entities. Since two iterations are never precisely repetitions in their deepest essence—they're composed of different atoms or occur at different time points—it is perception that abstracts both a relationship of shared identity and a relationship of difference.

At a minimum, a repeated element will sound different from its initial presentation by virtue of coming later and having been heard before. More subtly, it will sound different as a function of its position within the unfolding series of metric projection, a topic intriguingly explored in Hasty (1997). If one note functions as a beginning, the next might seem like a continuation—distinguishing the pitches phenomenologically, even if they look identical on the page. Even a string of repeated notes, then, sounds not like a series of undifferentiated hammer strokes, but rather like a hierarchically unfolding series of projections and realizations, such that each note in the sequence possesses different qualities— one might seem to start, one to continue, one to anticipate—simply by virtue of their succeeding one another in time. (The literature on subjective rhythmization explores a related phenomenon.) By duplicating surface content, repetition can draw attention toward these dynamic processes of projection, engaging listeners in the raw temporal processes of music.

Repetition need not be consciously identified to have marked effects on perception. When I teach Dido's Lament from the end of Purcell's *Dido and Aeneas* to university undergraduates, no one seems to be aware on first hearing of the ground bass's repetitions; once I explicitly point them out, however, everyone can usually agree that the endlessly looped descent contributed to some sense of fatality or doom. Although they didn't initially hear repetiveness, per se, they did hear certain expressive qualities that the repetitiveness engendered. In general, repetition functions with this kind of obliqueness; it gives rise to some impression that registers as an expressive quality, rather than as explicit recognition of repetitiveness. A classic example of the indirect workings of repetition can be found in the literature on the mere exposure effect (see Zajonc, 1968), a well-established finding that shows people prefer stimuli they've encountered before, even when they're unaware they've experienced them previously. People seem to gain increased processing fluency with each exposure, but in the absence of explicit knowledge that they've

*Figure 2.3*   Right- and left-branching repetitions. Reprinted with permission from Lerdahl and Jackendoff (1983), p. 184.

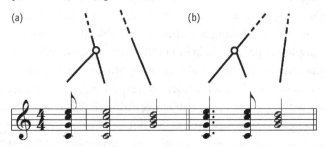

been reencountering the same stimulus, they misattribute this increased fluency to some positive quality of the stimulus itself (a phenomenon more fully explored in Chapter 5).

In *A Generative Theory of Tonal Music* (henceforth GTTM), Lerdahl and Jackendoff contemplate the status of the repetition of a single harmonic event, such as a chord. Schenkerian analysis might want to view such repetition as an embodiment of stasis. According to this reading, each iteration represents the same event at some background level of analysis, and no tensing or relaxing movement can occur between them. But Lerdahl and Jackendoff reject this view, noting, "it is impossible to hear absolute stasis, if only because events take place in time and hence form rhythmic relationships that produce tensing or relaxing events" (p. 184). Rather than serving to communicate stasis, they argue, repetition can serve to communicate either tension or relaxation, depending on the context.

They provide the example shown in Figure 2.3 to distinguish between "prolongational anticipation," where the first chord is heard as an anticipation of the second, relaxing into the downbeat, and "prolongational repetition, where the second chord is heard as a repetition of the first, and represents an intensification"—left and right-branching structures, respectively, within the prolongational tree theorized by GTTM. Indeed, this example, although it may at first glance seem trivial, highlights the difference carried by even the most immediate and literal of repetitions.

But Lerdahl and Jackendoff are careful to note that prolongational anticipations are only possible at local levels—"the opening tonic in a sonata-form movement," they claim, "is never heard as an anticipation of its restatement at the beginning of the recapitulation; rather, the beginning of the recapitulation is heard as a prolongational repetition of the opening.... Thus all large-scale prolongations are right branches" (p. 184–185). In this excerpt, Lerdahl and Jackendoff put forth a claim that repetition is experienced differently according to whether it occurs at a local or global level of the structure. But their strongest and most general claim is that in terms of the dynamics of musical motion, repetition always represents process rather than stasis; tension is always either building or receding across multiple iterations of the same material.

## Kinds of Difference

Repetition can occur at any level, of any entity, across any time-scale, within pieces, and between pieces. Some of these repetitions are more apparent to listeners, and some remain obscure. Repetition seems more identifiable the more the repeating element is perceived categorically. By categorical perception (cf. Harnad, 1987, and for a musical application, see Zbikowski, 2002), I mean the tendency to divide a continuous spectrum into discrete bins, such that a particular frequency, for example, is heard as a better- or worse-tuned A, or a particular wavelength is viewed as a more- or less-representative shade of blue. Pitch and duration are the musical characteristics most commonly understood to be perceived categorically. Although timbre might also qualify in some repertoires, in much of Western music timbre has been understood as a secondary sort of element, so that the repetition of a particular instrumentation accompanied by new pitches and durations seems less like a "repetition" than would a repetition of the same pitches and durations with a new instrumentation. Indeed, McAdams (1989) observes that transformations, such as variations, are most often (although not always) built on these dimensions. Some composers, György Ligeti for example, upend these norms and use textural and dynamic blocks as the principal compositional elements, a strategy that can shift impressions of what constitutes a repetition. His *Lux Aeterna* for 16 singers, for example, succeeds in elevating repetition of a particular timbral configuration to salience over repetition of particular pitches or durations. Although individual styles and pieces can surmount the tendency of pitch and duration to dominate the sense of what counts as repetition, the following discussion will focus on these dimensions because they are more commonly form-bearing in Western music.

Take, then, the smallest possible unit of repetition according to this scheme: the individual note. In the example from Mozart's C Minor Fantasy shown in Figure 2.4, the F#s needn't be repeated; it's easy to imagine an alternative where they've been replaced by a longer rest. The unnecessary repetition tunnels attention into the F#, such that when a D major chord enters underneath it, there's a sudden sense of expanse. It intensifies the sense of anacrusis, pointing attention at the downbeat of the next measure. It creates, paradoxically, a sense of muteness; after the repetition of the half cadence with its preceding gesture, and then the F# major chord, the insistence on the single note F# underscores

*Figure 2.4*  Mozart, Fantasy in C minor, mm. 24–27.

that we've reached the end of possible things to repeat, and this sense of having gotten stuck permits the D major harmony to enter as if from another realm.

Repetition of a single pitch is only noticeable, normally, when it is immediate, or almost immediate. Even in a simple tune like *Twinkle Twinkle Little Star*, the average listener probably wouldn't be aware that "twinkle" and "are" occupy the same pitch. Not only is pitch normally experienced relationally rather than in absolute terms, but it is also assimilated into gestures whose repetitions are much more recognizable than their component elements. For example, in a study where I had people press a button every time they heard something repeat, participants systematically missed repetitions of three- or four-note elements that repeated within changing eight- or ten-note gestures (Margulis, 2012). However, it is worth noting that repetitions that are not recognized can nevertheless play important roles in music perception. It has been observed that the Krumhansl Kessler tone profile (Kessler & Krumhansl, 1982), which tracks people's judgments of how well various scale degrees fit a tonal context, closely matches the typical distribution (raw frequency counts) of these scale degrees in tonal repertoire, suggesting that the raw frequency with which various pitches occur might contribute to the identification of key, even if these distributions aren't consciously available.

This example illustrates that to hear something as a repetition, a listener must first hear it as a *something*. In this way, repetition detection can be a useful methodology to investigate perceptual units: the segments of music that listeners treat as individual entities. As Hanninen puts it, "Repetition presumes recognition of a 'thing' that is repeated; to recognize this 'thing,' we must abstract the 'thing' from its context" (2003, p. 59). An individual note does not ordinarily rise to the level of "thingification;" only special treatment can promote it to this status.

John Rahn describes these perceptual processes in admirably precise language:

> Live repetition: how does it work? Let us ask a schema of bare repetition, A = {a, then-a}. The schema A itself is outside time, but it is a schema of a temporal experience: first I experience a, then then-a, which is a again. The context changes: a is not then-a.... A the global thing is the change of context. The change of context *constitutes* A and *reflects back into* each a... When we recognize a in then-a, we cognize a new the added context that makes a then-a, a new context that *is fused with* and *originally presented with* the a of then-a. In fact the a of then-a is secondary, derived, an abstraction from the primordially presented cognition of then-a. So recognition is derived from cognition: cognition gives then-a, then abstraction gives a-from-then-a, which we recognize as a. (But remember that recognition conditions cognition.) (Rahn, 1993, 50–51).

There's a lot to unpack in these ideas: first, repetition's role in segmentation, unit-definition, and "thingification" (according to Hanninen's scheme). To disagree slightly with Rahn, a *then-a* isn't strictly necessary to define an *a*, because other Gestalt-based cues (like proximity in pitch space or in time) or schema-based cues (if a segment matches a template in a particular style, or occupies a predicted span of time) can influence segmentation (Deliège, 1989, 2007; Krumhansl & Jusczyk, 1990; Krumhansl, 1996; Cambouropoulos, 2006). But if repetition does occur, it contributes to the definition of the segment as a relevant unit within the ongoing trajectory of the piece. Theorists in the Formenlehre tradition have identified this procedure as part of the basic strategy of thematic presentation in the Classical period; repetition shows the listener what should be considered the basic idea of a theme (Caplin, 1998). Second, Rahn implies that to identify a unit *a* out of its repetition within *then-a* necessarily involves a process of abstraction, or explicit cognizing, and third, he suggests that this recognition of *a* is inextricably linked with the larger context *A*, because it is

*Figure 2.5* Mozart, Piano Sonata in C, K. 330, I, mm. 1–9.

dependent on the existence of an *a* followed by a *then-a*. I would argue, however, that repetition can function more obliquely, guiding attention to different levels of the music, for example, without effecting explicit identification either of a unit *a*, or of the repetitive aspect of its larger context *A*.

In my 2012 study, discussed more extensively in Chapter 1, participants pressed buttons to indicate that something had repeated as short excerpts of classical music progressed. They heard each excerpt four times, performing the same repetition identification task during each presentation. For one particular type of repetition, there were no cases of correct identification in any of the four pieces, on any of the four repetitions. Repetitions of a smaller motivic element were never identified when they formed a part of a longer, more salient gesture that continued differently, even when the motivic elements were located in parallel positions within the larger units. Short motives of this type seemed to get assimilated into the larger units such that the higher-level contrast obscured the lower-level similarity.

Yet repetitions of shorter elements are salient in many other sorts of contexts. William Caplin has examined how the repetition of motives conspires to define the basic material of pieces in the classical style. Mozart's Piano Sonata in C K 330 (Figure 2.5), an example from his book, starts with an exact restatement of the basic idea, altered only by the addition of another repetition of the opening G.

This basic idea consists of a sort of tumble through an octave. It's possible to make sense of the immediate and nearly exact repetition in many ways (insistence, harmonic stasis, playfulness), but to me it mostly seems pleasant. It brings to the fore the particularly musical quality of metric directedness. (Other theorists and musicologists who have highlighted this often-overlooked variety of musical pleasure include Abbate, 2004—see especially p. 511—and Guck, 1996). As metric projections evolve, the high Gs, which were heard as a beginning in m. 1, possess a new element of continuation in m. 3. This transformation is subtly emphasized with the extra repetition of the G. Repetition often serves to elevate hypermeter, the larger-scale patterning of strong and weak beats, to an object of enjoyment and experience in and of itself. When the surface content merely repeats, the few things that do change—metric placement, for example—are rendered more salient. With a two-bar stretch foreordained, attention can shift even further into the future. In this way, repetition can function similarly to silence in some contexts, in the sense that they both relieve the burden of processing new information—in the case of repetition, by reproducing something already known, and in the case of silence, by removing all pitch content—so that some other thing can be attended to. The reduction of information at a particular level can form the basis for a host of metacommunicative functions, a topic explored in connection with the case of silence in Margulis (2007).

Repetition, however, frequently preserves the meter, whereas silence frequently disrupts it. In conversation, for example, repetition is sometimes inserted expressly to preserve the rhythm of the interaction. Johnstone (1987) analyzes classroom discourse in terms of this goal. When a chemistry teacher repeats some previous utterance—"mercury, so mercury"—while writing on the board, she preserves the rhythm of the ongoing discourse, when silence might have awkwardly disrupted it. The preservation of the governing rhythm is considered essential to successful communication (McGarva & Warner, 2003). Repetition is reassuring and unchallenging in a way that is quite opposite to silence—possessing less contrast with the surrounding context, it is simply less dramatically marked.

GTTM identifies parallelism as an important factor in the establishment of grouping structure, metric structure, time-span reduction, and prolongational reduction. Essentially, these rules capture the intuition that we try as much as possible to hear repeated material as a recurrence of the same "thing." If the same sequence of pitches and durations recurs, for example, we want it to start a group if the previous iteration started a group, and to initiate a metric downbeat if the first iteration did, and so on and so forth. All of the features that make a musical thing a "thing," we want to see preserved.

When confronted with repetitions that fail to conform to the principles Lerdahl and Jackendoff outline, listeners may simply find themselves unable to

*Figure 2.6* Haydn, Sonata No. 41 in A Major, Hob. XVI/26, II, mm. 1-20.

identify the occurrences as repetitions at all. For example, participants in my study on repetition detection (Margulis, 2012) failed to register m. 11 as a rep- etition of m. 10 when exposed to the passage shown in Figure 2.6, despite that they follow immediately on each other's heels within the amusing structure of the movement, according to which the second part restates the first in retro- grade. What explains the participants' failure to identify this repetition when other immediately successive repetitions of measure-length units (such as the ones in mm. 8 and 9) were identified without problem? Perhaps the acoustic differentiation between the performance of m. 10 and the performance of m. 11

was greater—performers tend to slow down at the end of phrases (m. 10), for example, but not at their beginnings (m. 11). But an alternative, if related, explanation simply observes that the notes in m. 10 serve as an ending thing, but the notes in m. 11 serve as a beginning thing. According to this explanation, syntactic function is so salient that the beginning-end distinction makes m.10 and m.11, for all intents, separate "things" despite their surface similarity.

Repetition tends to reify a passage—to set it apart from the surrounding context as a "thing" to be mused on, abstractly considered, and conceptualized as a unit. Rahn (1993) observes that the quality of being a musical "thing" generally depends on repetition, as "learning to be a musician always involves learning to repeat sounds, or more precisely, to repeat in a new sound some quality or complex of qualities heard in some previous sound.... Music, like science, is grounded on the repeatable experience" (p. 49). Rahn finds a paradox in this "thingifying," whereby each new repetition embodies both the abstraction of this "thing" as well as the totality of its new context.

Rahn sees constant enrichment, constant recontextualizing, as the core of our appetite for repetition in music. But this account leaves unexplained why this pleasure is concentrated in the art of music, and does not extend to the same degree to, say, literature. This is where, I would suggest, the limits of the capacity to abstract about music play a role. When a "thing" is communicated in speech, it is normally separable from the precise words used to describe it. For example, I could say: "The incumbent lost the election." Or, "The incumbent didn't get elected." Or, "People voted the incumbent out." Two special things seem to me to be the case. Number 1: we derive more or less the same information from these three statements. If asked to repeat the information, we might present it in one of the other forms than the one in which we originally heard it. The content seems separable from the vessel in which it was delivered. Number 2: This content is capable of being apprehended at a different time scale than the one offered by the spoken text. It takes a certain amount of time to say "The incumbent lost the election," but it does not take precisely this amount of time to reflect on this fact. To the contrary, this fact can be apprehended in a moment—it can be taken as an image, an atemporal visual representation of a despondent candidate, for example.

Neither of these characteristics holds for melody. The closest thing to Number 1—deriving more or less the same information from three differently worded statements—might be variations, but it's clear that varying a theme changes its content in a way that varying the wording of a fact does not. And the existence of earworms speaks against Number 2—once a melody gets going in your head, even involuntarily, it tends to make its way to a cadence rather relentlessly, occupying precisely the amount of time it would take to actually hear that melody performed. To return to *Twinkle Twinkle Little Star*, if I asked you to imagine the tones on which "what you" are sung, you probably have to start at "Twinkle" and go through note by note until you get to "what you." Now I want to know when this note recurs. You'd probably have to sing still further, until you got to "high." You can't duck in and out of music, midphrase—you have to mentally "sing through" until you get to the spot you want. This apparent fact, that music cannot be retrospectively grasped without a mental or actual replay, could serve as a foundation on which both the excessive use of and excessive appetite for musical repetition might be understood.

In Figure 2.7, a Tambourin by Rameau, repetitions establish a basic unit of two-bars size, displaced by a half measure with respect to the meter. Mm. 3 and 4 repeat the rhythm of mm. 1 and 2, but thereafter literal repeats take over. Mm. 5 and 6 repeat mm. 1 and 2. Mm. 7 and 8 complete the parallel period by repeating mm. 3 and 4, but adjusting the cadence so it ends on the tonic. Mm. 9 and 10 present a new unit that preserves the established rhythm. Mm. 11 and 12 repeat this unit verbatim. These units (9-10 and 11-12) repeat a salient element in the melody—an appoggiatura-resolution figure—that lasts half a measure, drawing attention closer to the temporal surface. This focus is rewarded when measure 13, 14, and 15 narrow the dominant window of repetition from 2 measures to 1. The resulting perceived acceleration leads back into the restatement of the opening, which widens the temporal plane to 8 measures.

As this example illustrates, one important function of repetition is its capacity to influence the unit understood to be of concern. When the size of the repeating unit changes, from half a measure to 8 bars, attention can burrow in and then widen out, so that there's almost an impression of distance—things seem close when the repeating unit is small, and more distant when the repeating unit is large (cf. Feld, 2005). A smaller repeating unit can create a more intense impression, as if the music were bombarding you again and again from close proximity, but when the repeating unit is large, a broader landscape becomes apparent. During a longer repeat, the barrage of new stimuli retreats for a moment, allowing the listener to step back and survey her musical surroundings. Without new material to process, she can reflect on what happened previously or what might happen much further down the road. By modulating subjective impressions of landscape and distance, repetition can play an important role in the expressive trajectory or narrative of a piece.

The Rameau example also illustrates the obvious but important fact that repetition can occur proximally—when the repetition immediately succeeds its model—or distally—when something different intervenes between a model and its repetition (Meyer, 1973 terms the latter case "return"). The one-measure descents are proximal—they occur one after another, in immediate succession—but the restatement of the opening period in m. 17 occurs after eight bars of contrasting material. It is distal repetitions of this type that are often thought

*Figure 2.7* Rameau, Tambourin, mm. 1-29.

to be important in defining a piece's form, unlike immediate repetitions of the sort that could be notated with repeat signs, which have a more checkered reception history.

Moving out from notes and motives, repetition also often occurs at the level of the phrase, and frequently involves a change of cadence. Consider the opening of *Wilder Reiter* (Wild Rider) from Schumann's Op. 68, a typical parallel period in which the first phrase is altered its second time around to make the cadence more conclusive. In my experience, this cadential alteration fuses the phrases together such that it is hard to remember one of the versions as canonical—rather than thinking of "this four-bar phrase," one tends to think of "this eight-bar period"; I would hypothesize that earworms from this piece would be more likely to cycle through mm. 1-8 as a single loop, rather than mm. 1-4 or 5-8. The consequent in this excerpt sounds so much like a continuation of the first phrase, rather than a "starting again" of it, that its repetitive nature is somewhat obscured. When it occurs on the repeat, the downbeat character of the opening of the phrase has been transformed to acquire an afterbeat, continuative quality that makes it more difficult to recognize as "the same." Moreover, the new cadence seems to be implied already, so that at the start of the repeat, I feel it leading inextricably to the tonic, despite that the only model I know went to the dominant. This "going-to-the-tonic"-ness also transforms the sound of the repeat, even its opening, such that although I can identify the repetition involved, I do not expressly experience it as a "repeat." Lidov (2004) observes that "phrases which are repeated first with a dominant and then with a tonic ending...provide the most natural expositions of the tonic-dominant opposition as an abstract principle" (p. 26); in the absence of other changes, the cadential difference comes to the fore.

Contrast this with the opening of another piece from the same collection, Schumann's *Frohlicher Landmann* (The Happy Farmer). Because the opening four bars repeat without alteration, they possess a stable identity in and of themselves, and don't fuse together into an inevitable eight-bar unit as strongly as in the case of the period. It's possible to imagine the theme, and stop after four bars. Additionally, because these measures repeat exactly, the second statement sounds less like a continuation, and more like an immediate restatement of the opening. The downbeat quality of the first measure is much more strongly preserved, to my ears, and the passage reads like a phrase and then an affirmation of the phrase, rather than like a single larger subject. Schumann uses exact repeats with some frequency at the start of pieces from this collection, perhaps partly to help passages that are otherwise quite simple or indistinct rise to the level of a theme.

Consider No. 18 from the collection, *Schnitterliedchen* (The Reaper's Song). It starts with a melody made up of lilting triplets set against a C major drone.

Nothing of harmonic importance "happens," and the surface rhythm consists almost entirely of eighth-note triplets, but there is some rhythmic interest at the next metric level, where movement to F in the alto and an accented statement of the drone, tied past the downbeat of the next measure, articulates a syncopation-like emphasis on the second beat of the measure. When these four bars are immediately restated, and then again eight bars later (an interlude which is itself composed of four bars that repeat), the goal is clearly pleasure, not the transmission of information. The repetitions are *involving*—like a call and response, they trace out a musical path and then re-present it for the listener to follow. Musical repetitions on the level of the phrase often seem like something just short of an invitation for the listener to sing along (dismaying, perhaps, in the case of the example titled Reaper's Song).

After the opening section, the texture thins to a single voice and arpeggiates alternating subdominant and tonic chords in continuous eighth-note triplets. Not only is the four-measure unit immediately repeated, but also within that unit, the second two measures almost entirely repeat the first two. There could hardly be less content.

The most distinctive part of the passage is the melodic movement from D to C, with the D appearing first as an unprepared upper neighbor against IV and again at the same metric point (but within the context of a different contour) against I. The leap between the preceding note and the D can be understood as a small-scale grouping boundary, and the contour of the melody over the I chord makes this boundary more prominent than in the measures articulating the IV chord. This difference creates a kind of rhythmic curving, a type of ambiguity and play that the statements and restatements seem to accentuate. With repetition, the measures come to sound more subtle to me, not less, as their grouping ambiguity unfolds. Multiple repetitions of apparently simple things tend to increasingly involve the listener with any shading, complexity, or rehearing the passage can sustain.

## Part Repeats

A third form of repetition, found midway between recurrences of individual gestures, explored above, and the replay of entire pieces, explored in Chapter 5, is the repetition of large sections. Such repetitions can be immediate, as in the case of a repeated exposition in sonata form, or gapped, as in the case of a repetition of the theme in a rondo form. Hepokoski and Darcy (2006) observe that the earliest norm in eighteenth-century sonata form was to enclose both the exposition and the development-recapitulation in repeat signs. By 1790, it had become rare to repeat the second part, and not uncommon to omit the exposition repeat, especially in lighter works and overtures. For music written after this time, Hepokoski and Darcy claim, repeating the development-recapitulation, or failing to repeat the exposition in a serious work, is "exceptional and need[s] to be considered as [a] consciously expressive choice" (p. 20). Although a section repeat from a sonata written in 1765 might differ expressively from one written in 1800, the majority of contemporary listeners likely lack appreciation for the distinction, making the expressivity of the decision harder to convey.

Conventional part repeats, Hepokoski and Darcy explain, embody ideals of balance.

> The emphatically architectural construction calls attention to the genre's ordered formality... One of the structure's implications would have been that this culture [Enlightenment culture] had devised a rational, balanced means to shape and contain the fluid, raw, elemental power of music. By extension, the process probably also represented the controlling or harnessing of those impulsive, instinctive, libidinal, or 'uncivilized' elements within ourselves. (p. 21).

Hepokoski and Darcy explicitly argue against the viewpoint articulated in the Green (1979) textbook on form—that part repetitions are " of little significance in formal analysis" (p. 82)—claiming instead that "repeat signs are never insignificant" (p. 21). But precisely what significance they might carry is unclear. They reject the Schenkerian view that some repeats are important because of their role in the unfolding of a central line, and emphasize the primary role of section repeats as "generic identifiers" (p. 21). They warn against omitting repeats on the basis of the misapplication of later nineteenth-century perspectives, which tend to assume that "all unaltered repetition [is] an aesthetic error. It may be... that saying the same thing twice was what the composer had in mind" (p. 21).

Indeed, the aesthetics of the section repeat is a persistently unresolved issue. One need only look to the 1882–83 edition of the Proceedings of the Royal Musical Association to find Ferdinand Praeger raging against the practice, as chronicled in Chapter 1. A hundred years earlier, Andre-Ernest Modeste Grétry, a composer of comic opera, voiced almost the same objections as Praeger:

> A sonata is a discourse. What would one think of a man who, after cutting his discourse in two, would repeat each half? (For example) "I went to your home this morning; yes, I went to your home this morning, in order to discuss some business with you; in order to discuss some business with you." That is just about the effect that repeats in music have on me (Grétry, 1789, quoted in Broyles, 1980, p. 343).

But nineteenth-century theorist and composer Ebenezer Prout speaks for the opposition:

> If you hear an orator speak, or if you hear the first act of a drama, it is in a language intelligible to all; every word conveys a distinct and definite impression at once. There is no occasion to repeat that; you know perfectly well the first time what the orator has said; but music is a much more vague and indefinite language—it does not speak to us, at least to me, with the same distinctness and directness as a written language. If anybody asked me what I supposed a Beethoven Sonata meant, I could not put it into words to save my life; no more could most of you, although you were fully sensible of the charm of it. But if you hear a new work there is this advantage to be obtained of hearing it twice: the ideas are much less distinctive in the language of music than of speech, and, therefore, there is more gained by familiarity with them (Praeger, 1882-83, p. 6-7).

The axis along which both of their arguments turn is a comparison with language. Grétry aspires for music to embody the same constraints and affordances as speech. In arguing the opposite position, Prout nevertheless adopts similar aspirations. Like Grétry, he views music as a kind of language, albeit one whose semantic indeterminacy makes repetition necessary.

These shifting views on repetition's role in music were associated with shifting compositional practice. Cole (1969) identifies a sudden increase in the usage of rondo forms after 1773, an increase roughly contemporaneous with the decline in immediate section repeats of the sort previously found in binary forms, as chronicled by Broyles (1980). It is clear that repetition that is not immediate has a different role in historical and aesthetic theories and practices of music; Sisman (1993) argues that the two—immediate versus gapped repetition—should even be described with different terms. The question of the different functions and perceptions such repetitions afford may be of greatest interest to the enterprise at hand. In the case of an immediate repeat, for example, the music itself often makes little acknowledgment of the connection between the section and its repeated versions—it is unclear how the two are meant to relate, or whether the repetition should be acknowledged and evaluated from the perspective of formal analysis. In a movement like a rondo, however, the music often makes explicit reference to the fact that the listener has become familiar with the theme. For example, in the last movement of Beethoven's Piano Sonata Op. 13, the return is prefaced by an elaborate dominant prolongation, scalar flourish, and fermata, all of which serve to foreshadow and articulate the impending repetition. Because the listener knows how the theme starts, she can be teased with elements of its opening motives.

But it is not only the degree to which the repetitions are absorbed into the syntactic and formal structure that makes the gapped repetitions of a rondo seem different from the part repetition in binary forms; it is also the temporal separation of the recurrences. The passage of time at different magnitudes (minutes or even days or years, such as might occur between hearings of a familiar song) can transform the way repetition works—an empirical issue that remains largely unexplored.

Richard Middleton (2006), one of the few writers to attempt to confront the pleasure of musical repetition head-on, places each instance of repetition on a spectrum ranging from "musematic"—the immediate repetition of short elements—to "discursive," the kind of larger-scale section repeats just discussed. Garcia (2005) grounds the pleasure of musematic repetition in the process of listening, of forging an individual attentional path through the looping elements.

> A persistently-looping, dense collection of riffs provides a dense layering of textures without pre-determining the listener's path of focus. In this manner, a listener is able to construct his/her own process(es) of attention, creating a unique sonic pathway and manifesting a form of mastery over the ordering of these looping elements...looping allows the listener to plot pathways between these points of attention, mapping out a landscape of shifting creation pleasure while prolonging the process pleasure of an ever-changing same (Garcia, 2005).

*Process pleasure,* then, can be located in the repetitive unfolding of the musical surface, but it is precisely and paradoxically this repetitiveness that affords a separate *creation pleasure* in the mind of the listener, who can now inventively connect different time points within the stimulus to generate novel, changing experiences.

Rebecca Leydon (2002) summarizes Middleton's position in this way: "Middleton argues that a purely musematic strategy will achieve a kind of 'psychic resonance' for listeners, while discursive strategies will require more of an '*investment* of energy' *from* listeners. His account of discursive structures as 'requiring energy' intersects with Cumming's account of syntax as the site of intentionality." She develops this perspective into a theory about repetition's role in the construction of musical subjectivity, particularly in repertoires that could be described as minimalist:

> The creation of internal contrasts between musematic and discursive structures is one way that repetitive music can forge particular subjective identities. If the degree of "volitional will" of the musical subject is correlated with the sense of hierarchical organization, then the features

of a particular hierarchy, such as its depth or granularity, will afford and constrain the musical subject's identity in particular ways. Music that confounds hierarchic listening altogether because of a preponderance of undifferentiated "riffs" may suggest a "will-less" or "automatized" subject. Hierarchies that are shallow, with few levels, may suggest a tentative volitional state. In more highly stratified textures with differentiated levels of musematic and discursive parsing, the subject may be understood as more "willful," provided the strata are perceived as hierarchically interlocked. Particularly deep or complex hierarchies or situations in which metrical relationships between figure and ground are ambiguous may suggest a split subject or a plurality of willful subjects (Leydon, 2002).

Lidov (2004) similarly acknowledges a spectrum of functions for repetition—noting that while it often serves to delineate and segment, it can also "create a hypnotic continuity which is opposite in its effect to segmentation. Meyer has noted that repetition increases tension, but that when sufficiently prolonged, the tension yields to saturation, which has its own expressive values (1956, p. 136, 152)" (p. 29). Part of the issue is clearly the way that functions and responses change as repetitions continue—threefold repetition (when the punchline normally appears in American jokes—see Zinoman, 2012) is different from twofold, but six times is different yet again, and thirty times still more different. From a discursive perspective, a single repetition is enough to establish a pattern, but from a musematic perspective, many more may be desirable. Perceptual changes across repetitions are often nonlinear—enjoyment, for example, seems to peak after a moderate number of repetitions, but decrease thereafter—a topic explored in Chapter 5.

Lidov contrasts formative repetition, which is "conventional and logical and does not attract attention…[it] defines the units of a musical work" (p. 30) with focal repetition, "which is a self-referential type that focuses attention on the fact of repetition, per se" (p. 29). He argues that repetitions that cross "larger segmental boundaries" are necessarily focal, because they are so "striking."

Aside from boundary crossing, another factor that can turn repetition focal is three-or-fourfold repetition—repetition that extends beyond a model and its copy. Focal repetitions, for Lidov, "have a strong power to evoke the feelings of situations typified by repetition: activities that go on and on, rituals, compulsive actions, getting stuck 'in a rut,' emphatically accented speech, dancing, or laughing," by virtue of drawing attention to the act of repetition itself. When repetition extends beyond the three-or-four mark, Lidov postulates that it acquires a new function, that of "textural repetition" and "cancels out its own claim on our attention and thereby refers our focus elsewhere, to another voice or to a changing aspect" (p. 35).

It is interesting that a rudimentary form of some of the distinctions made here can be found in Praeger's 1882-83 tirade against part repeats: "My contention [Praeger clarifies] does not apply to rhythmical compositions—e.g., dances, marches, etc. The case stands entirely different here. In rhythmical compositions of this class, the music itself holds but a subordinate position. It is but the supporting accompaniment of rhythmical evolutions, supplying the necessary and unchanging accents of the physical movements" (p. 2). Despite the general rigidity of his argument, Praeger finds room to acknowledge that repetition can have entirely different functions depending on the style and aesthetic aims at hand. It is clear that empirical studies of repetition in music must carefully acknowledge and consider the style within which the stimuli are situated. It would be fascinating to investigate how listeners without explicit knowledge about a style or its history abstract different categories and perceive repetition differently. What are the musical cues that encourage a kinetic response to a particular instance of repetition, but a syntactic response to another?

It is self-evident that not only different pieces but also different styles and genres feature different degrees of repetition. For example, DeVoto (2004) observes of Debussy that "the direct repetition of phrases in succession" is "the single outstanding characteristic of form in all of his [Debussy's] works" and estimates that "between 60 and 70 percent of all phrases in Debussy are repeated in this way, a far higher percentage, it seems to me, than in any other composer" (p. 188). DeVoto goes on to marvel at the skill with which Debussy renders these repetitions nonobvious. How do different composers in different periods and different styles employ repetition differently? What conditions conspire to make some of these repetitions more salient than others? The former concern is a domain for which corpus-based analysis could prove particularly useful. We recognize that Reich is more repetitive than Beethoven, but to what degree and in what respect? What about Beethoven versus Schubert? Does the degree of internal repetition within a piece affect how fast enjoyment peaks over repeated listening, and how quickly song fatigue sets in? Are pieces consistently more repetitive toward the beginning, in the presentation phase of the material, or toward the end, in the recapitulatory phase (see Ollen and Huron, 2004)? Are there typical syntactic repetition structures, of the sort Lidov theorizes? These are all questions that would be relatively easy to answer with the quantitative analysis of data that already exist in the form of scores.

It is important not to overestimate the role that repetition might play in defining musical styles and syntaxes. Semioticians such as Jean-Jacques Nattiez and Nicolas Ruwet have attempted to discard the constructs of theory and rebuild an understanding of various musical styles from the ground up, through the cataloguing of different repetitive elements and their hierarchic position, establishing a more objective basis for the workings of musical structure. But even Ruwet himself acknowledged that the abstractions that emerge in cultural descriptions of music are not reconstructable through this supposedly neutral form of repetition analysis (Ruwet, 1975).

## Repetition and Source Segregation

One enterprise in which repetition may play a defining role, however, is source separation—an old and important problem in auditory perception. Given that sound waves strike the eardrum as composite waveforms, representing the sum of the waveforms created by individual sound sources (such as a friend's voice, the hum of the air conditioner, the voice of a person at a nearby table), how does the brain separate out the individual sources from the audio mixture? Theoretically, there are an infinite number of ways to decompose a composite waveform into its possible contributing components, but practically, the brain uses Gestalt-like principles and knowledge about the real world to perform these calculations rapidly and with amazing accuracy (Bregman, 1994). With seeming effortlessness, we listen to our friend's voice across the table, experiencing it as entirely individuated from the surrounding buzz, despite that in reality all of these sounds hit our ears together as a mixture.

A similar problem applies when listening to music. When are the trombones heard as their own distinct source and when do they seem to blend with the rest of the orchestra? In pop music, there is often a clear perceptual separation between the melody and the accompaniment; listeners have no trouble identifying the line with which they should sing along and relegating other sound to the background. Rafii and Pardo (2011, 2012) observed that if a computer were able to automatically separate the melody from the accompaniment in an audio file, it would open up new technologies ranging from karaoke applications to singer identification. They suggest that since many pop songs are based on a varying melody pitched against a repeating accompaniment, the detection of periodicities in the signal could help separate foreground from background. They term this technique "REpeating Pattern Extraction Technique (REPET)."

Indeed, Volk and van Kranenburg (2012) found that the repetition of short characteristic motifs was the feature most computationally relevant in categorizing Dutch folk songs into tune families. These small-scale repeating elements were more relevant to categorization than similarity within global features, such as melodic contour. Like Pardo and colleagues, Volk and colleagues exploit this kind of repetition detection in the generation of algorithms for Music Information Retrieval.

Although the use of repetition detection in source separation might seem to be an expedient technique more relevant to computer systems than to human cognition, behavioral evidence suggests that people do in fact use the detection of repeating patterns in auditory stream segregation (McDermott, Wrobleski & Oxenham, 2011). Specifically, McDermott and colleagues found that a newly generated sound impossible to detect within a single mixture could be identified if it recurred more than once within different mixtures. Distinct from many other cues in source segregation, this mechanism "does not require prior knowledge of sound characteristics" (p. 191). Repetition, in other words, can teach a listener how to hear a sound, in the absence of any explicit information. It is this ear-guiding quality of repetition that makes it so useful as a musical technique.

# 3

## Attention, Temporality, and Music that Repeats Itself

Poetry and Eloquence, it has accordingly been often observed, produce
their effect always by a connected variety and succession of different
thoughts and ideas: but Music frequently produces its effects by a
repetition of the same idea; and the same sense expressed in the same,
or nearly the same, combination of sounds, though at first perhaps it
may make scarce any impression upon us, yet, by being repeated again
and again, it comes at last gradually, and by little and little, to move,
to agitate, and to transport us.

—Adam Smith, 1795

To this point, musical repetition has been viewed as a particular kind of *object*.
But it can also be viewed as a particular kind of *behavior*. Some examples: hit-
ting the repeat button in iTunes, cycling through the same CD again and again
in your car, revisiting the concert of a favorite performer every night he's in
town. All of these instances represent repetitive behaviors related to listening.
Musical repetition can also be understood as a consequence of behaviors related
to composing. According to this perspective, in-score repetitions are traces of
a compositional act, artifacts of a composer's conscious or unconscious choice
to use repetitive structures in her work. In some collaborative, participatory
kinds of music making where the lines between composer and listener blur, the
use of repetition is both a kind of performative and a kind of receptive act, a
choice both to repeat and to relisten. In all of these cases, receptive or performative, when repetition is recast as behavior, questions about musical repetition
become questions about repetition-related acts. Consequently, the psychology
of other sorts of repetition-related acts can be brought to bear on the psychology
of musical repetition.

Repetitive or repetition-seeking behaviors can fall within scopes broadly construed as normal or pathological. The former category might include ritual, trance, habit, and childhood play; and the latter might include addiction, obsessive-compulsive disorder, echolalia and echopraxia (the mimicking of others' vocalizations and movements) as they sometimes present in autism, schizophrenia, Tourette syndrome, and perseveration, defined as the involuntary and prolonged maintenance of an activity—a condition that sometimes emerges after right hemisphere damage. Repetitive behavior disorders are understudied in comparison to other psychiatric conditions such as mood and anxiety disorders (Stein, Christenson & Hollander, 1999), despite that their prevalence rates match or exceed those for better-studied conditions (Woods, Miltenberger & Flach 1996). This chapter examines the existing literature in an attempt to understand the general psychological mechanisms that might drive the prevalence of repetition in the musical domain.

## Ritual

Humans engage in a wide range of ritualized behavior, from family rituals surrounding bedtime or dinner to highly formalized religious and cultural rituals involving large groups of people. Anthropologists, who study ritualistic behavior in people, and ethologists, who study it in animals, generally define ritual as collective action that is repetitive, scripted, and stereotypic. Psychologists, on the other hand, have tended to define it in terms of the pathologically repetitive behaviors that arise in conditions such as obsessive-compulsive disorder. Boyer and Liénard (2006) observe that normal, nonpathological ritualization emerges during certain stages of childhood development, but psychologists have paid little attention to it, despite that understanding this normative occurrence might help illuminate its pathological counterpart.

Regardless of its etiology, ritualized behavior shares certain features: it tends to be compulsory and high-cost (consuming of time or resources). It tends to be rigid, valuing precise adherence to the details of past performances. It entails goal-demoted behavior—action sequences that are drawn from the typical repertoire, but reenacted outside the context of their ordinary use. Ritual involves a highly unusual degree of internal repetition and redundancy, and a restricted range of topical themes (Boyer and Liénard, 2006). Anthropologist Roy Rappaport (1999) views ritual as a critical index of a person's internal state and intentions, a way of enacting—literally placing into action—beliefs and commitments that language might make subject to dissemblance. I might claim, for example, that I'm a dedicated Catholic or a devoted Jew, but if I spent hours in recitation of the rosary or in prayer at the Western Wall, I would have substantially strengthened my case. One purpose of ritual, then, is to manifest publicly some subjective, internal qualities of self. Another purpose, chronicled by psychologist Matt Rossano (2012), is to transmit social norms. This transmission often takes place with the full emotional force of group-synchronized behavior (see McNeill, 1995). Wiltermuth and Heath (2009) experimentally manipulated whether or not subjects participated in a ritual-like activity before observing their performance in an economic game that involved the option of extending trust and cooperation to co-players. Subjects who had participated in ritual-like motor behavior played the game more trustingly and cooperatively than their counterparts who hadn't, reinforcing the notion that ritual actions encourage prosocial norm following.

Music, like ritual, emancipates things (in this case, sounds) away from their ordinary, goal-directed purposes, and, like ritual, often involves relatively strict replication (as in individual performances of Bruckner's Ninth Symphony or Leonard Cohen's *Hallelujah*), as well as high levels of internal repetition and redundancy. This similarity argues for a common purpose, or perhaps a common origin, between the two. Indeed, in three key areas, ritual and music have been hypothesized to serve similar ends: to foster prosocial normal following and strengthen social bonds (studies have shown that music can promote the release of oxytocin, a hormone related to bonding that is also released during breastfeeding and sex; Freeman, 1995; Nilsson, 2009); to shape and publicly reveal personal identity (musical interest peaks in adolescence, when the enterprise of finding and solidifying a social identity is most intense; North and Hargreaves, 1999); and to unleash the euphoria of joint, synchronized movement (Koelsch, 2010).

These commonalities suggest that scholarship on repetition in ritual might help shed light on the role of repetition in music. Repetition has been understood to serve the process of goal-demotion in ritual contexts. If a ritual washing, for example, involves excessively repeated gestures of wiping, gestures which are themselves repeated on the already-clean object during the next day's performance, then the fact that these gestures lack an everyday, pragmatic goal—like actual cleaning—is significantly underscored. Attention is drawn instead to the movements themselves. Since close observation of movements often involves mental simulation of them, this new focal point aids in the generation of a sense that the actions are virtually shared. The shift in attention itself can elicit a sense of profundity, sacredness, or transcendence, as everyday goals are set aside, and new insights and perceptions are allowed to emerge. Moreover, as carefully controlled and replicated motor movements never happen by accident, the deliberate repetition powerfully signals intentionality, revealing to the external world the internal commitment of the participant. By following rules strictly and attempting to reproduce past enactments as closely as possible, the participant also persuasively manifests the presence of an invisible social community, made evident by its impact on the diligent actions of the participant.

Many instances of musical repetition can be understood to achieve similar ends through similar means. Goal demotion, for example, can be promoted in various ways by musical repetition. The very act of repeating a passage in the first place emphasizes a certain nonteleological attitude, intimating that something within the sound itself, rather than an aim toward which things are driving, should be the focus of attention. And when a passage with a certain syntactic function is repeated—a drive toward the final tonic, for example—the effect is not only to delay the musical goal but also to highlight the expressive function of the passage in question, beyond its basic syntactic role.

Schubert often repeats passages an unusual number of times, and at unorthodox places within the form, leading critics such as Donald Tovey (1927) to question whether Schubert is technically capable of handling large-scale musical structures (an attitude that reflects the tradition of skepticism toward repetition). But others, including Theodor Adorno (1928/2009) and Scott Burnham (2005) have examined Schubert's repetitive practice with an ear for its powerful aesthetic effects. In an analysis of repetition within the second theme of Schubert's String Quartet in G Major, Op. 161, Burnham remarks on the ritualistic repetition of the melody, which is restated verbatim by each of the players, starting with the first violin, and moving successively through the second violin, viola, and cello. He points to "a sense of singularity here, a kind of self-sufficiency, an intensive coherence that does not necessarily point beyond itself. What to do with such a singularity? Repeat it" (Burnham, 2005, p. 33). Burnham's account highlights several ritual-like aspects: the rugged intentionality implied by the highly controlled repetitions, the almost palpable sense of a subjectivity reaching out to gather listeners in, and the goal-demotion away from syntactic function and toward the very "surface materiality" of the tune.

Goal demotion can operate in a manner even more directly evocative of ritual when music repeatedly samples or mimics a real-world sound, such as the infant squeals in Aaliyah's *Are You That Somebody*, the gunshots and cash register clanks in M.I.A.'s *Paper Planes*, the coppery metal clangs in Caribou's *Bowls*, or the cash register noises in Pink Floyd's *Money*. In each of these cases, the repetition musicalizes the samples—shedding them of their real-world associations, functions, and goals, and allowing their rhythmic and melodic qualities to rise to the foreground. To be sure, just as ritual washing retains the semantic reference of cleansing, all of these examples explicitly point to real-world actions and objects even as they work to demote their ordinary functional context, but this dual resonance marks another connection between the effect of repetition in music and in ritual.

Boyer and Liénard (2006) identify during ritual "a special attentional state that focuses on low-level properties of...actions. The action-flow is parsed in smaller units than is usually the case" (p. 601). Psychologist Jeffrey Zacks and his colleagues have examined the ways people normally parse continuous experience into a sequence of events, identifying three basic levels of representation: gestures (on the order of a few seconds), behavioral episodes (longer events, such as taking a shower or tying your shoes), and scripts (extended phenomena, such as dining at a restaurant or attending a party). People tend to spontaneously recall events at the middle level, the same level that it is most natural to describe in terms of goals (Zacks et al., 2001); in fact, an excessive focus on events at the lower, gestural level can indicate pathologies such as frontal lobe damage or schizophrenia (Janata & Grafton, 2003). Boyer and Liénard note, however, that ritual expressly drives attention down to this level, resulting, they claim, in an overload of working memory that induces a special mental state. When the mid-level of representation, at which gestures are connected into goals and chunks, is suppressed, the information going into working memory is much more fragmented and challenging to encode (Zalla et al., 2004). Repetition can drive attention down toward levels of nuance, microstructure, and expressive timing: another point of contact between repetition in music and in ritual.

Just as the repetition in ritual can powerfully communicate human intentionality, giving the impression that a careful order has been imposed on the otherwise entropic world, studies have shown that repetition in music can be received as a kind of handprint of human intention. In my recent study (Margulis, 2013), more thoroughly discussed in Chapter 1, participants consistently rated the modified excerpts as more likely to have been crafted by a human artist, suggesting that the mere insertion of repetition can create an impression of intentionality.

Repetition can evoke not only the solitary hand of the individual artist, but also the collective hands of a community or social group. Just as repeating rituals with careful adherence to a set of rules reveals the invisible eyes of the group of people who've generated and stewarded the tradition across time and place, so can repeating musical acts—especially when they involve the coordinated effort of large groups of people, like a symphony orchestra—connect the present moment to thousands of previous moments and to the people who have made them possible and shared their sense of value. Repetition works to draw out the signature of the individual as well as his or her connection to the surrounding community.

Turning from anthropology to ethology, the process of ritualization in animals similarly involves gestural elements forming a part of a larger goal-directed action, simplified and taken out of context to communicate something to another animal—often, availability for mating. In their ritualized form, these abstracted gestures are often exaggerated and performed in rhythmic repetition (Morris, 1957).

Dissanayake (2006) draws compelling parallels among animal ritualizations, rituals in human culture, and musical practice, theorizing a shared evolutionary origin. She observes that in many cultures, it is impossible or unnatural to conceptualize music outside the context of associated body movements. Indeed, although technology has flattened much musical practice and transmission into a digital, exclusively auditory form, passive listening continues to robustly activate motor areas of the brain (Haueisen & Knösche, 2001; Zatorre, Chen, & Penhune, 2007; Chen, Penhune, & Zatorre, 2008). Because sound carries traces of movement, it can take on the imprint of gesture that is so fundamental to ritual. Obsessive-compulsive disorder and related pathologies involving repetition and ritualization have been theorized to arise from damage to areas that subserve motor control. An investigation of the biological substrates of these disorders might shed light on mechanisms that may also relate to repetitive behaviors in nonpathological contexts, such as musical listening.

## Obsessive-Compulsive Disorder and Related Pathologies of Repetition

Normal behavior includes a fair amount of repetition in the form of routines: overlearned motor programs that can run largely unconsciously, such as in the act of brushing your teeth or starting a car (Eilam, Zor, Szechtman, & Hermesh, 2006). But several pathologies—including obsessive-compulsive disorder, autism, and schizophrenia—produce repetitive behavior that ranges from nonfunctional to detrimental, and is referred to contrastingly as "ritual." It remains controversial whether ritualization represents an exaggeration of normal routinization processes or whether it may be a different process entirely. Figure 3.1 depicts the levels of event structure identified by Zacks et al. and discussed above: gestures (on the order of seconds), episodes (mid-length events at the level descriptions spontaneously refer to), and scripts (longer occurrences, comprised of multiple subparts).

The arrows on either side illustrate the attentional shifts engendered by routinization and ritualization. Routinization pushes attention up to the level of the script and longer-term goal, allowing for the automatization of component episodes, while ritualization tunnels attention down to the level of individual gestures, making it more difficult to achieve larger-scale goals. For example, in the routine of getting dressed, a person might execute the individual episodes (putting on socks, buttoning a shirt, etc.) without conscious attention. This routinization is highly functional, reducing attentional demands and allowing

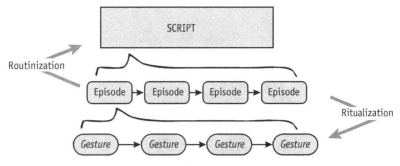

*Figure 3.1* Routinization versus ritualization. Reprinted with permission from Keren et al., 2010.

for the easy attainment of a goal. Ritualization, by contrast, involves excessive explicit attention to individual gestures that are ordinarily performed without special thought.

Nonhuman animals exhibit repetitive behaviors that can range from normal, as in the case of fixed-action patterns (or FAPs)—instinctive patterns related to important functions such as mating—to pathological, as in the case of stereotypies—highly repetitive, nonfunctional behaviors that can arise under conditions of stress, such as being caged. A useful example of normal repetitive behavior is bird song, the learning of which has been shown to depend on an avian brain circuit that corresponds to a cortico-basal ganglia loop in mammals (Graybiel, 2008). Pathological stereotypies, similarly, have been shown to arise from problems in the basal ganglia. In caged parrots, for example, stereotypy arises from disinhibition of the behavioral control mechanisms of the dorsal basal ganglia (Garner et al., 2003). Cage stereotypies in other species have also been attributed to basal ganglia dysfunctions (Cabib, 1993; Cooper & Dourish, 1990; for a review, see Eilam, Zor, Szechtman & Hermesh, 2006).

The basal ganglia, shown in Figure 3.2, are a collection of tightly interconnected nerve cells deep within the cerebrum, consisting of three primary parts: the caudate nucleus, the putamen, and the globus pallidus. They participate in cortico-basal ganglia loops, whereby input from the cortex enters the putamen, and output from the globus pallidus proceeds through the thalamus to return to the motor cortex. The basal ganglia play an important role in voluntary movement, as well as in implicit, procedural learning (learning *how* in contrast to learning *what*), especially learning related to repeated behaviors such as routines and habits.

In humans as in animals, repetitive disorders have been traced to dysfunction in this region. Pitman (1989) attributes human compulsions to activity in a phylogenetically primitive basal ganglia-based habit system with clear connections to the animal system described above. Basal ganglia problems have been

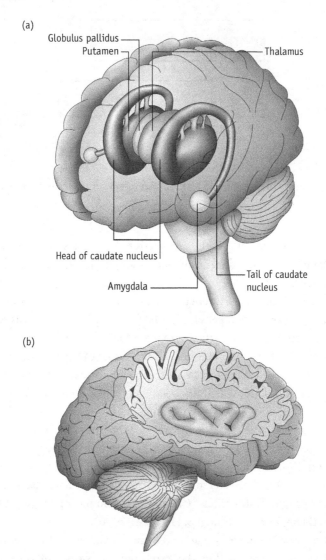

*Figure* 3.2  Location of the basal ganglia in the human brain. Reprinted with permission from Macmillan Publishers Ltd: Nature Reviews Neuroscience, copyright 2010.

implicated in Tourette syndrome (Kalanithi et al., 2005), OCD (Graybiel & Rauch, 2000), and the repetitive behaviors sometimes found in autism (Sears et al., 1999).

Another pathology, aphasia, has been linked to the basal ganglia through its most successful treatment. While people ordinarily think in terms of logic and semantics, with utterances emerging as sequences of acoustic signals, this connection has been interrupted for aphasics. They are unable to put together the appropriate motor sequences to form an intelligible speech stream. One of the most productive treatments for this condition is melodic intonation therapy (Norton et al., 2009). During treatment, patients repeat sung words and phrases while being tapped in rhythmic synchrony on the left hand. Recent work by Stahl et al. (2011) suggests that rhythm, rather than singing per se, accounts for the therapy's efficacy, and that the therapy depends crucially on long-term memory and motor automaticity. Furthermore, aphasics in this study who had suffered basal ganglia lesions benefitted from rhythmicity even more than patients with other kind of deficits. The kinds of expressions most often used in melodic intonation therapy are stock, formulaic expressions—ones that are repeated a lot in everyday conversation, and have presumably been best automatized as motor routines. By this account, melodic intonation therapy works by piggybacking on overlearned sequences, underpinned neurologically by the basal ganglia.

Repetitive behaviors that arise normally rather than pathologically have also been linked to the basal ganglia. Graybiel (2008) lists five characteristics of habits. According to her account, habits are (1) learned; (2) repeated until they become rigid; (3) performed automatically, outside conscious thought, allowing attention to shift elsewhere; (4) typically comprised of an "ordered, structured action sequence that is prone to being elicited by a particular context or stimulus" (p. 361); and (5) by nature either a pattern of thought or a pattern of overt motor activity. Together, "these characteristics suggest that habits are sequential, repetitive, motor, or cognitive behaviors elicited by external or internal triggers that, once released, can go to completion without constant conscious oversight" (p. 361).

The ability to execute and control sequences—chunks of serially ordered behavior—is critical to cognition. Finney and Palmer (2003) found that performers' memories for musical sequences are stunningly accurate, with an error rate under 3 percent, despite highly complex demands in temporal and motor control. Gabrielsson (1987) found that performers were able to replicate subtle expressive inflections such as microtiming with incredible accuracy across repetitions. Encoding actions as sequences allows people to chunk movements such that the start and finish are specially tagged, but the intervening actions can be performed automatically, without conscious control. This automaticity allows attention to be allocated elsewhere during the course of the sequence, with control intervening at the endpoint to select the next activity. Broadly, this distinction is consistent with a distinction between two important mental states—one devoted to exploring and evaluating, and another devoted to exploiting and executing. From the perspective of natural selection, it is easy to imagine the necessity of both systems: exploration includes finding and procuring food, and execution involves eating it.

Studies recording neural activity in monkeys have identified firing patterns that seem to mark the beginning and endpoints of sequences (Fujii & Graybiel,

2003; 2005), and similar studies in rats have found neural firing patterns that are concentrated at the start and end of maze runs, a kind of action sequence (Barnes et al., 2005). For very well learned sequences of this sort, "human neuroimaging studies have…emphasized the role of the basal ganglia" (Zatorre, Chen & Penhune, 2007, p. 548). Graybiel (2008) identifies with exploration episodes where neural activity in the sensorimotor striatum within the basal ganglia is variable across the course of a task, and identifies with execution episodes where neural activity in the region becomes locked to the start and endpoints of a task—as happens across repetitions of the behavior. Graybiel sees this shift as the neural signature of "the process by which action sequences are chunked for representation as a result of habit learning" (2008, p. 377). The end result is a chunked sequence that can unfold automatically, surrounded by boundary markers subject to intervention and control.

Habits, for better or worse, arise when this intervening control step is skipped; when an organism stays in the exploitation/execution mode, without stepping aside to evaluate. The rough neural correlates of evaluation and goal selection line in the prefrontal cortex (Miller & Cohen, 2001), and the rough neural correlates of sequence execution lie in the basal ganglia (Lehéricy et al., 2005; Nakahara, Doya & Hikosaka, 2001; Boecker et al., 1998). During habit formation, the prefrontal cortex becomes increasingly inactive, and the basal ganglia increasingly active, reflecting a shift from goal- to habit-based processing (Wood and Neal, 2007).

The basal ganglia underpin not only the learning of motor sequences, but also the learning of nonmotor sequences: ordered series of events that don't involve any overt movement. Vakil et al. (2000) used the serial reaction time task to demonstrate that people with lesions restricted to the basal ganglia exhibited deficits in processing both motor and nonmotor sequences. During the serial reaction time task, lights flashed in a specific series of locations on a computer screen, and participants either tracked their location by pressing keys in associated spots on the keyboard (in the motor condition), or (in the nonmotor condition) by responding whenever the light appeared in one particular position among the four possible. Unbeknownst to the participants, the lights repeatedly flashed through the same sequence of positions, until a certain point at which they began to flash in a random order. Across repeated trials, participants demonstrated increasing implicit awareness of the sequence with faster reaction times to the light positions. By contrasting performance on the sequenced series with performance on the random one, experimenters could identify what portion of this benefit was due specifically to sequence learning, rather than to general improvement on the button-pressing task. Participants in the control group—those with normally functioning basal ganglia—showed significantly faster reaction times to flashes appearing in the familiar sequence than flashes appearing randomly, but participants in the group with basal ganglia damage were not advantaged by sequence learning for either the motor or nonmotor condition. Basal ganglia lesions prevented them from both learning implicitly while performing action sequences, and learning implicitly while passively tracking sequences in the environment.

In addition to playing a role in sequence learning, the basal ganglia have repeatedly been shown to contribute to music listening. Grahn and Brett (2007; 2009) used neuroimaging to implicate the basal ganglia in beat perception—the complex process of extracting a regular meter from a messy acoustic signal. As Grahn observes, perceiving a beat entails interrelating units of time as multiples of each other (rather than as discrete independent units), a process that possesses a clear connection to the kind of chunking necessary for the formation of procedural sequences. Further fMRI work (Grahn & Rowe, 2013) established that the basal ganglia's role in beat perception has to do with actively predicting the beat, rather than merely identifying temporal regularities.

What does it mean that the circuitry that underlies habit formation and the learning and execution of sequence routines also underlies the process of beat prediction in musical listening? Series of tones become sequences insofar as they are repeated. Within a piece, especially in an unfamiliar style, repetition defines what will count as a unit: what musical events will fuse together and function as a thing — a discrete, coherent entity — in the unfolding theater of the piece. Beats create the temporal grid that makes this structuring possible; they lay out predictive spans, the temporal skeletons on which music can hang. When the basal ganglia is engaged with projecting the beat, it is also engaged with projecting musical sound, since the beat is never abstract but always appears in the guise of a musical surface. In fact, beat induction—the process of inferring the meter from a piece of music's acoustic signal—is notoriously difficult to model. In attempting to create a computer program that could tap to the beat in apparently straightforwardly metric examples, Desain and Honing discovered that the phenomenon we experience as the beat arises from a complex set of auditory cues ranging from surface characteristics like loudness and duration to characteristics that present deeper processing demands, like harmonic stability, parallelism, and phrase structure (1999). Thus, the discovery that the basal ganglia are active in the projection of the beat can be understood as a discovery that the basal ganglia are involved with the projection of musical patterns themselves.

Psychologists often categorize knowledge into two primary forms: declarative and procedural, with declarative signifying knowledge about *what*, and procedural signifying knowledge about *how*. For example, knowledge about why a plane is flyable would be declarative, but knowledge about how to fly a plane would be procedural. The basal ganglia, extensively connected to motor regions, have been conceptualized as an important seat of procedural knowledge. They are also an area critical to disorders of repetitive behavior. How might this functional overlap be understood to relate to the prevalence of repetition in music?

Music has consistently been shown to recruit motor areas not just in active performance, but also in passive listening (for a review, see Zatorre, Chen & Penhune, 2007). Scholars and everyday listeners alike default to movement in attempting to describe musical experience: "The melody shot up quickly"; "The violins soared," and so on. The experience of music often seems like the experience of some sort of motion, a thing that is virtually enacted rather than declaratively known.

Phrases, in fact, can be thought to have important similarities to motor sequences. Just as repetition makes it possible to encode a series of movements as a fluid sequence that can be performed without conscious attention, repetition makes it possible to encode musical phrases as fluid sequences that can be imagined without effort. It is easiest to recognize that phrases get encoded this way when questions are posed about moments in a musical experience, and we realize that we have to mentally reenact a complete sequence to access an intermediary moment (e.g., are "oh" and "you" sung on the same pitch in the opening of *The Star-Spangled Banner*?; see DeBellis, 1995). The sequential nature of musical encoding is also evident in earworms—tunes that get stuck in our head. Earworms are invariably chunks that proceed (often frustratingly) from a start to an endpoint; timbres and chords aren't "catchy" in the way a tune can be. The catchiness arises from the chunked and sequential nature of tunes; once they interest an ear, they play themselves through to a point of rest.

Reencountering a passage of music involves repeatedly traversing the same imagined path until the grooves through which it moves are deep, and carry the passage easily. It becomes an overlearned sequence, which we are capable of executing without conscious attention. Yet in the case of passive listening, this movement is entirely virtual. The sense of being moved—of being taken and carried along in the mode of a procedural enactment, when the knowledge was presented by simply sounding in a way that seemed to imply a more declarative mode of understanding—can be exhilarating, immersive, and boundary-dissolving: all characteristics of strong experiences of music as chronicled by Gabrielsson and Lindström (2003).

The SEM (Strong Experiences of Music) project (Gabrielsson & Lindström, 2003) solicited reports of peak musical experiences from more than nine hundred listeners, and analyzed the descriptions to identify characteristics that were broadly common from one person to the next. Most relevant to the present account are findings that peak musical experiences tended to resist verbal description; to elevate arousal, and instigate action tendencies—an impulse to move in some way or other; to elicit quasi-physical sensations, such as being "filled" by the music, or being drawn out of the body; to alter sensations of space and time, including out-of-body sensations, percepts of disappearing boundaries and collapsing time; to bypass conscious control and speak straight to feelings, emotions, and senses; to effect an altered relationship between music and listeners, such that the listener feels penetrated by the music, or merged with it, or feels that he or she is being played by the music; to cause the listener to imagine him or herself as the performer or composer, or experience the music as executing his or her will; to precipitate sensations of an existential or transcendent nature, described variously as heavenly, extraterrestrial, ecstatic, or trance-like.

These sensations can be explained as consequences of a sense of virtual inhabitation of the music engendered by repeated musical passages that get procedurally encoded as chunked sequences, activating motor regions and getting experienced as lived/enacted phenomena, rather than heard/cognized ones. It is repetition, specifically, that engages and intensifies these processes, since it takes multiple repetitions for something to be procedurally encoded as an automatic sequence. Indeed, Pereira et al. (2011) show that prior exposure to a piece can be an important prerequisite for deep emotional engagement.

## Trance, Flow, and Musical Pleasure

Ethnomusicologist Monique Ingalls has collected examples of trance induced by repetitive music, ranging from Sufi spinning in India to Contemporary Pentecostal trancing in the American South to the trancing of bissu (transvestite priests) in Indonesia. Gilbert Rouget (1980) and Judith Becker (2004) have systematically investigated the phenomenon of musical trancing, and been careful to acknowledge that the practice arises differently in different times, places, and cultures. But in many different circumstances in many different places, one kind of behavior that has been linked with repetitive music is trancing. If we can assume that trancing is an intensification or exaggeration of ordinary experiences of music, rather than a phenomenon of an entirely different ilk, then a consideration of repetitive music's role in trance may help us understand more about the perceptual processes ordinarily involved in listening to repetitive music. Becker observes that "in trance, the inner languaging stops (Friedson 1996: 19). Similarly, for 'deep listeners', simply playing or listening to music alone will halt the inner language. As an inhibitor of the inner language, deep musical listening parallels trance" (2004, p. 29). Invested, engaged listening, according to this account, mirrors the elements of trance. Herbert (2011) links the familiarity of music that has been repeated to its tendency to induce what she views as "everyday trancing" (a dissociation from surroundings paired with a deep absorption with sounding music), because unfamiliar sounds raise vigilance and conscious awareness, elements antithetical to trance. The more familiar a piece is, the more a listener can respond automatically, allowing for the suppression of explicit thought and an increased sense of bodily involvement with the music.

Becker (2004) defines trance as

> *a bodily event characterized by strong emotion, intense focus, the loss of a strong sense of self, usually enveloped by amnesia and a cessation of the inner language. Following James, I wish to include that trance is an event that accesses types of knowledge and experience which are inaccessible in nontrance events, and which are felt to be ineffable, not easily described or spoken of* (p. 43).

Supporting the notion that trance represents one point along a continuum of musical experiences rather than a truly separate phenomenon, many of these characteristics overlap significantly with those chronicled by Gabrielsson and Lindström in their account of strong experiences of music. Trance, in fact, is mentioned as a possible characteristic of strong experiences of music. Becker's description of trance simply brings some of these characteristics to further prominence, particularly the qualities understood to surround the loss of a sense of self: a kind of amnesia, and a cessation of inner language. Both of these qualities can be understood to reflect a shift from a state engaged with cognitive, declarative kinds of representations to a state engaged with embodied, procedural ones; the kind of state, I have argued, that repeated sequences of tones encourage us to enter, by exploiting circuitry devoted to sequence learning. The experience of an external force (namely, sound) engaging these kinds of representations can contribute to a sense of transcendence, a sense of being played by the music, or a sense that the boundaries of the self have dissolved into the surroundings. Because repetition allows the sequence to be gone through automatically, without attentional control, a person is free to marvel at the nonverbal, physical response she is sustaining in response to objective sound. With sufficient reduction in executive monitoring, she can enter a trancelike state, where other cognitive kinds of percepts (inner language and explicit memory, for example) fall away.

A less extreme version of this same kind of process underlies much everyday musical pleasure. Pereira et al. (2011) used fMRI to establish that emotion-related limbic and paralimbic regions as well as reward circuitry were more active for familiar than unfamiliar music; the study's authors interpret these results as evidence that familiarity (i.e., repetition) is a critical factor in engaging listeners emotionally with music. Interestingly, familiar music also triggered increased activation in the basal ganglia and the motor cortex, further supporting the hypothesis that repetitions of music encourage encoding as automatic sequences.

Consuming, pleasurable musical experiences also connect to a highly satisfying state described by Mikhail Csíkszentmihályi (1997) as "flow." When someone has achieved a state of flow, bodily and temporal awareness recede, and a person finds himself totally immersed in the activity at hand. Music performance is explicitly mentioned as an example of an activity during which this state can arise, but I would suggest that music listening can produce the same state. Indeed, Csíkszentmihályi (Nakamura and Csíkszentmihályi, 2002) later came to articulate this possibility, and Herbert (2011), Diaz (2011), and Lamont (2011, 2012) have all recently examined it. Flow seems to occupy a place on the spectrum between ordinary music listening on one end and full-blown trance on the other, exhibiting many of the properties of both. By recruiting motor circuitry and engaging representation as automatic sequences, repetition facilitates the generation of this state, fostering an intimate connection to the music while bypassing conceptual cognition and allowing the sound to seem "lived" rather than "perceived." As discussed in Chapter 1, a recent study (Margulis, 2010) showed that participants without special musical training reported increased enjoyment of excerpts of Beethoven String Quartets when they were presented on their own rather than when they were prefaced by information about the expressive or structural content of the music. Listeners seemed to prefer an unmediated, "lived" experience of the sound, rather than a more "cognized" one, invested in drawing connections between the acoustic phenomena and some conceptual entities. In the inimitable words of Leonard Meyer, "listening to music intelligently is more like knowing how to ride a bicycle than knowing why a bicycle is rideable" (1973, p. 17). One distinctive joy of musical listening comes from a kind of procedural immersion rather than a more declarative understanding. Repetition is an important element that encourages this kind of attending.

Garcia (2005) builds his account for the pleasure of repetition in Electronic Dance Music (EDM) on the notion of function or process pleasure—pleasure that arises from the act of doing something rather than achieving some ultimate goal. He contrasts process pleasure with satiation pleasure, using the example of baking a cake: although the act of eating it might bring satiation pleasure, the act of baking it could bring process pleasure. For Garcia, repetition itself constitutes a kind of process, affording involvement and mastery by way of dancing or listening. Although these qualities are particularly prominent in the ebullient looping of EDM, they are present to some degree in even much more reserved styles that feature musical repetition, such as the Classical rondo; and even in styles that themselves feature little repetition, if our behavior in relation to them (e.g., multiple replays of a recording) entails lots of repetition, we become connected to the sound in a way that feels almost physical.

# Repetition in Early Childhood

Although disorders of repetition have received some attention from neuro-scientists and psychologists, repetitive behaviors that arise during the normal course of development have received relatively little scientific attention (Evans & Maliken, 2011). Yet detailed rituals characterize mealtime or bedtime in the lives of over 80 percent of toddlers (Evans et al., 1997; Leonard et al., 1990). Anyone who has spent much time with children under the age of six will recognize that an impulse to repeat is a very normal part of childhood; children will demand to rehear the same story past the point of all adult tolerance, and sternly correct attempts at improvisation—"Wait, you skipped that part!" or "That's not what the bear said!" If you play a game with a child of this age—take "horsey" for example, where the small person plays a gleeful rodeo rider and the adult provides the ride—you can count on demands for repetitions, and exact repetitions at that. You will be asked to start at the same corner of the room, lean back for a dismount at precisely the same section of sofa, and say "whoa, Nelly" in exactly the same tone of voice at exactly the same point. Ethologist Konrad Lorenz (1966) chronicled this tendency in a passage considering the frustration of geese when forced to break a habit; he observed that their frustration recalled that of children who becomes desperate when a storyteller diverges slightly from the familiar text of a fairy tale.

What is the function of this appetite for repetitive behavior? And why does it appear so strongly in children but recede in adults? Horst, Parsons, and Bryan (2011) presented children with novel words in two conditions: (1) embedded within different stories, or (2) embedded within a single story. Over the course of one week, they either heard diverse stories featuring the new words, or repetitions of the same story. In each condition, they heard the new words the same number of times; the difference was the context in which the words were embedded, which could be either different or the same. Intuitively, it might seem that hearing new words in multiple contexts would be most advantageous for vocabulary learning, but this study found that children in the varied context condition entirely failed to learn the new words, whereas children who had encountered them within repetitions of the same story had not only learned but also successfully integrated them into their everyday vocabulary.

Similarly, Simcock and DeLoache (2008) showed that children exposed to illustrations of a sequence of actions leading to the construction of a rattle imitated the sequence more successfully when they had been exposed to the illustrations four rather than two times. Crawley et al. (1999) showed that pre-schoolers exposed to the same TV episode five times (a number that might cause a parent to shudder) performed far better on comprehension questions related to the program than children who had only seen it once. Horst, Parsons, and Bryan hypothesize that repeated contexts facilitated word learning because they required fewer attentional resources, leaving room for the children to focus on the novel words.

A stronger, less careful interpretation of these data could argue that repetition *in general* allows for the freeing up of attentional resources, such that attention can rove to different levels of the stimulus—up to higher-level, structural features (such as plot and character, in the case of the repeated TV show), or down to lower-level, detailed features (such as novel words, in the case of the repeated tellings of a story). Since so much remains for small children to learn, repetition provides an opportunity for them to master aspects of their environment they are typically too attentionally taxed to grasp. This view represents a subtle recasting of the typical account of the childhood appetite for repetition, which centers on the pleasure that can be drawn from familiarity and expertise—the pleasure of being able to predict things about an environment and feel safe. By way of contrast, the account I'm presenting here suggests that the pleasure derives not from familiarity and safety of the old, but rather from the excitement of learning and the new: namely, the new elements that become available to perception and cognition when attentional resources are freed from merely tracking entirely new events. Children experience the joy of engagement with richer and more interconnected aspects of the stimulus—a type of play that often gets relegated in adulthood to the domain of the aesthetic.

Figure 3.1 traces the attentional shifts that accompany repetitive behavior, shifts that either move up within the temporal hierarchy, enabling the individual to grasp larger-scale relationships, or move down within the temporal hierarchy, confronting him or her with detailed, low-level attributes that often get ignored. Music presents adults with a socially circumscribed space within which pleasure and play are valued and encouraged (DeNora, 2000). The kind of free mulling-over and deep digesting that children might do with any old stimulus, adults will often generally restrict but allow to emerge in the circumscribed domain of aesthetic experience, such as musical listening.

But there are many domains in which aesthetic attending is relevant—so why does repetition so uniquely characterize music? The kind of sequence learning underpinned by the basal ganglia, also the seat of many pathologies of repetitive behavior, requires not just that a stimulus unfold in time, but also that its temporal ordered-ness be relevant: if the notes in Mozart's 40th Symphony or the sounds in Donne's Sonnet 14 were scrambled and replayed in a new order, the result would be something else entirely—something we not only wouldn't recognize as Mozart or Donne, but might not even recognize as eighteenth-century music or as an utterance in the English language. It is possible, however, to absorb Miró's *Women, Bird by Moonlight* in any order: starting by looking at the red bits in the middle and moving out, or looking first at the star and then moving your gaze over toward the figures, or standing far away to take it all in and then moving closer to focus on particular parts. In examining and reexamining this painting from all these different vantage points, the stars must not inherently come before the figures, or vice versa—the temporal ordering of the experience is not fixed.

This point is well-illustrated in Chapter 1. If portions of a famous image were blacked out, it might be easy to imagine the missing parts; if, however, a famous tune were stopped too early, before a point of cadence or rest, it would not only be easy to imagine the absent continuation, but almost impossible *not* to do so. When temporal ordering is fixed, repetition welds the distinct component occurrences together into inseparable chunks, such that perceivers "listen ahead," with the expectation for forthcoming events literally alive in the present moment—expectations that are felt and experienced rather than cognized or articulated. Repetition effects this temporal welding—and this temporal connectedness, in turn, whets an appetite for further repetition. As examined in Chapter 5, repeated exposures have been thought to generate a certain processing fluency that can be misattributed to the stimulus itself, resulting in increasingly elevated judgments of pleasingness as familiarity increases. The likelier case is that when a temporal sequence is involved, more than just processing fluency increases—people attain a kind of temporal suspendedness, where the present moment is more obviously colored by the immediately preceding ones, and where future moments are more obviously implied within the present. This sense of temporal extendedness can be pleasantly expansive, and work to set up the sort of peak experience chronicled by Gabrielsson and Csikszentmihaly.

Work by Grahn, Henry, and McAuley (2011) implies that temporal sequencing is particularly effective in the auditory domain. In their study, they cued a beat either in the auditory or the visual domain, while using fMRI to watch how beat sensitivity in these two modalities emerged in the brain. Not only were participants less sensitive to the beat when it was presented in a visual rather than auditory sequence, but also areas in the basal ganglia were more active when an auditory instead of a visual sequence had initially cued the beat. The authors conclude that even when trying to abstract a beat in the visual domain, people generate an internal auditory rhythm representation. Immersive, predictive participation in temporally ordered sequences seems to be a behavior more linked with the auditory than the visual domain.

Yet unlike images, words are auditory stimuli that take place in temporal sequence, just like music. Why do passages from sonnets and stories feature less repetition than music, and why do they invite rereadings or rehearings less compulsively than passages of music? One possible explanation is that language entails meaning: words function to represent ideas, objects, and phenomena outside themselves, phenomena that populate the real world—in short, language has a semantics. Verbatim memory—memory for the precise words used to express a thought—is surprisingly poor (Gernsbacher, 1985), with people tending to paraphrase when they are asked to repeat utterances, so that the gist is correct but the precise wording is off. Memory for music, contrastingly, involves no equivalent kind of paraphrase. If asked to repeat a song after hearing it for the first time, people are likely to replicate a snippet, rather than attempt a summary of the whole thing (it's unclear, in fact, just what such a summary might entail— the structural tones? Just the highpoints?). Phonemes and words are hopelessly bound to sense-making—a challenge for drama involving music, since plot must ever move forward—but music wants to repeat itself. In opera, this problem was traditionally dealt with by relegating all the action to recitative—a sort of musical quasi-speech, often with minimal accompaniment and no catchy tunes. For a proper song to take place—an aria—the action has to freeze, as a character steps forward to reflect on the situation. This reflection generally occurs outside narrative time, making it possible for the same lovely melody to return many times, without the pressure to move to something new, as would generally be necessary if the plot were advancing.

Words hold meaning—they serve as vessels for it—whereas musical sounds, by some accounts, *are* the meaning. At a minimum, they lack a separate semantic association that is fixed enough to render the signal carrying it discardable or exchangeable. And although translation from language to language is imperfect, translation from music to music is impossible. Rather, even when music conjures up particular referents by imitating birdsong or alluding to a particular topic, much more is going on than an evocation of the high style, or the Turkish style, or a particular dance. And conversely, when music uses snippets of speech, as in Steve Reich's *Different Trains*, which features recordings of interviews with various figures associated with the composer's cross-country train trips as a child, the repetitions often encourage listeners to approach the stimulus musically; although a residue of the speech's "meaning" remains, elements of the prosody, the contour, and the rhythm are foregrounded (in the case of the Reich, by means of imitation from a string quartet). When these elements rise to central importance, the speech is being approached musically. In this way, it needn't take the profound perceptual shift of the speech-to-song illusion to convince a person that repetition musicalizes speech; a simple thought experiment is enough to illustrate that repetitions rhythmicize speech and elevate its acoustic characteristics to unusual prominence. None of these effects are desirable in everyday uses, where language is used to relay information and a foray into the acoustic properties would represent a real distraction (as in the case of aphasia).

# Repetition, the Overlearned Sequence, and Musical Pleasure

Broadly speaking, musical repetitions push processing down from the more cognitive, conceptual regions of the frontal cortex and into the more motoric, automatic basal ganglia. Encoding passages as sequences, where the first bit is tightly connected to the second, which is tightly connected to the third, and so on until a point of rest, allows an entire phrase or section to be passed through with a degree of automaticity, such that the listener's attention is free to move up or down in the temporal hierarchy. Both the sense of embodying an external stimulus in the way that you'd ordinarily embody a physical action, and the playful exploration made possible by the attentional shifts, are intrinsically pleasant, and set up the kind of circumstances within which the strong musical experiences reported by Gabrielsson can happen. In *Dry Salvages* from *Four Quartets* (1968), T. S. Eliot describes a "music heard so deeply/ that it is not heard at all/ but you are the music/ while the music lasts." This sense of extended subjectivity sounds a lot like the kind of experience that can arise from the sequential encoding of repeating music.

When a musical passage is repeated and encoded more and more robustly as a sequenced unit, it serves as a literal hook, compelling a person to execute the sequence imaginatively until a resting point is reached. Music, in these cases, can seem to play the person. Since music comes from other people—composers, performers, collaborators—and is often experienced in a social setting, with other people jointly moving to the beat or listening together, this sense of being played from outside can feel intensely bonding and communal, and serve to construct a sense of shared subjectivity. Musical repetitions, in other words, depending on the surrounding circumstance and the preparatory set brought to the experience, can effect a sense of boundary-collapsing communication that can awaken a range of experiences from mildly pleasurable to totally redemptive.

# 4

# Earworms, Technology, and the Verbatim

Few people are spared the at least occasional experience of being gripped by the obstinate unfolding of an imagined line of music. Although the sound might not exist at the present moment in the real world, or be audible to anyone else, it can seem compellingly, maddeningly real. An episode of this sort often seems more like the reliving of a tune than the simple remembering of it. If I *remember* hearing a concert performance of Brahms's Second Symphony, the memory might include something about the hall, the view from my seat, how many movements there were, the perfume of someone in the row behind me, a bit of lush orchestral timbre, and the expressive resonance of the piece. These recollections emerge jumbled together, without a clear temporal order that I could relate, let alone the temporal ordering in which they originally occurred; and they emerge in a flash, the memory occupying a duration far shorter than the duration occupied by the actual event. But if the second theme gets stuck in my head, it's a totally different experience—I seem not to remember, but rather to *rehear* the entire thing, note by note, in clear temporal sequence, and over an amount of time that roughly matches the duration its actual performance might have had. In this sense, it is more like an imaginative reconstruction than a memory. But a quality of this experience that distinguishes it from most imaginings as well as most memories is its repetitiveness: once the tune comes to an end, it loops around and starts playing again from the beginning. On some of its replays, I might be driven to sing along, or hum a bit, or tap the rhythm on the table, and it's usually only when the music breaks into the external world in this way that I become aware of the extent to which it has ensnared my mind.

This odd cognitive phenomenon, although quite common, remained unstudied until recently, and even the handful of studies that approach the topic have remained at the descriptive level, failing to provide a theoretical account. There is, however, no shortage of words in general circulation that attempt to capture the experience, as Beaman and Williams (2010) demonstrate. Germans call it *Ohrwurm*, and the English language has adopted the translation of this word, earworm. It can be called *musique entêtante* in French and *canzone tormentone* in Italian, which translate respectively to "stubborn music" and "tormenting songs" (Halpern and Bartlett, 2011). Among scholars, Kellaris (2001) refers to it as cognitive itch, Levitin (2006) as stuck song syndrome, Sacks (2007) as sticky music, and Liikkanen (2008; 2012) as involuntary musical imagery (INMI).

Liikkanen (2008) surveyed 12,420 Finnish Internet users about their experience with INMI. An amazing 91.7 percent of them reported getting a tune stuck in their head at least once a week. 33.2 percent said a tune got stuck in their head at least once a day, and 26.1 percent said it happened several times a day. The fact that more than 1 in 3 respondents identified earworms as a daily occurrence, and more than 1 in 4 reported experiencing them several times a day, suggests that the phenomenon is not only widespread but also relatively frequent. Steven Brown (2006), a neuroscientist at McMaster who studies the arts, chronicled his own "perpetual music track," reporting that short musical fragments repetitively loop in his mind on a near constant basis. The pianist Kirill Gerstein has also reported pervasive musical imagery in the form of a vivid and continually looping soundtrack that continues even underneath conversations. Extreme versions of involuntary musical imagery, like those chronicled by Brown and Gerstein, feature the same kind of fragmentation and repetitiveness as typical earworms. Brown reports that the fragments tend to last between five and fifteen seconds, and loop repetitively, sometimes "for hours on end," before moving to a new fragment (Brown, 2006).

The unusual repetitiveness of musical imagery parallels and exaggerates the unusual repetitiveness of actual music in the world. The relationship between earworms' repetitive looping and the uncommon repetitiveness of actual music seems striking, yet to my knowledge this connection has not been pointed out or investigated, except to observe that earworms can be induced by frequent relistenings to particular tunes.

It would be tempting to believe that the kind of repetition afforded by technologies of recent and semi-recent invention—the stuck needle on a phonograph, the tape loop, the digital sample—had spurred this epidemic, provoking some new and distinctly twentieth-century malady, but Mark Twain chronicled the experience in his short story *A Literary Nightmare*, published in an 1876 edition of *The Atlantic Monthly* (and discussed in Beaman and Williams, 2010). This story, which describes the gradual possession of an entire community by a damningly catchy jingle that gets stuck on mental repeat in all of their imaginations, was handily published one year before the invention of the phonograph by Thomas Edison in 1877, evidencing that the phenomenon of the earworm existed before the dissemination of technologies that mimicked and perhaps exacerbated it.

Yet technology unquestionably makes possible a degree and pervasiveness of repetition that was previously unheard of. This affordance is reflected in the tendency of contemporary art music either to suffuse itself with or entirely reject repetitiveness. Technology made it impossible to remain neutral or unreflective about repetitiveness; in twentieth-century styles it was either pushed self-consciously to the foreground (in the case of minimal music) or expressly avoided (in the case of serial music, for example). This state of affairs has been well investigated by cultural theorists. Notably among them, Robert Fink (2005) chronicles how repetition in minimal music "can be interpreted as both the sonic analogue and, at times, a sonic constituent of a characteristic repetitive experience of self in mass-media consumer society" (p. 3-4). Fink cites Jacques Attali's treatise on the political economy of music and the all-consuming repetitiveness of mass production—"the replacement of the restaurant by pre-cooked meals, of custom-made clothes by ready-to-wear, of the individual house based on stereotypical designs, of the politician by the anonymous bureaucrat, of skilled labor by standardized tasks, of the spectacle by recordings of it" (1985, p. 128).

Fink's take represents a revisionist account, developed in response to the tendency of cultural critics influenced by Freud to find timeless human proclivities—either Thanatos, the death drive, or Eros, the life instinct—in minimalist music's repetitive structuring. Fink wants instead to acknowledge something very historically specific—namely, a culture of mass consumption—in the sound structures of twentieth-century music. As a pervasive cultural experience, Fink identifies the "pure control of/by repetition" as "a familiar yet unacknowledged aesthetic effect of late modernity, sometimes experienced as pleasurable and erotic, but more often as painfully excessive, alienating, and (thus) sublime" (2005, p. 4).

Rahn (1993) presents a different perspective on the Freudian reading of repetition that is worth quoting at length:

> This process of continual repetition, continual change-of-context constituting meaning, creatively folding a life back over its traces as it unfolds, is a source of great satisfaction, aesthetically desperate and desperately aesthetic, for without this process, without hope of telos, there would be no life. Who among us is ready to die? To be ready to die would be not to be living. As long as one is living, one's life is unachieved, the final reconfiguration un-folded-back to give meaning to the whole, to make a whole. Therefore no one can die happy who is still really living, who is committed to the project of repetition, of

making sense of changes-of-context. Death is not a change of context;
it is the end of changes of context and the end of meaning....

A piece of music for Mary is the life Mary lives alongside of her life.
Because music is temporal, Mary can experience it as she experiences
(abstracts, constructs) her own life, as an ongoing project of the repetition that is changes-of-context that is meaning. The depth and subtlety
she asks of the music will be the depth and subtlety she has brought her
own life to. If a piece of music cannot sustain her interpretation, perhaps
because its terrain is perceivably limited –closed—and thus unlifelike,
she will turn away. She will be attracted to pieces of music whose terrain
leads her into ways of refolding, of replication (Deleuze, 1988), that
can teach her about her life. Aesthetic desperation is always looking for
ways to go on. Music is both temporal and abstract enough to show her
the delineaments of telos, the physiognomy of hope (p. 53-54).

Rahn depicts music as a kind of sandbox or playground in which the pervasive
process of making sense of repetition through continual changes of context can
be experienced on its own, "alongside" ordinary life. In a sense, the account put
forward by this book, although markedly different from the Freudian account, or
from Deleuze, or Rahn, nevertheless has more in common with these than with
Fink's, in that it holds a tendency toward repetition in music to represent some
sort of unified psychological principle, rather than an incidental byproduct of a
set of cultural or historical circumstances. And although the historical and cultural shape the psychological as much as the psychological shape the historical
and cultural (Nisbett, Peng, Choi & Norenzayan, 2001; Shore, 1998), it can be
expedient to talk in terms of one or the other. I'm advancing the argument that
basic psychological tendencies constrain musical uses of repetition. According
to this perspective, technology is a force that interacts with these fundamental
tendencies, exaggerating them, or creating an opportunity for exploitation. In
the same way that modern technologies related to food production hijack appetite tendencies that evolved long before taquitos were invented, modern technologies related to sound production can hijack perceptual tendencies that were
in place before the technologies were invented. Sociocultural factors like those
outlined by Fink no doubt impact the use and experience of repetition not only
in twentieth-century music but also in the music of any time and place; the claim
here is that particular perceptual tendencies, largely invariant from culture to
culture, also serve as a constraining and generative force in the shaping of musical practices.

Yet the relationship among technological affordance, perceptual experience,
and compositional intent can be quite complex. Jonathan Kramer has argued
that composers in the early twentieth century, particularly Arnold Schoenberg,

foresaw that their music would be recorded and thus replayed, and in response to intuition about this future practice, reduced the amount of repetition within the works themselves. This kind of logic relies on the theory that there is some ideal, medium amount of repetition that can be instantiated either *intraopusly*, within the piece itself, or *extraopusly* (terms from Narmour, 1990), in the way the piece itself is used and repeated. According to this theory, highly repetitive music would bear fewer repeated listenings, but highly nonrepetitive music would bear more. The psychoaesthetics literature of the 1970s, explored in Chapter 5, systematically engages with this hypothesis. More recently, Novis and Wong (2011) use measures of fractal content to examine the role of complexity in the relationship between repeated exposure and preference, suggesting that increased complexity (i.e. less internal repetition) makes replaying musical excerpts more tolerable.

It is worth noting that even if Kramer is correct that technology has given rise to musics that avoid repetition more than previous styles in history, it has also given rise to musics that embrace it more—consider the role of Steve Reich's mid-1960s experiments with tape loops in the development of minimalism. Reich discovered that if he placed two copies of the same tape loop (a segment of magnetic tape with its ends connected to each other) on two different reel-to-reel players, the loops would go in and out of phase with each other, a happenstance that formed the basis for early works like *It's Gonna Rain* (1965) and was also influential on later works such as *Clapping Music* (1972).

Katz (2004) observes that the repeated motives in minimalist pieces are often about two seconds long, the amount of time it takes an LP record to complete a single rotation, adding further resonance to pejorative contemporary accounts that accused the style of sounding like a broken record. In the Bronx in the 1970s, hip hop artists began experimenting with a similar process, also called looping, that involved switching between copies of a single LP record placed on multiple turntables such that a particular fragment could be repeated for an extended period. This practice, Katz notes, came to form the basis for much of the instrumental accompaniment in rap — evidence of how the affordances of recording technology were shaping repetitive practices in diverse styles.

The influence of recording's capacities continued in the decades to follow. Spurred on especially by the production of the E-mu SP-1200 sampler in 1987, the practice evolved from the manual establishment of drum loops to the digital manipulation of samples, ultimately yielding the highly sample-based aesthetic of hip hop and rap in the 1990s. In the domain of self-styled art music, around the year 1950 composers in the US (with Vladimir Ussachevksy) and in France (with Pierre Schaeffer and Pierre Henry) simultaneously began to experiment with electronic, tape-based music, leading, in the case of Ussachevsky, to the founding of the Columbia Experimental Music Studio, and, later, the Columbia-Princeton Electronic Music Center.

Pierre Schaeffer famously overheard a scratch on a record in the late 1940s and instead of moving the needle forward, attended explicitly to the resultant loop. He called it a *sillon fermé*, or closed groove, and came to value the "purer" way it allowed him to engage with the sound. When wrested from its ordinary ephemeral position in an ongoing temporal context, the sound could be contemplated and attended to for its own fundamental sonic characteristics. It was the change in orientation made possible by this accidental, technology-enabled repetitive exposure to a particular sound that led to the invention of the compositional style known as *musique concrète*. Once the looping engendered by the scratch had revealed the gestural and musical potential of arbitrary sounds, Schaeffer reasoned that all sorts of ordinary sounds not typically considered musical might carry this potential if used in a way that highlighted their "purely" sonic aspects. For Schaeffer, repetition served to musicalize things that had previously not been understood to carry aesthetic affordances.

Schuftan (2007) links the shift in perception that repetition permitted for Schaeffer with the use of repetition in contemporary hip hop. Consider the following account of the way mechanical repetition can expose musicality in a passage, even when no such musicality was expressly composed into it:

> Sometimes I'll put a loop on and let it play for, like, two or three days…When you do something like that, you get to hear all the different parts and pieces and elements of it that you never really heard before…It probably sounds strange to a lotta people, but you get to hear stuff that the musician didn't try to put in there. You know what I mean? It's just in there. (DJ Kool Akiem, quoted in Schuftan, 2007).

This quotation traces the way excessive repetition musicalizes qualities of a loop that may have initially seemed incidental, driving attention to otherwise perceptually inaccessible qualities of the sonic surface.

There can be no question that recording technology fundamentally shaped musical practice in the second half of the twentieth century. Technology (instruments, most directly, and transportation, affecting which cultures intermingle and co-influence one another) has always been a force in the development of musical styles, but since recording technologies are essentially repetition machines, the advent of these capacities is particularly relevant to practices of repetition in music. It could be argued, in fact, that by placing repetition front and center, and in particular by placing mechanically generated repetition front and center, these technologies engendered not only musics that engaged creatively with this capability (like minimalism), but also musics that rejected it on philosophical or aesthetic grounds. Whichever stance a composer took, she

could not be unconscious of, or neutral about, the potentiality of repetitiveness—it had to be reckoned with.

The split into the embrace or avoidance of repetition spurred vitriol on all
sides, with Pierre Boulez famously telling the *New York Review of Books* "today's
type of minimalist and repetitive music appeals to an extremely primitive perception...If an audience wants to get high with this kind of music rather than
with another product, that's OK with me. But I don't consider that a very high
level of enjoyment" (Boulez, 1984). This sentiment captures the notion that
repetition, while enjoyable, is not very *interesting*, and the kind of enjoyment it
engenders is base and unsophisticated. Nevertheless, it's interesting that even
composers passionately committed to avoiding repetition in their own music
do not dispute the idea that repetition can be pleasurable; they simply fail to
identify this type of pleasure as worthy of pursuing. Thus, the existence of a style
of musical composition that self-consciously rejects repetition is not proof that
a fundamental psychological principle related to musical repetition does not
exist; rather, composers of this school are so aware of such a principal that they
make it their central desire to thwart it.

## On the Mechanical and the Imagined

The advent of recording technology brought a precise, concrete kind of repetition into the objective soundscape that shadowed the involuntary, imagined
kind of repetition that characterizes earworms. This new similarity between the
organization of sound in the real world and its internal, imagined occurrence
can contribute to a sense of extended subjectivity, as if previously internal habits
of auditory imagery have been pulled into shared, external, three-dimensional
reality. While this sense of pulling what seemed subjective and individual into
sounding, shared reality can seem pleasant and expansive, it also introduces the
possibility of complicated feedback and interrelations. On the one hand, tech-
nologically engendered repetition can seem ecstatic and expansive—but on the
other hand, the mechanical basis of this experience might come to seem danger-
ous or suspiciously consuming. Repetitiveness exposes the razor edge between
internal and external, human and mechanical, private and public in a way that
can either be interpreted as sublime or degenerate.

Are earworms really as pervasive as this account claims? Liikkanen's (2008)
study suggests that more than 90 percent of people experience involuntary music
imagery at least once a week, and more than 25 percent of them experience it
several times a day. Bailes (2007) used a different methodology, contacting participants at random intervals over a week-long period and asking them to report

their experience of musical imagery at the moment they received the request. The prevalence rate varied widely among participants, but was still surprisingly high, with the participant who experienced the least frequent imagery reporting it on 12 percent of the sampled occasions, and the participant who experienced the most reporting it on 53 percent of them. Between ten percent and half of randomly selected moments throughout the day, in other words, were moments when people were experiencing musical imagery.

The highest incidence of musical imagery occurred during "time filler" activities such as waiting in line, and more often in social contexts than when people were alone. Participants were generally aware of the imagined music, but it was not the focus of their attention, and the experience typically wasn't unpleasant. The most vivid part of the imagery was the melody and the least vivid was the harmony, leading Bailes to favor the expression "tune on the brain" over "music on the brain" (p. 565).

An earworm most frequently consists of a looping tune—a looping sequence of notes rather than a looping progression of harmonies or a looping chain of timbres. Bailes points to the important role of the vocal system in musical imagery, and speculates that its lack of a capacity to simulate different timbres physically may have constrained the ability to vividly imagine timbres during earworms. But research has shown that performers possess motor routines (such as fingering patterns or breathing techniques) associated with the timbre of their instrument of expertise (see Margulis et al., 2009), raising the possibility that imagined music for their own instrument might retain timbral vibrancy. In response to an open-ended question about "how complete their imagery was," most participants in Bailes's study described "the image as a repeated fragment...very often the chorus of a song" (p. 562). Song choruses are not only the most frequent musical segment to show up in an earworm, they are also the musical segment most people can readily sing. What sounds people can vividly imagine are related to what sounds they can actually produce, a fact that highlights the close relationship between musical imagery and the motor system.

Beaman and Williams (2010) carried out a diary study in which participants were asked to record earworm occurrences whenever and wherever they happened. Sixty percent of the incidences that people reported consisted of small sections of the music—usually the chorus of a song, but occasionally some other fragment. All reported earworms came from music that had been previously familiar to the participants, suggesting that "only overlearned tunes are available to be 'replayed' as earworms" (p. 649). The authors speculate that repeated exposure is an important contributor to overlearning, but that "simple and repetitive tunes" might facilitate it over the short term. If you listen to a nonrepetitive song often enough, it might show up as an earworm, but tunes from repetitive music might emerge as earworms even before the song has been replayed very often.

In an analysis of a large body of self-reported earworm descriptions from anonymous callers to a BBC radio show, Williamson et al. (2012) identify recent and
repeated exposure as the two most dominant earworm triggers; however, they
note that factors beyond overlearning must also intervene, given that professional musicians who spend hours practicing and re-practicing the same pieces
appear not to experience an associatively extreme quantity of earworms.

The most in-depth account of the "loopiness" of involuntary musical imagery
comes from Steven Brown's detailed 2006 report of his own personal experience with pervasive musical imagery. His name for the phenomenon, "perpetual music track," highlights the way that audio technology has influenced our
conceptualization of even imagined experiences of music. Since the music in
film scores frequently hovers over a scene without any sign of its actual physical sources (e.g., we understand that the melody sweeping over the battlefield
scene didn't come from violins on the front line), we are quite used to the idea of
music permeating a scene without being physically present within it. This parallel makes it easy to think about imagined music as a kind of soundtrack; or, conversely, it is possible that the ease of imagining music in this way made it more
natural than it would otherwise have been for invisible soundtracks to become
so common in cinema (cf. Cooke, 2008; Tan et al., 2013).

The perpetual music track described by Brown possesses at least one characteristic that distinguishes it from music you'd be likely to hear at the movies: it is
composed largely of "short musical fragments that get looped repeatedly upon
themselves" (p. 25). This loopiness is extensive; Brown reports that sometimes
a short fragment will cycle ceaselessly in his mind for hours at a time. At other
times, one fragment will loop for a while before inexplicably jumping to a new
one, which itself begins to loop. "The boundaries of the looped fragments . . . are
in general quite fuzzy. However, they correspond more or less to phrase boundaries in the music, where the end point of the fragment is usually more stable
than the starting point" (p. 30). By Brown's estimate, fragments have a minimum
length on the order of a few measures, and will loop either at that core level (say,
the level of a half-phrase), or at a larger level that includes the core segment (say,
the level of the phrase or section). The endpoints of the looping fragments are
almost always the same; it is very rare for a fragment to cut off midway through.
The looping is often accompanied by finger movements (Brown is a pianist)
that reflect the contour of the melody, or by tapping or other rhythmic motions;
moreover, Brown notes that his breathing pattern often synchronizes with the
rhythm, proceeding as if he were singing the line himself (regardless of whether
the imagined melody is actually sung or played on an instrument).

Brown expressly contrasts the loopiness of musical imagery with the "stream-
iness" of verbal imagery. Inner speech doesn't tend to jump around and loop
repeatedly like musical imagery, a distinction that leads Brown to theorize that

musical and verbal imagery "may have different underlying natures" (p. 37). He attributes this possible distinction to differences between the typical characteristics of music and speech, respectively. He cites Lomax to the effect that "music is much more formulaic, redundant and repetitive than language (Lomax, 1968)" (p. 30) and that "song may be recognized and defined as more frequently redundant at more levels than any other kind of vocalizing (Lomax, 1968)" (p. 37).

Contrary to Brown, I make the case throughout this book that the repetitiveness of musical imagery and actual music, rather than one being influenced by the other, are two manifestations of a general property of the cognitive musical capacity. Furthermore, modern recording technology has allowed composers and performers to play with this characteristic in a "knowing" way that is consistent with what Jonathon Kramer calls the "attitudes" of postmodernism (Kramer, 2002). These attitudes include a kind of ironic distance that can emerge when cognitive predispositions (e.g., toward musical repetition) become available for playful use and consideration within the music itself.

A cognitive tendency so closely tied to motor systems, and so squarely removed from conceptual and rational kinds of thought, can naturally arouse suspicions; particularly when its repetitive structures so powerfully evoke systems of mass production and a threatening mechanization (as explored in Fink, 2005 and Auner, 2003). Auner raises the example of the last utterance of the dying HAL in *2001: A Space Odyssey*, observing that its repetitiveness (*I can feel it. I can feel it. I can feel it.*) encapsulates the horror of a kind of erasure of the human (p. 112). He quotes W. G. Sebald's description of a brand of physical disgust that can arise in response to inadvertent repetition in behavior or conversation—a sensation that is likely familiar to many. I recall one occasion when I was collecting data for a project, ushering participant after participant into a soundproof booth in a room where other researchers were working at various workstations. As I repeated the same instructions to each participant, and answered the same questions that tended to arise mid-experiment with the same language while my colleagues worked away in silence at their computers, I found myself almost irresistibly drawn to slight variations in the order or wording of my statements, disturbed by something inhuman and sinister in the experience of hearing the same words coming out of my mouth again and again. The same sort of squeamish feeling can arise when a person retells a story you've already heard, especially if the retelling includes verbatim locutions. Part of this discomfort is attributable to the fact that verbatim repetitions violate Gricean conversational maxims (see Grice, 1991) to reduce redundancy and remain maximally relevant, making the speaker seem boorish or improperly socialized. But part of it is attributable to discomfort at the idea that thoughts are not our own, spontaneous, soul-engendered entities, but rather products of some invisible, subconscious script: it's a fear about automaticity and loss of control.

While verbal repetition, especially verbatim verbal repetition, can raise these sorts of fears, the execution of motor scripts often fails to trouble us in the slightest. I'm not at all worried that I use the same movements every time I brush my teeth, or that I move about the kitchen every morning in precisely the same sequence assembling a cup of coffee, using the same gestures, and following an identical series of steps. In fact, it is only when these routines are interrupted that I am even aware of them: if the mug is not on the shelf as expected, or the toothbrush fell on the floor. The repetitiveness of imagined and real musical stimuli have more in common, I would argue, with the inconspicuous repetitiveness of these routines than with the highly marked form of repetitiveness that can occasionally occur in language. Even when the linguistic repetition is goal-directed and necessary (as in the repeated instructions to experiment participants)—not different in function from the kind of repetition that occurs in the case of tooth brushing or medicine preparing—it's salient and unsettling.

## The Verbatim

Reyna and Brainerd (1995) posit a "fuzzy-trace theory," attributing two separate kinds of mental representations to people: verbatim traces and gist traces. Verbatim traces record surface details, but gist traces bypass the surface and encode the underlying semantic content. Gist traces more frequently form the basis for reasoning. In a series of papers, notably Brainerd and Kingma (1984), these authors and their colleagues showed that children were able to perform well on reasoning tasks even when their memory for the specifics of the initial premise information had degraded. This disassociation between surface retrieval and reasoning ability led to the notion that verbatim and gist information are encoded separately, and stored in parallel. The verbatim trace decays rapidly, but the gist trace can last for long periods of time (Brainerd & Reyna, 1996). When asked to recall a story or a sentence, people often paraphrase, reflecting a tendency toward gist over verbatim memory (Gernsbacher, 1985). Elementary school students asked to retell the gist of a story were more fluent and used fewer and shorter pauses than students asked to retell it verbatim (Schoenpflug, 2008). Field (2004) observes in a survey of the literature that it "appears that listeners and readers jettison surface form as soon as possible in favour of a more easily stored conceptual representation" (p. 319). Hunter (1984) claims not only that people lack the kind of memory that would allow them to reproduce prose verbatim, but also that they lack the kind of memory that would allow them to recognize whether a reproduction was verbatim in the first place. In his assessment, it wasn't until the technology of written text emerged that this kind of reckoning became possible. He terms the inability to accurately distinguish whether a speech, saga, or story actually constitutes a word-for-word repetition of its previous telling "verbatim insensitivity."

Although older children are adult-like in the sense that they employ a predominantly gist-based memory, young children rely primarily on verbatim memory (Reyna and Brainerd, 1995). In what I would argue constitutes a behavioral reflection of this cognitive difference, children crave repetition—they want to hear the same stories again and again, and will often protest vehemently if specific words are omitted or altered. These twin qualities—enhanced verbatim memory and elevated appetite for repetition—also characterize responses in adulthood to a particular domain: music.

Calvert (1991) and Calvert and Tart (1993) examined how changing whether information was presented in spoken or sung form affected the accuracy of gist and verbatim memory. Sung information elicited better verbatim recall, but spoken information elicited better gist recall. This parallels previous findings that children's verbatim recall for nursery rhymes—a category as music-like as text gets—surpasses their verbatim recall for prose passages (Johnson & Hayes, 1987), but their content recall for nursery rhymes lags behind their content recall for prose passages (Hayes, Chemelski & Palmer, 1982). Children's memory for educational material presented during the television program *School House Rock* followed the same pattern: songs improved verbatim memory, but spoken presentations improved comprehension of content (Calvert, 2001). Wallace (1994) showed that singing a text rather than speaking it also improved verbatim recall in adults. More recently, Tillmann & Dowling (2007) and Dowling, Tillmann & Ayers (2001) adapted a paradigm from an early study that demonstrated poor verbatim memory for linguistic sentences (Sachs, 1967) to study verbatim memory for music. Their work revealed that verbatim memory for musical phrases, in contrast to linguistic sentences, was quite good and not subject to the same kind of deterioration over time.

The comparison between memory traces for language and for music only holds if the paradigms used to study them each are deeply similar. Sachs presented people with a short story and asked them to distinguish between a sentence drawn from early in the narrative and various foils. Foils came in two varieties: entirely novel sentences (featuring both different words and different meanings than any found in the story), and paraphrases (sentences with different words but the same meaning as some found in the story). Increasing temporal delay between the story presentation and the task led to increasingly poor performance in discriminating the original from the paraphrase. Temporal delay did not, however, damage performance in discriminating the original from a different sentence. Participants remembered the gist of what had been recounted, and could easily identify when a sentence featured a meaning different from any found in the story. They couldn't, however, recall surface detail—a paraphrase of an original sentence was as likely to be identified as belonging to the story as the actual sentence with the original wording.

In the Dowling studies, listeners heard a minuet from the classical period and were asked to discriminate a target phrase from near the beginning of the piece from either an entirely new phrase or a similar lure that preserved the melodic and rhythmic contour but changed the pitch level or texture. Even with increasing delay, participants remained good at distinguishing the original phrase not only from the different one, but also from the similar lure. Their memory, in other words, was quite verbatim in nature, linked to specific attributes of the original stimulus, rather than to its gist. The Sachs studies on speech and the Dowling studies on music preserve elements of experimental design as much as possible given the differing natures of the material, lending credence to the notion that their contrasting results expose a real contrast in mental representation.

What accounts for this difference in the nature of musical and linguistic memory? Gernsbacher (1985) suggests that as a written story unfolds, readers build substructures in order to integrate information, sustaining all the relevant details in working memory until a point of closure. At this point, all the surface information is discarded so that a new substructure can be initiated; only the thematic content, which continues to be relevant, is held in mind. Field (2004) reviews a number of studies that provide evidence that people jettison verbatim content at structural boundaries (p. 318). It's simply no longer relevant. Yet in musical contexts, aspects of the surface remain relevant across closural boundaries. Motives are played with, rhythms are echoed, pitches are returned to. The prevalence of musical repetition underscores the importance of the surface. Musicians often speak about repetition in didactic terms: repetition teaches the listener what the basic materials of the piece are. Repetition tells the listener what will constitute the piece's basic idea—not what gist-like point should be derived from this idea, but rather what the idea itself *is*, at its surface.

Tillmann and Dowling (2007) show that memory for the surface details of a particular phrase decreased across delays for phrases embedded within a prose story, but not for phrases embedded within a poem. This finding parallels that of Dowling, Tillman & Ayers (2001), which showed that delays did not diminish memory for the surface details of musical phrases embedded within larger pieces. In fact, delays not only failed to diminish verbatim memory for poetry and music, but also actually resulted in fewer false alarms to the similar lure. Time seemed to allow for a better representation of the phrase's specific details, making it easier to distinguish from phrases constructed to be similar in gist. This trend represents not just an absence of the one found for prose, but actually its opposite. Krumhansl (2010), moreover, has shown that listeners can identify the emotional tenor, style, decade of release, and even artist and title from extremely brief 400 ms clips of songs popular between 1960 and 2010. The information in these clips often contains no more than a kind of grain or timbral configuration and includes none of the elements typically considered essential to a piece of music's identity: the sequence of notes constituting its theme, the rhythmic progression constituting its temporal signature, the harmonic unfolding constituting its basic structure. The clips convey only a verbatim snippet, and this scant information is sufficient to trigger surprisingly sophisticated kinds of recognition, contributing further evidence to the unique relevance of verbatim representations to music.

The relationship between poetry and music has been variously explored, overstated, and backed away from (for a contemporary account with a perceptual bent, see Lerdahl, 2001). Tillmann and Dowling attribute the shared pattern of verbatim recollection for poetry and music to the joint use of rhythmic and temporal features (such as rhyme and meter) that limit the possibilities for word choice and thus enhance memory for the original words. Whatever the mechanism, this investment in the surface makes repetition more likeable in poetry and music; repetition, in contrast to variation, repositions before the listener precisely the thing the listener is to care about: the phrase itself (Hatten refers to the "irreducible significance of the surface" (1994, p. 160). But in prose, where the investment is in the *meaning*, restatement in different words might get the listener closer to what matters, while verbatim repetition might mire them in the surface, a distraction from the intended semantic essence. The phenomenon of semantic satiation chronicled in Chapter 1 exemplifies this danger; verbatim repetition draws attention down to the component phonemes, or letters, or notes—something unwelcome in many prose contexts but desirable in types of music and poetry.

Aside from poetry, verbatim memory for language is also enhanced when the utterance has high interactional content, as in a joke, insult or catchphrase (as opposed to a transactional, informative statement). In these cases, words serve more clearly as a kind of action, a parry or riposte, and memory for the words represents memory for the action rather than for some encoded semantic association. The rhythm and temporal structure explanation fails with regard to enhanced verbatim memory for jokes and insults; although some sorts of jokes possess this kind of structure, insults as a rule do not. Their verbatim memorability may be enhanced when such a structure is invoked ("*Junie* and *Jonny sittin'* in a *tree*"), but this structure itself doesn't seem to provide a full account of the verbatim boost for this kind of utterance.

High verbatim memory, rather than (or in addition to) benefiting from temporal structure, seems to reflect an implicit commitment to the idea that something valuable resides in the surface content. It can be taken as an index of the value assigned to the actual details of the stimulus over and above some abstract content for which those details serve as a vessel. Just as the significance of a poem often resides in specific word choices and their nuanced associations and connotations, as well as in their interrelationship, the significance of an insult often resides in the specific word choice and the timbral nuances used to utter it. These elements are the most resistant to conceptual capture, and thus benefit most from repetition.

## Technology of the Verbatim

Hunter (1984) observes that the technology of writing made possible not only a kind of verbatim repetition of text that hadn't previously been possible, but also a kind of verification mechanism that was new: it was now possible to *check* whether the repetition had indeed been word for word. Audio recording technology makes possible an even more intense record of the verbatim: replication that is not simply word-for-word, but syllable-for-syllable, cough-for-cough, flub-for-flub—repetition at a kind of grain that goes finer than the word down to the nuances of spoken expression.

Very early in its history, by at least 1900, the phonograph was being marketed as a specifically musical device. The kind of verbatim replication it made possible was from the start more closely aligned with music than any other kind of sound. But Picker (2001) highlights the anxiety and disorientation that this technology produced:

> Quite suddenly in the late 1880s, throwing voices became easy, but lost was the control that the ventriloquist had always had over placement and timing. With such fiendish possibilities, the operation of the phonograph carried inherent risk, for the playback process was open to manipulation by anyone with access to the controls. Having made a record, how would it be used, and when, where, and for whom would it be played? (p. 769-770)

While the sound might be reproduced note for note, its geographic and social setting could become alarmingly labile. This transformation gradually ushered in a fetish for music as an abstract weaving-together of sounds, rather than music as a discrete social act. The psychological proclivity for musical repetition in conjunction with the technological affordance of audio reproduction gave rise to new ideas about what constituted music, ideas most nakedly espoused in formalist approaches to music listening and composition but prevalent in subtler forms throughout twentieth-century music (see Lippman, 1994). These developments can be best understood as the result of psychological tendencies interacting with technology and culture in complex feedback loops that constrain, in turn, listening behavior, compositional/productional behavior, technological invention, and user behavior; as each of these elements changes, it feeds back into the network and alters the others. A contributing force underneath all of these behaviors is the appetite for musical repetition—an appetite that might be exploited or inhibited by various cultural and technological forces, but that remains a limiting factor.

As has been well explored by Philip (2004) and Katz (2004), the mass dissemination of classical music recordings had significant effects on musical composition and performance. Philip traces how recording technology facilitated the development of standard instrumental sounds with newly universalized practices of vibrato and tuning, as well as the development of a new performance ideal valuing accuracy in terms of notes and rhythms. This new ideal eroded numerous idiosyncratic but common practices, including the heavy use of portamento (sliding from note to note on string instruments), hand asynchrony (deliberately misaligning in time the left and right hand on the piano), and wild within-piece tempo variation.

In Charles Rosen's 2005 article on Philip's book in *The New York Review of Books*, he mentions his own repeated listenings to Schnabel's recording of Mozart's Piano Concerto in C Major, K. 467, noting that "a sudden rhythmic hurrying of the second theme...was interesting and effective when I first heard it; now I wait for it [to] come and it is an irritant." This observation raises several interesting issues, including whether listeners respond differently to expressive inflections across multiple hearings, and whether musicians, aware of this danger, might perform differently when recording. Rosen seconds Philip's observation that pianist Rudolf Serkin's recordings "are less interesting, less spontaneous than his best concerts"—presumably a result of the performer's effort to avoid a potential transformation across rehearings from the spontaneous and expressive to the mannered and annoying. Similarly, Rosen avers, Horowitz's recording of Prokofiev's Seventh Sonata is "considerably more prudent than his live renditions."

In 1966, Glenn Gould published a lengthy article in *High Fidelity* arguing for his previously announced and already controversial position that recordings would make live performances extinct. Comments on the subject by leading figures in the music world were included in the margins, including this one by Aaron Copland:

> For me, the most important thing is the element of chance that is built into a live performance. The very great drawback of recorded sound is the fact that it is always the same. No matter how wonderful a recording is, I know that I couldn't live with it—even of my own music—with the same nuances forever.

These remarks actually touch on a central issue in music theory, cognition, and aesthetics—the notion of expectation, which has been viewed as central to music and emotion (Huron & Margulis, 2010). Stretching back to Leonard Meyer in the 1950s, whose work was influenced by Dewey's conflict theory of emotions (1895), there has been a notion that musical affect arises when an expectation is set up and then thwarted. Since Meyer, there has been much theoretical and empirical study about what kinds of expectation exist, how they are elicited, and what effect it might have on the listener if these expectations are fulfilled or denied (Huron & Margulis, 2010 reviews this work). Part of the appeal of live performance, especially in an age of recording, lies in the introduction of unexpected nuance and expressive inflection—waiting milliseconds longer than is conventional before a resolution, or voicing a chord slightly differently than is standard. Yet as the quotations above make clear, these same kinds of performance choices—the very ones that make live performance worth hearing—can be reduced to caricature when recorded and subjected to multiple replays. With their strict renditions on recording, performers seem to seek a reconfiguring of the perceptual landscape such that recordings will become a kind of common, expectation-setting body of reference against which performances can then play, choreographing affective experiences by subtly deviating from the straightness found in typical recordings.

But almost everyone has an anecdote about coming to love a particular recording in youth or adolescence, listening again and again to the same performance, only to be disappointed by every live performance of that piece in which different things happen with the timing, or in which a disappointingly "right" note is played when the recording featured a pleasantly "wrong" one. When most everyday listening happens through recordings, and when most recordings feature a high level of technical cleanness and expressive restraint, these practices do not serve as a kind of neutral background on which more individualized live performances can stand; rather, they come to define the set of expectations listeners bring to new musical experiences. Live performances come to be experienced as particular instances of a more general body of "music," where music is understood as something akin to a set of platonic forms—a body of recordings whose sources might lie not only in the drawing of a bow across a string or the movement of air through a cylinder, but also in digital editing and manipulation. This represents a full reversal from early ideas about the relationship between performance and recording, when cassette tapes were marketed for their fidelity to live performance: "Is it live, or is it Memorex?" (Katz, 2010). If musical enculturation—the largely implicit process of coming to make sense of a particular culture's musical soundscape—tends to happen largely out of various kinds of contact with recordings, then expectations are set by the range of what is normal and what is possible in the corpus of recorded sound, not by the range of what is normal and possible in live performance. This set of recording-shaped expectations, implicit in the minds of listeners at live performances, significantly defines the culture within which the live performance is understood.

*Figure 4.1*  Pamina's aria from Mozart, *The Magic Flute*.

Repetition as a fact of musical practice and usage, in fact, has traditionally posed the biggest challenge for the expectational account of musical affect. This problem, termed "Wittgenstein's puzzle" (Dowling & Harwood, 1986), asks how, if deviations from expectation produce affect, music can continue to remain moving after multiple hearings, when listeners clearly know what to expect? Or, as Meyer puts it:

> If a work has been heard already, we will know what is going to happen and, in later hearings, the improbable will become probable, the unexpected will be expected, and all predictions will be confirmed... But is not precisely the opposite the case? The better we know a work—the more often we have heard it—the more we enjoy it and the more meaningful it becomes (1967, 46).

Whether it is in fact the case, as Meyer claims here, that repeated exposure systematically increases enjoyment will be returned to in the next chapter. For the moment, the principal point is that moving musical events often continue to seem affectively powerful even when we've encountered them enough times for surprise, as ordinarily construed, to be an unlikely explanation.

Bharucha (1987) proposed that the solution to Wittgenstein's puzzle lies in the fact that there are two types of expectations, schematic and veridical. Schematic expectations arise from familiarity with typical practice, but veridical expectations arise from familiarity with what happens in a specific piece, even if the thing that happens is odd. For example, if a person knows the aria in Figure 4.1 well, she knows that the dominant chord at the end of the excerpt's third measure resolves deceptively to VI, rather than proceeding to I as is typical. But even if this listener's veridical expectation targeted the Eb major chord (VI), her schematic expectation would continue to predict a G minor chord (i), on the basis of what typically happens after a cadential dominant. Thus, a person can continue to be surprised in one way, even when she's utterly "in the know" in another. This duality has been argued to explain the preserved sense of deception and affective charge in deceptive cadences, even when they've been heard many times in overfamiliar repertoire.

The urge to create ever more elaborate deviations has been identified as a driving force behind stylistic change in music. A gambit that was unusual and highly charged at one time (say, the diminished seventh at the start of the nineteenth century) can come to seem ordinary and ineffective after repeated use (say, the diminished seventh by the end of the nineteenth century). Composers must then find new ways of deviating from expectations, since these expectations have broadened to encompass the thing (e.g., the diminished seventh) that initially functioned as a deviation but has now become a standard part of the vocabulary. Arguably, recording technology allows this progression to happen faster; more people can listen more times to the latest thing, causing a more rapid saturation in the efficacy of any new, deviating element, and precipitating the need for the ever-speedier invention of new ways to thwart predictions. The possibility for increased repetitiveness made possible by technology, in other words, can be hypothesized to accelerate stylistic change.

While our appetite for repetition in music is no doubt spectacular, and outpaces our appetite for repetition in many other domains, our response to repetition is still distinctly nonlinear—repetition doesn't seem to enamor us more and more of a piece *indefinitely*; rather, at some point, our affections reach a maximum and then decline with further repetition. Thus, composers and performers have a very real challenge, especially given current technology-enhanced modes of listening practice, in identifying the sweet spot between performances that are too standard and familiar and performances that are too new and unfamiliar. How much will the typical listener rehear this rendition? How many similar things have they typically already heard and reheard? These kinds of questions form part of the subterranean ground of musical concerns that emerge in the guise of musical intuitions and taste.

For example, when a performer takes on a piece heavily associated with a particular recording, say the Goldberg Variations (commonly associated with Glenn Gould's landmark recordings) or certain Scarlatti Sonatas (commonly associated with recorded performances by Vladimir Horowitz), elements of his or her performance can be understood to obliquely refer to these "standards." If Gould sped through a variation, or Horowitz used extreme dynamic contrasts in a particular passage, a contemporary performer might expressly slow down the same variation, or attenuate the dynamic extremes and highlight a rhythmic contrast in the same passage. In this way, the repetition afforded by recording technology can redefine what is tacitly understood to form the background culture within which the performance is taking place, causing distinct changes in performance practice. It can also, more worryingly, result in a deeper divide between the cognoscenti and the uninitiated, the former of whom may have spent years familiarizing themselves with basic recordings. This familiarization sets up a network of expectations that performers (themselves surely well steeped in this body of work) can play with; while highly satisfying to "super-fans," these deviations may be unrecognizable to newer parts of the audience, who lack the familiarity with standard recordings that would allow them to erect the expectations the performances are thwarting. Chapter 6 explores the relationship between performance and repetition in more detail.

# 5

# Relistenings

Repetition is a topic of interest not only for the way it characterizes material within individual pieces, but also for how it characterizes the way we listen (and relisten) to them. The repetitive aspect of music is multiplied many times over by ordinary listening behaviors, as we return again and again to our favorite pieces. Sometimes relistenings are involuntary, as when radio stations and airport concourses impose replays on their listenership. But whether voluntary or captive, relistenings have broadly, if not perfectly, predictable effects. The number of repeated exposures, crude though that measure seems, has a startlingly clear relationship to the complex construct of "musical pleasure."

To get a sense of the relationship between pleasure and relistening, imagine a song you hated the first time you heard it—on the radio, or in a lobby somewhere. But as it keeps getting played and replayed, every time you overhear it, its allure subtly grows. It becomes harder not to tap, or nod, or sing along a bit. Eventually, it might even sneak its way guiltily onto your playlist. In the end, however, if you've heard it too many times over a short span of time, you may once again start to realize why you hated it in the first place. This example, which might seem painfully familiar, points to an interesting characteristic of repetition—it works one way at first, and then another way later. In many cases, it increases pleasure for a certain period and then reduces it. The relationship between exposure and enjoyment, in other words, is nonlinear.

It seems remarkable that such a simple thing—hearing a piece again—can have significant and reliable effects on as complex a phenomenon as enjoyment. Jakobovits (1966) saw the way patterns of radio playtime reflected this relationship, and designed a study that documented the reception of songs that *Variety*, a weekly magazine on show business, listed on the Hit Parade, an index of radio airtime. By examining the dynamics of the songs' position on the list, he was able to explicitly connect radio playtime with the psychological mechanisms put forth in the Wundt curve (Figure 5.1). The Wundt curve's inverted U traces the initial increase in pleasure ("hedonic value") across repeated exposures, and

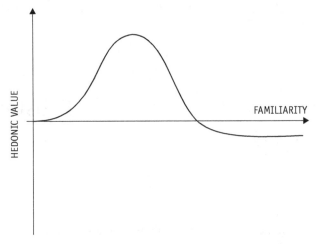

*Figure 5.1* The Wundt curve traces a nonlinear, inverted-U relationship between hedonic value (pleasure/liking) and stimulus familiarity.

the ultimate decrease once the exposures have become too numerous—a trend documented for all types of stimuli, but particularly evident in the real-world example of a typical song's introduction, saturation, and retirement from radio play. One needn't consult only the Top 40 cycle for evidence; ever since Zajonc's work on mere exposure in the 1960s, psychologists have known that the prior presentation of a stimulus affects preference for it later. This relationship has been identified as more robust for complex, ecologically valid stimuli such as actual music, over simpler, laboratory-based stimuli such as computer-generated beeps (Szpunar et al., 2004). Richer stimuli offer the kind of intricacy that allows a listener to derive more from repeated exposures.

Schellenberg (2008) makes the clearest contemporary case for the centrality of repeated exposures in cognitive and affective responses to music. Historically, most experiments that explore this topic took place in the 1960s and 1970s. The psychoaesthetics literature of that time, reviewed in Berlyne (1974), investigated the effect of repeated exposures on preference for various types of stimuli. The Wundt curve illustrates the relationship identified by the studies: familiarity initially yields increasing pleasure (or "hedonic value"), but ultimately yields increasing displeasure.

Two mechanisms have been posited to account for the inverted U-shaped preference response across repeated exposures; Szpunar, Schellenberg & Pliner (2004) provide an excellent overview of both. The perceptual fluency model (Bornstein & D'Agostino, 1994) explains that people misattribute the processing facilitation associated with a familiar stimulus to some positive attribute of the stimulus itself (Mandler, Nakamura & Van Zandt, 1987). Pleased by their own processing fluency and the sense of acumen and power it confers, but unaware of the origins of this sensation, they assume that the triggering stimulus itself (rather than the repeated presentation of it) possesses some special, pleasing quality. According to this account, the tail part of the inverted U, where pleasure decreases, can be understood as a consequence of increased conscious recognition—as people become aware that the perceptual fluency results from prior exposure, they stop misattributing this effect to the stimulus. Berlyne (1971) proposes a different explanation for the inverted U: the ascending part arises from an evolutionarily conditioned preference for the familiar, based on the notion that if a stimuli was previously encountered and you lived to encounter it again, it's inherently preferable to the unknown. The descending part of the U, on this read, stems from a different evolutionarily conditioned preference that favors novelty-seeking; if an organism never explored its environment, it might miss opportunities and lose the capacity to deal with change. The full inverted U reflects the interaction of these two opposing impulses, the positive learned safety effect on the one hand, and an aversion to boredom on the other.

The timescale of the satiation effect varies with the complexity of the stimulus. In the most ecologically valid study to date, Szpunar, Schellenberg & Pliner (2004) presented listeners with repetitions of fifteen-second excerpts from orchestral and chamber music of the Baroque, Classical, and Romantic periods. These excerpts were short enough to induce a complete range of exposure-related responses in a single experimental session. Although responses to full-length works might be more interesting, time constraints make it impossible to repeat them a sufficient number of times in a single session, and logistical constraints make it difficult to retain participants across multiple sessions. Szpunar, Schellenberg & Pliner (2004) confirm the intuition that ecological validity strengthens the satiation effect—the more complex and ecologically valid the presented object, the larger the initial increases in liking as the structural complexity gradually becomes manageable. But, even for very difficult stimuli, after the complexity has been absorbed, boredom intercedes and satiation reduces pleasure. Tan, Spackman & Peaslee (2006) further underscore the role of complexity in responses to repeated exposures, finding that repeated hearings increased liking for patchwork compositions (comprised of sections of actual pieces that had been extracted and reinserted in random order) but not for intact compositions (where the sections occurred in the typical order). Both of these findings tend to support a third explanation, the one generally advocated here: repeated listenings engage listeners with the stimulus at different levels, connecting them with new aspects of the same sound. Very simple stimuli don't offer enough at either end of the hierarchy—timbral richness, or large-scale structure—to reward new perspectives. Understood in this light, it's not a piece of music's familiarity, per se, that is rewarding, but rather the kind of involvement that familiarity affords.

Hunter and Schellenberg (2011) asked whether personality traits might affect the way individuals respond to repetition. A reanalysis of data from past studies in Schellenberg's lab revealed that although at the group level—averaged across all responses—their participants showed the typical inverted-U response to music across repeated exposures, fewer than half exhibited this response pattern individually. They designed a new study to investigate whether personality might account for some of the variation in response patterns among individuals.

In the new study, participants again exhibited an inverted-U response across exposures at the group level, but Schellenberg found an intriguing interaction between the pattern of responses and "Openness-to-Experience," one of the personality dimensions identified by the Big Five Inventory—capturing an appetite for new experiences, a willingness to reevaluate traditional political or moral beliefs, a vivid imagination, intellectual curiosity, receptivity to inner emotional states, and a predilection for aesthetic experience (see John, Naumann & Soto, 2008). People who scored high on Openness-to-Experience tended to like pieces less and less with repeated exposure, but people who scored low on Openness-to-Experience tended to like them more and more over the same period.

These data reaffirm that musical enjoyment is a complex construct, dependent on at least the following factors: situation/context (Is the music being heard in a club, at a wedding, or in a fluorescent-lit lab?); a person's "listening biography," the sum of previous exposures to, knowledge about, and experiences with music of different styles and traditions (Wong, Chan & Margulis, 2012; Wong et al., 2011; Wong, Roy & Margulis 2009); personality (Does the person value new experiences and intellectual challenges? Does she prefer to attend aesthetically or leave music in the background?); mood at the start of the listening session; intrinsic features of the music, including structure, style, content; and general psychological characteristics, such as limitations on memory, pitch perception, and so on.

This chapter, and this book in general, aims to understand as much as possible about the very last factor, the psychological constraints and affordances that affect experiences of repeating music. Still, it is important to acknowledge that all of these factors interrelate in complex ways, and it is not always possible to eliminate the impact of other forces even in the best controlled experiments. For example, using strange beeps as stimuli to attempt to control for familiarity with the materials may inhibit people from relating to the music holistically as "real" music; presenting real-world music as stimuli in a soundproof booth may not elicit the kind of orientation to music that would emerge in a more naturalistic setting; collecting data in a real concert hall (as is now possible in several concert halls around the world, including at McGill University in Montreal where individual seats have been wired for data collection) may be problematized by associations participants carry over from previous experiences in the space; and these are but a smattering of the kinds of challenges faced by people trying to understand more about the psychology of music listening. Moreover, although it is reasonable to think that you might get a read on a person's enjoyment by asking him directly, methods reliant on this kind of explicit report suffer from a tendency for participants to provide the result they think the experimenter is looking for (Jolicoeur & Kosslyn, 1985).

Hunter and Schellenberg (2010) address these possibilities carefully in their discussion of the effects of personality on music liking across exposures. They acknowledge that people high on the personality trait of Openness-to-Experience may have listened differently, with more focused attention, causing the music to become familiar faster than if it had been relegated to background sound. Moreover, they note that people high on this personality trait may have been more familiar with the kind of classical music used as stimuli in the study, particularly since Rentfrow & Gosling (2003) and Rentfrow & McDonald (2010) have shown that people with high Openness-to-Experience scores tend to gravitate toward more "elite" genres such as classical music. Although this supposition was not supported by a main effect of liking (the people who scored high on Openness-to-Experience didn't show overall higher liking ratings for the music than people who didn't), they may have used the scale differently relative to their own body of listening experience. In short, Hunter and Schellenberg's study demonstrates that the laboratory idealization of the Wundt curve must be applied conservatively to actual cases of aesthetic experience in the real world; all kinds of variables, including personality, mediate its effects.

One of the beguiling things about the inverted-U response to repeated exposures is its seeming robustness across different modalities (visual, auditory) and different stimuli (pop music as in North & Hargreaves, 1995; classical music as in Hunter and Schellenberg, 2010; and strings of beeps as in Vitz, 1966). Can it really be that there's some predictable trajectory for experiences of liking across exposures to these highly different phenomena? Orr and Ohlsson (2001) question in particular the role of musical style in these responses, noting that complexity is an important modulator of preference effects (a subject well explored in Beauvois, 2007), but may influence liking differently in different styles. Participants in their study listened to improvisations in jazz and bluegrass and rated both the music's perceived complexity and their liking for each excerpt; results showed an inverted-U response for excerpts in a bluegrass style, but not for excerpts in a jazz style. Using a similar methodology but enrolling expert performers as subjects, Orr and Ohlsson (2005) established that the relationship between perceived complexity and liking did not hold for experts. They provide several possible explanations for this difference, favoring the notion that experts have developed deep criteria for engaging with stimuli in their own domain, and that these criteria override the complexity concerns that generally influence responses.

Orr and Ohlsson's studies didn't investigate familiarity or repeated exposures; instead, they looked at complexity, which has also been shown to engender inverted-U patterns for liking similar to those found when familiarity is varied (there is, however, a relationship between these two phenomena—as listeners are reexposed to a piece, its perceived complexity decreases). Their work further reinforces the notion that many different factors, such as the distinct expectations people bring to a particular style, can modulate the real-world effects of even well-established laboratory phenomena. What's surprising is not that experiences like aesthetic appreciation and human enjoyment have their origins in many different things, but rather that generalizations about them can be made at all.

With the broader agenda of using different methodologies and more ecologically valid stimuli to research the effects of repeated exposures to musical pieces, Patrick Wong and I chose a twenty-minute orchestral piece that was unfamiliar to all of our participants—Bizet's *L'Arlesienne Suite No. 1*—and supervised their exposure to this work over headphones in the lab on five occasions across a period of ten days (Wong & Margulis, 2008). After every exposure, we asked them to perform a set of tasks. For a subset of participants, we also used fMRI to assess changes in neurophysiologic response before their first exposure, at the midpoint of the exposures, and after the final exposure. Participants' enjoyment ratings showed the expected inverted-U curve, but more interestingly, the ratings at one session were highly correlated with the number of earworms that participants reported having endured when asked at the start of the next session. What hidden factor might have mediated the relationship between enjoyment and earworm frequency? Perhaps listeners who enjoyed the piece paid more attention while listening, making the material more available for later recall. Perhaps listeners who reported enjoying the piece were more virtually engaged by it and experienced a higher degree of physical connection—in other words, participants who felt physically *played by the piece* might not only have enjoyed it more, but were also more susceptible to the music hijacking their motor circuitry in the form of an earworm.

Participants were also asked to perform a number of descriptive tasks after each hearing—to detail the kind of film the music might accompany, describe the piece as they would to a group of friends, or provide a review of the piece for an online database. The descriptions participants provided in response to these three questions were coded for level of analysis and level of engagement. Level of analysis coding reflected the degree to which participants' descriptions

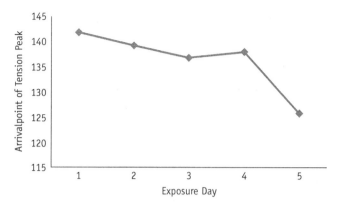

*Figure 5.2* Arrival point of moment of peak tension in Bizet's *L'Arlesienne Suite No. 1* across 5 days of exposure. Perceived tension peaked earlier and earlier as listeners came to anticipate the tensest event *before* it happened.

demonstrated an analytic partitioning of the piece, while level of engagement coding reflected the intensity of personal involvement contained in the descriptions' language. Interestingly, analytic attending peaked on the second exposure day, but engagement actually diminished for that hearing, not peaking until the last exposure on Day 5.

One way to understand these data is to hypothesize that on Day 2, when participants showed a high level of analytic partitioning of the piece but a low level of personal involvement, they were working to absorb the piece's structure, a process that made engagement more difficult. Only after this analysis had been sufficiently internalized could it recede into the background, allowing personal engagement to reemerge and intensify, enriched by the new familiarity with the underlying structure.

Participants were also presented with several shorter excerpts from the exposure piece and asked to move a slider to indicate fluctuations in perceived tension as they progressed. The mean tension highpoint for each excerpt on each day—the moment at which participants perceived musical tension to be at a maximum—was identified from the participants' tension slider responses. These tension peaks, representing the intensity of the tensest moment in each excerpt, decreased in height linearly across exposure days. The affective impact, in other words, appeared to diminish with each exposure—a moment that seemed maximally intense on the first hearing seemed progressively less so with additional exposures.

Figure 5.2 plots the time point of the arrival of these tension peaks (not their intensity). Across the course of the exposures, the tension peaks came earlier and earlier. Increasingly familiar with the work, listeners were able to predict the arrival of the maximally tense point rather than simply wait for it and respond.

This trend implies that repeated exposures are actually able to reshape the time course of affective engagement with a piece of music. The height of the tension peak and the time point of its arrival were positively correlated. This correlation suggests that when people are *reacting* to a tense moment in the piece (late time point of arrival), that moment seems more intense to them (high tension peak), but when they are *anticipating* a tense moment (early time point of arrival), that moment seems less intense (low tension peak). Direct experience of a tense musical event seems to have a bigger impact than the imagination and anticipation of that event. It is an open question how these shifts in tension responses feed into composite experiences of musical pleasure, but they support the general notion that people hear differently across repeated exposures, such that reencounters with the same acoustic stimulus do not replicate the same perceptual experience.

David Huron has observed that although people claim to listen to "all kinds of music," the track play statistics on their iPod often reveal that they listen again and again to one kind of thing. In *Sweet Anticipation* (2006), he uses data from *Billboard Magazine* in the early 1990s to estimate that five albums in the typical listener's collection "account for some 90 percent of their self-programmed listening" (p. 241). Moreover, he observes that these pieces themselves typically contain a large amount of repetition, so by factoring in the prevalence of repeated hearing, as well as the prevalence of within-piece repetitions, Huron calculates that about "99 percent of all listening experiences involve listening to musical passages that the listener has heard before" (p. 241).

Perhaps this practice could be an artifact of some kind of situational constraint, rather than a direct preference for familiar music—for example, perhaps individuals prefer a certain set of qualities in their music, and the only way to reliably access music with these qualities is to revisit pieces known to have them. According to this scenario, it is conceivable that people would rather listen to a constant stream of new music featuring their preferred qualities, but lacking access to this ideal music generator, simply revert to their old favorites. Technology now exists, however, that can approximate the qualities of an ideal music generator, providing an inexhaustible stream of music that is unfamiliar but consistent with individual listeners' preferences. After listeners enter one or more seed songs or artists, Internet music services like Pandora and Spotify generate a station full of similar music. As the listener offers feedback on the recommendations, the station (theoretically, anyway) moves closer and closer to perfection.

Pandora is very good at predicting preference, and has a nearly limitless supply of music. Yet every Pandora station I've created or listened to still features a lot of replay. I suspect that the same pieces get replayed on individual stations not because the service has run out of similar music, but because people prefer it. I also suspect (understandably, Pandora won't disclose any part of their algorithms) that Pandora knows that people like the kind of music that they like, but they like it even more when it's familiar.

The suspicion that listening behavior (and Pandora DJing) is really driven by a preference for repetition—rather than by some situational constraint related to a lack of access to likable new music—could be tested even without access to Pandora algorithms. If a large enough sample of people were administered a survey about music preferences in which they checked off boxes next to songs they liked, a cluster would no doubt emerge within which preferences largely overlapped. The body of overlapping preferred songs for these participants could then be fed into Pandora, which would produce a stream of new songs similar to the ones enjoyed by the selected subgroup of participants. Two groups of songs that were unfamiliar but which conformed to the participants' preferences could be chosen from the stream: Group A and Group B. Half of participants would be exposed to a set of songs consisting of one presentation of each song in Group A and multiple presentations of each song in Group B. The other half would be exposed to a set consisting of one presentation of each song in Group B and multiple presentations of each song in Group A. If listeners were asked to rate their enjoyment after each song, these ratings should steadily increase across sessions for songs in the group that had been replayed (Group B for the first half of participants, Group A for the second). A study with this design could make a clearer case for the role of relistening in musical enjoyment if participants were found to prefer familiar music even in comparison to novel music featuring the same likeable qualities.

Another possible strategy for teasing apart the likeability of particular musical characteristics from the amount of exposure to them would be to construct some experimental music stations using the same materials: songs that an Internet music service predicted would be liked by the people whom the survey showed to share preferences. Each station would feature music the listeners are predicted to like, but the stations would vary according to the frequency of song rotation. One station would never repeat a song once it had been played; another would repeat a song every eight minutes; others would fall somewhere in between. The amount of time participants spent listening to their station could serve as an implicit measure of preference, and the amount they reported enjoying it could serve as an explicit measure. The prediction would be that people would listen longer and report higher enjoyment for stations that featured higher degrees of repetition—further contributing to the demonstration that familiarity itself, rather than a set of desirable musical qualities, materially influences preference.

In some sense, the implicit evidence for a relationship between repeated exposure and liking provided by widespread musical behavior is more compelling than the evidence collected in laboratory settings. The top-40 cycle on radio stations, where particular songs are played repeatedly for a certain amount of time before being pulled from circulation, and the common habit of listening and relistening to favorite records before retiring them for a period, are both good evidence for a sort of inverted-U relationship between familiarity and liking. The interesting questions are why this relationship is so particularly evident for music, and what the mechanism or mechanisms behind it might be.

## Replay

Cone (1977) examines repeated listening through the metaphor of three archetypes: a First Reading "based on total or partial ignorance of the events narrated" (p. 79) that "is purely experiential: one knows only what one experiences (i.e., is being told)" (p. 80); a Second Reading, in which "mystery and suspense are banished" and there is "no emotional involvement" (p. 79); and a Third Reading, or "Ideal Reading" (p. 81). "The Second Reading aims at an analysis," Cone writes:

> [and] treats the story, not as a work of art that owes its effect to progress through time, but as an object abstracted or inferred from the work of art, a static art-object that can be contemplated timelessly. Paradoxically, the Second Reading achieves its goal when it ceases to be a reading at all—when it becomes the pure contemplation of structure (p. 80).

Temporally, in the Second Reading, "the trajectory of thought is zigzag, or even discontinuous, constantly shifting back and forth between the planes of memory and experience" (p. 80). It is only in the Third Reading that experience once more gains supremacy—

> The reader follows the actual narration; but this time he is in a position fully to enjoy the journey, for he is now both confident of his direction and aware of the relative importance of each event along the way. He cannot fully suppress what he already knows, for he travels at the same time on the plane of memory; but he tries to ration what he knows in such a way as to make the path of experience as vivid and as exciting as possible (p. 80).

Cone's Third Reading privileges a certain kind of abandon; the listener must possess enough information to have the capacity to orient to relevant features, but can't be mired in the explicit work of identifying them. How does a Third Reading emerge? And how does temporal zigzagging occur—how is it possible to have knowledge of what will happen in a piece and still be swept away by it?

The 2008 Wong and Margulis study described above shows that a listener's level of analytic involvement with the piece (as calculated by counting the number of overt contrasts and sections in their descriptions of it) peaked on the second day of exposure, the same day their level of intensity of engagement with the piece (as calculated by the intensity of their language in the descriptive task) was at its lowest. This confluence of characteristics is reflective of Cone's Second Reading, in which a conscious engagement with conceptualized thought about the piece interferes with the kind of unmediated vividness achievable in a Third Reading, when the analysis has been sufficiently internalized. Repetition might be understood to tacitly orient a listener to different features and temporal scales such that a successful Third Reading can emerge without explicit study and analysis. While repetition may not be enough to take a listener to a Third Reading in all cases, it seems clear that for many casual listening contexts, relatively passive exposure is enough. Few listeners explicitly analyze their favorite music, but many nevertheless come to have deep and rewarding experiences with it. Repetition itself can work to involve listeners with music in rich, new ways.

In a 2010 experiment, I brought listeners without special training into a sort of Second-Reading encounter with excerpts from Beethoven String Quartets by prefacing them with written information about their structural or dramatic content. Participants reported enjoying the music less when it had been preceded by such information than when it had been presented fresh, with no preliminarily conferred knowledge. One explanation for these results is that participants who didn't receive special information enjoyed a kind of First Reading: fully sensorial, if somewhat ignorant. When they were provided information, it approximated the experience of a Second Reading, with a listener's attention moving in zigzags between conceptual thought about the piece and actual auditory experience of it; this aspirational kind of experience, directed at trying to synthesize modes of knowledge and achieve understanding, represents hard work and is typically experienced as less pleasurable.

These particular data can't inform Cone's last reading type, the third and supposedly ideal reading, in which knowledge about the piece has been so well mastered and successfully internalized that a person can return to a direct, sensorial experience of the sound, an experience that has nevertheless been enriched and transformed by knowledge gained during the less pleasant Second Reading stage. Neuhaus, Knösche & Friederici (2009) looked at the phenomenon of structural hearing, the process of listening for phrase patterns—a Second Reading kind of endeavor, entailing for example the explicit identification of a connection between two themes—and found that people tended to view pieces with an ABAB phrase structure as hierarchical and those with an AABB phrase structure as sequential. They also judged pieces in ABAB form as more coherent. These assessments were made via verbal report after the piece had ended.

Event-related potentials, changes in electrical activity recorded as the piece progressed via electrode caps placed over the scalp, showed no shifts related to these decisions in real time, suggesting that in normal musical encounters, considerations about structure are indulged in not during the ongoing trajectory of the piece, but after it ends. Listeners without special training, when asked to engage analytically with a piece in a Second-Reading kind of way, may do so between rather than during listenings. There seems to be something about *just* listening that is compelling, even when an analytic task is involved. People seem to like to listen and then think, rather than try to listen and think at the same time.

If one way to get from a First to a Third Reading is via a Second Reading stage comprised of explicit information about the piece (gained by analyzing, reading an analysis, or taking a class), another is via a Second Reading stage comprised exclusively of rehearings. The argument here is not necessarily that passive relistening without explicit study or examination is the *best* way to get to a maximally satisfying Third Reading musical experience (although this may be the case for some styles); it's simply that passive exposure, in some cases, *can* take a listener from a slippery first exposure to a more traction-filled experience. This account takes start and endpoints from Cone, but its characterization of the Second Reading stage departs radically from his, offering an alternative to get from stage one to stage three—an alternative that may be dependent on musical style, social context, personality, and other factors, but that, I argue, represents a fairly common route for many listeners.

In this account, the mechanism for the movement from stage one to three is not a kind of back and forth zigzag between perception and conception as a person consciously wrestles with a piece's structure and content (the pleasure of the experience a temporary casualty), but rather a steady and unconscious improvement in musical orientation, such that a person becomes more entrained with the piece without even realizing it's happening. The primary contrast here is between a conscious and committed grappling motivated by the intent to learn, with the ultimate goal of a more pleasurable listening experience in the future, and a casual reengagement with the piece motivated by the intent to take pleasure in the immediate moment, a byproduct of which might be implicit learning and an even more pleasurable listening experiences in the future.

## Implicit Learning

How might this experience of implicit learning work? There's something suspicious about the idea, like a TV commercial for a machine that "exercises" your abs while you lie about and read. Yet many varieties of implicit learning have been shown to take place during simple exposure to auditory stimuli. The statistical learning literature, for example, demonstrates that listeners track the event-to-event probabilities within musical styles unconsciously—but reliably. In the classic studies regarding this phenomenon (Saffran et al., 1999), both babies and adults were shown to have the ability to extract the three-note "words" within an otherwise undifferentiated stream of tones simply by tracking transition probabilities between the sounds. Since no special constraint governed word succession (any three-note word could follow any other three-note word), but within-word transitions were highly constrained, low probability transitions marked "word" boundaries. This research followed up on a study with the same design, which used sequences of syllables as stimuli (Saffran, Aslin & Newport, 1996) and showed how robust statistical tracking by eight-month-olds who had been exposed to only two minutes of syllable streams could account for processes of word segmentation in language learning.

Relatedly, statistical learning studies of music reveal a latent kind of absolute pitch representation in the general population (Saffran & Griepentrog, 2001). Although absolute pitch, the ability to identify a pitch independent of context or relationships with surrounding pitches, is generally held to characterize only 1 in 10,000 listeners (see an overview in Chapter 2), recent studies have shown that various degrees of "near" absolute pitch, or "enhanced pitch memory," or absolute pitch without labeling (the ability to store and represent individual notes without the ability to assign particular names to them) are more common. For one thing, babies seem to have reliable access to absolute pitch information, an ability that decays with age, presumably as listeners come to tune into the relative pitch information relevant to most Western music, where *Happy Birthday* remains *Happy Birthday* regardless of whether the starting pitch is a low C or a high A—the defining characteristic is the intervallic relationship *among* the pitches (see Figure 2.2).

Indeed, when Saffran, Aslin & Newport's 1999 study demonstrated that eight-month-old infants tracked the transition probabilities between individual pitches, it incidentally revealed that they must also have tracked the individual pitches themselves. Without a robust representation of G3, for example, they wouldn't have been able to track the probability that G3 would occur after B3. In addition, Levitin (1994) showed that people without absolute pitch or special musical training spontaneously sang the first notes of familiar songs on the correct pitch, or within a semitone of it. Moreover, people can recognize when familiar TV theme songs have been transposed to the "wrong" key (Schellenberg and Trehub, 2003), or when the dial tone has been played too high or too low (Smith and Schmuckler, 2008). Creel and Tumlin (2012) tracked eye movements to shapes that had been associated with particular melodies to demonstrate that ordinary listeners spontaneously employed both absolute and relative pitch information. Saffran and Griepentrog (2001) examined pitch perception across the lifespan, demonstrating that both infants and adults have some varieties of relative and absolute pitch at their disposal. Infants, however, tend to default to absolute pitch representations, and adults to relative ones.

Statistical learning is critical to understanding the effect of rehearings on experience, because it demonstrates that listeners are able to learn a lot about a piece without knowing that they're learning anything. The level of sophistication and robustness with which people can abstract statistical properties from auditory stimuli demonstrates that repeated presentations of a piece of music or of music within a particular style, absent any verbal construct or conscious thought, are sufficient to orient a listener in ways that matter. Listening to music is at the same time learning *how* to listen to music, without special effort or exertion.

This is not to say that special effort and exertion can't result in even deeper, more rewarding kinds of musical learning. And statistical learning is not the only mechanism that allows listeners to gain implicit knowledge about a piece or repertoire. Most of the studies in the statistical learning literature use stimuli that are clearly distinct from actual musical styles—a monophonic, unbroken series of isochronous tones not following typical tonal patterns, for example. This allows for the cleaner construction of a "microenvironment" with its own rules, uncontaminated by knowledge about what happens in the larger musical world. For example, in the statistical learning studies, it was possible to track transition probabilities after G3 within the stimulus without contamination by knowledge about what generally happens in music after G3. But typically, listeners employ knowledge about not only what tends to happen within a particular piece, but also what tends to happen within the general style to which that piece belongs. These schemata can be very general or very specific according to a listener's prior experience (what Patrick Wong and I have called a person's "listening biography"). For example, when presented with a Schumann duet, people with varying levels of previous experience might bring a schema either for classical music (if they don't have much experience with the genre), for nineteenth-century music, for lieder, or for Schumann songs (if they have lots of experience with very similar repertoire). A new piece of music is apprehended not merely with information presented across its duration, but also with information garnered from past experiences with similar music.

Simultaneously, then, a person might be tracking the transition probabilities within a new piece, and applying the probabilities tracked in other similar pieces—and, depending on what percentage of experience with that genre the current listening session represents, adjusting these general probabilities with information from the new piece. Narmour (1990, 1992) believed the way these probabilities changed with each new listening experience was sufficient to explain Wittgenstein's Puzzle, described in Chapter 4. According to his account, every time a person listens to a piece, he does so against a slightly different landscape of what generally happens in music. This new set of norms subtly changes implicit notions of what might be most expected in the piece, and thus also subtly changes its expressive trajectory, since according to Narmour, music's affective qualities stem from the ways it fulfills and thwarts expectations. Although it seems implausible that this interplay between background norms and rehearings accounts for much of the pleasure of repeated listenings, it is worth noting this complex relationship between ideas about what happens in a specific piece and ideas about what happens more generally in a style.

Although the studies described above abstract the transition probabilities between individual notes for the purpose of controlled research, actual music perception involves an engagement with transition probabilities between many different kinds of entities at many different levels of the structure: between intervals, and motives, and timbres, and themes, and sections, and rhythms, for example. In an information-theory study of music, Andy Beatty and I (Margulis and Beatty, 2008) engage with the question of which entities listeners might track, hypothesizing that they might attune to the parameters with an optimal level of variability—the parameters that are not too predictable but also not too unpredictable. In a piece for solo piano, for example, the instrumentation never changes, which makes timbre an unrewarding domain to shift attention toward. These parameters might change from style to style. In other words, it is an unrealistic simplification to imagine that the probabilities listeners track are restricted to individual notes. The succession of durations, or of dynamics, or of gestures comprised of certain configurations of notes and durations and dynamics, are equally—and in some cases more—probable candidates for careful statistical tracking. Much more research needs to be done to connect the kind of statistical learning documented in laboratory settings with the full extent of implicit learning a person might sustain over the course of repeated listenings to a piece.

Repetition of a particular piece, broadly construed, can be understood to shift the expectational set or schemata a listener brings to the music from a general backdrop of similar pieces toward a much more constrained framework: the microworld of the specific piece. Repeated encounters with a piece gradually and implicitly teach a listener how to hear it on its own terms. For example, Schubert's Moment Musical Op. 94 No. 4 contrasts a restless C#-minor A section comprised of unbroken sixteenth notes in perpetual motion with a central B section in Db -major (the parallel major) featuring a distinctive rhythmic lilt drawn from dance. The piece has a typical ternary ABA structure, with a two-measure recollection of the central motive from the B section in the coda after the final A.

As discussed in my paper on musical silence (Margulis, 2007a), the A section contains a primary theme that tends to fold in on itself, the dominant at the end of the four-bar hypermeasures resolving back into the hypermeasure's

*Figure 5.3* Measures 170–180 of Schubert, Moment Musical, Op. 94 No. 4.

tonic opening, with slight modifications (see m. 4 to 5, for example, or m. 55 to 56). But at the transition to the B section and in the passage shown in Figure 5.3 (the transition to the coda), the dominant is abruptly broken away from. A measure of silence, lengthened by a fermata, saliently disrupts the looping before the entrance of the B theme in D#-major, played pianissimo.

Repeated hearings underscore the contrast between this continuation and the one typical to the piece's A sections by steadily erecting a microworld in which the movement from the hypermeasure-ending dominant to the hypermeasure-beginning tonic forms one pole, and the movement from the same dominant through a measure-long pause to the opening motive of the B section forms another, noticeably oppositional in both rhythm and modality. As a person is exposed and reexposed to this piece, the universe of possible continuations to this dominant shrinks from *anything* to A's tonic or B's move to the parallel major. Especially against a background of familiarity with classical music—in which B sections are often contrasting, silent gaps often perform this interruptive kind of function, and major and minor modes are often set against one another in this way (particularly in nineteenth-century music)—the opposition constructed within Op. 94 No. 4 can emerge across repeated hearings as more clearly etched and prominently delineated.

One consequence of the gradual absorption of this opposition across repeated hearings is that each hypermeasure-ending dominant carries both its possible continuations latently within it; the restless looping of the A section, rather than standing innocently for itself, comes to be marked against its eventual breaking. It no longer represents simple and straightforward looping, but rather looping set deliberately against the possibility of its disturbance by the B material. And conversely, the more deeply repeated exposures establish the groove of the initial looping, the clearer the disruption marked by the entry of the middle section.

It is this kind of process through which repeated listenings gradually make possible a Conian kind of Third Reading experience. The piece's internal logic and particular workings come to be absorbed in ways that help listeners make dramatic and expressive sense of the material without the need for explicit study (which is not to say that explicit study can't convey additional insights not absorbable through passive listening). Repeated listenings can also serve to entrain us to the piece in ways that increase our identification with it, subtly bonding us to the music's temporal and motoric path.

## Entrainment

There's a large literature on social and interpersonal entrainment in general, as well as on its specific manifestation in music (see Clayton, Sager & Will, 2004 for a nice overview). Studies show that conversation partners tend to gradually and subtly entrain their gestures, body movements, and speech prosody to each other across communicative episodes (Shockley, Santana & Fowler, 2003), with more successful entrainment serving as an index of more successful communication—such synchronization happens less, for example, over the course of a bad date than a good one (Hove & Risen, 2009). Entrainment to music is often readily apparent even in the staid environment of a classical concert hall; subtle foot tapping, torso swaying, and head nodding can be seen to converge increasingly on the beats, often without any explicit awareness of this process.

Keil terms the motoric aspects of music perception "kinaesthetic listening," and talks about listeners who feel "the melody in their muscles" (Keil, 1995, 10). Overt tapping or swaying is often only the surface manifestation of a deep sense of internal movement generated by musical listening (see also Cox, 2011 and Hatten, 2004). Listeners often have some sense of executing the sounds themselves, whether by semi-realistic imagined guitar strumming or piano playing or some more metaphoric, less literal sense of embodying the sound. Across repeated listenings, the particular sonic and temporal trajectory of the piece grips and regrips motor circuitry, solidifying a kind of motor routine that makes the music increasingly feel like a familiar *way of moving*, rather than merely a familiar series of sounds. The more this happens, the more the music seems to dissolve boundaries, occupy your subjectivity, and connect your inner sensibilities with the outer world: important parts of the pleasure of repeated listening.

The ability to entrain to temporal structures in the environment is a prerequisite for the kind of mirroring that happens in dance (Calvo-Merino et al., 2005) and in the rhythmic exchange of gestures and coos characteristic of parent-baby interactions (Jaffe et al., 2001). Mari Riess Jones's theory of dynamic attending (1976; Jones & Boltz, 1989) explores the way that attention is allocated not only to specific points in space (as in the case of looking in the direction of an event of interest) but also to specific points in time. Jones et al. (2002) present data showing that judgments about pitch were more accurate when the target pitch occurred at a temporal interval that preserved the established rhythm of the excerpt. Listeners, in other words, engage in anticipatory attending, allocating attention in advance to expected time points in the future. This strategy enables them to process music more efficiently, devoting additional attention to moments where events are likely to occur, but it also allows them to tap along, or join in. Repetition allows for increasingly successful predictive attending, and the resulting entrainment mimics the condition of successful social interactions and easy communication. Some of the pleasure of repeated listenings might stem from the way they form a sort of shortcut to this sense of social ease.

Music scholars have referred to elements of this state as *groove*: a felt, kinesthetic sense of the predictable elements of the temporal structure within a particular episode of music making (Keil & Feld, 1994; Pressing, 2002). Intriguingly, music performers have often used the same term, groove, to refer to a particularly pleasant mode of playing in which the generation of beautiful music seems effortless (Berliner, 1994). Janata, Tomic & Haberman (2012) surveyed 215 people about the term groove, and results converged around two points: groove involves a tendency to move, and groove is pleasurable. According to the definition that emerged from their survey, "the groove is that aspect of the music that induces a pleasant sense of wanting to move along with the music" (p. 56). Responses also suggested that groove tends to make people feel as though they were "a part of the music," providing further evidence for a link between the ability to successfully predict elements of the musical structure and the kind of extended subjectivity that has been identified as a hallmark of strong experiences of music. Indeed, Janata, Tomic & Haberman (2012) explicitly associate the tight sensorimotor coupling characteristic of groove with its role in flow as defined by Csikszentmihalyi (1997). By progressively making more and more of a piece's temporal structuring available to prediction and representation across repeated exposures, multiple hearings can facilitate a kind of sensorimotor coupling referred to as groove or flow and broadly valued as pleasant.

A tradition of music appreciation well examined by Burnham (1995) views the particular sequence of notes penned by Beethoven in a symphony or sonata as inevitable and perfect—people subscribing to this line of thought often claim "you couldn't change a note." Although this attitude turns up most frequently in relation to the music of Beethoven, Burnham documents the way that people came to listen to other music, even music that well predated the composer, in this way. While this aesthetic attitude might strike us in 2013 as impossibly nineteenth-century, it colors informal and formal discourse about classical music even now. Although traditions with a more vibrant contemporary practice of improvisation and oral transmission admit more regularly of variation from performance to performance of the same piece, recording technology has influenced nearly every style and genre to the extent that it is common to hear people register disappointment that their favorite improvisational band's live performance deviated from their canonic reference recording.

Regardless of how we might or might not be intellectually committed to the ideas just described, there's something about rehearing the same piece exactly the same way again and again that lulls us into a sense of its special "rightness." On first hearing, the sounds might seem to have been put together haphazardly, but each time we go down the musical path etched out by the piece, its track gets deeper and deeper, such that we fall down it more and more easily, until it carries with it some sense of inevitable rather than accidental reality. This is an inevitability we *feel* rather than believe. And since we know that musical pieces are not natural objects but rather artifacts of a human urge to communicate, express, and create, feeling that a piece is inevitable and right amounts to an appealing sense of someone else's (the composer or performer) artistic act *precisely matching* our own sensibilities. It can be intoxicating to feel that a piece created by another person is fundamentally *right*; we don't generally stop to ponder that excessive literal repetition might have led to or at minimum enhanced this sense of perfection.

Some of the effects of repetition, including an emergent sense of inevitability or rightness, can depend on a lack of awareness that repetition itself is mediating the experience. It might be harder to sustain an impression of transcendent communion with an artist if the listener recognizes that the sense of inevitability—the need for this note to move to this other one in precisely the piece's way—stems as much from having heard the music trace that path many times as from a deeply shared sensibility. Some support for this notion comes from data showing that the mere exposure effect, Zajonc's (1968) finding that the simple re-presentation of a stimulus could increase subjective ratings of it, not only held but actually intensified when the stimuli were presented subliminally, outside of conscious awareness (Kunst-Wilson & Zajonc, 1980; Bornstein, 1989; Bornstein & D'Agostino, 1992; Monahan et al., 2000; Hansen & Wänke, 2009).

As described at the start of this chapter, the mechanism commonly proposed to account for this curious effect is processing fluency: the previous presentation, although not sufficient to trigger conscious recognition, resulted in an improved capacity to handle the stimulus on its re-presentation. Without awareness of the prior exposure, this improved fluency is misattributed to the stimulus itself.

Even when stimuli are presented sufficiently often or in a sufficiently prominent context for listeners to be aware of the repetition, some vestige of this effect might endure. So long as people are not expressly aware of the extent of their prior experiences with a piece, they are particularly liable to misjudge repetition effects as consequences of particular stimulus characteristics. The sheer number of exposures may not be the only factor affecting the delicate balance between exposure, preference, and conscious recognition. The same number of exposures spread out over a longer period of time, or relegated to less salient contexts (e.g., background music at a bar instead of a deliberate play on the iPod) may elude the deleterious effects of conscious recognition across additional hearings. There may be some optimal pattern of presentation frequency. While this question remains unsolved in the laboratory, everyday practice provides some insight: the sudden emergence of a favorite song, years unheard, on a streetside radio can bring a distinctive burst of pleasure—due without doubt partly to nostalgia and a sense of uncanniness at the intact reappearance of an entire song when all the circumstances surrounding it have changed—but also due to the long dormant period during which the ancient overuse of the tune was forgotten. I'll sometimes listen to a song I enjoy three or four times in a row, but at some sensible point an awareness that I'm going to ruin it for myself forever sets in, and I move along to something else. These everyday choices and behaviors evidence the practical intuitions about the relationship between repetition, temporal spacing, and enjoyment.

It's important to distinguish the psychoaesthetic kinds of patterns that have been identified in relation to many different kinds of stimuli—shapes, sound effects, pictures, and music—from the sorts of patterns that seem to hold more specifically for the domain of music. There's a big difference between granting a specific triangle measurably higher preference ratings when asked to do so in a laboratory setting and voluntarily returning again and again to the triangle in an everyday situation. None of the stimuli chronicled in the psychoaesthetics literature lie on the receiving end of the kind of excessive, real-world pursuit of repetition that music does.

Musical repetition benefits from more than the kind of processes identified in the psychoaesthetics literature. It also benefits from its occupation of the motor circuitry, from the multiple temporal levels of structure available for engagement as attention shifts across exposures, and from the opportunity for increased virtual embodiment it affords. All of these benefits are intuitive rather than conceptual, procedural rather than declarative, felt rather than cog-nized. Acknowledging the effects of repetition means acknowledging that wide swaths of musical pleasure stem "from the kishkes," bypassing language and con-ceptualization. It's ironic that after scholars worked hard to make music seem language-like and win acceptance as a legitimate domain of scientific inquiry, applying scientific methods to the study of music might reveal that it's closer to another nonsense than another language, that its appreciation might lie in the body as much as in the mind, and that the idea that we "feel" music may be nearer to the truth than the idea that we "think" it. Precisely what Ferdinand Praeger feared!

Pereira et al. (2011) used fMRI to investigate people's emotional responses to song excerpts from the pop/rock repertoire, discovering that emotion-related limbic and paralimbic regions as well as reward circuitry were all more active for familiar than unfamiliar music and leading the authors to conclude that familiar-ity is a crucial factor in engaging people emotionally with music. Familiarity cor-related more closely with the activation of these emotion-relevant regions than liking did. Every time people are exposed to a piece, they acquire in addition to the various types of procedural and implicit memories discussed throughout this volume, *both* kinds of declarative memory—not only a semantic memory related to the music itself, but also an episodic memory of *themselves listening* to the piece. It's hard to disentangle the effects of the first kind of memory from the second; some of the increased emotional engagement may stem from pro-cesses related not to the piece itself, but to autobiographical memories triggered *by* the piece.

With these limitations in mind, it's interesting to observe that in Pereira et al.'s study, the basal ganglia were also selectively activated in response to familiar music. The authors note that these results are consistent with Rauschecker and Scott's (2009) theory about the function of the dorsal path in their dual-stream model of audition. According to the elaboration of this model in Rauschecker (2011), the premotor cortex and basal ganglia are recruited when incoming sounds match expectations developed by previous exposures.

Rauschecker emphasizes that the brain's method for storing sequences of sounds remains unknown; tantalizingly, however, we *do* know about a sys-tem that must control processes in finely tuned temporal sequence: the motor system.

> While the motor cortex provides the origin of axons projecting to the spinal cord for control of muscles, it is commonly assumed that subcortical entities such as the basal ganglia or the cerebellum set up the patterns reflecting temporal sequential structure of motor acts (Rauschecker, 2011, 20).

In other words, these regions could form the seat of the representation of temporal sequencing.

Leaver et al. (2009) examine this hypothesis head-on, by investigating anticipatory imagery during silence. They observe that when two musical excerpts frequently follow one another, as in the case of songs in a cycle or tracks on an album, the silence between them is often irrepressibly full with anticipated imaginings of the start of the next piece. When my children were very young and we listened to the same CDs over and over again in the car, the last twenty seconds of every song were entirely eclipsed by shouts of (for example) "Baby Beluga is next!" Their anticipation was so intense that it papered over not only the pause, but also the end of the preceding song. It was clear that their listening was passionately future- rather than present-oriented, invested more in the sequencing from one thing to the next than in the individual thing itself.

Leaver et al.'s study implicated the basal ganglia in the learning of auditory sequences. After hearing a melody during a training session, when participants imagined the next melody in the sequence, they relied on the basal ganglia—but when they imagined the next melody in the sequence for actual, long-familiar melodies, they didn't depend on these subcortical areas. This pattern of activation seems to suggest that the basal ganglia are especially relevant to the active formation of representations of temporal sequence. The authors observe that the basal ganglia analogues in songbirds have been identified as critical to sensorimotor song learning during development (Brainard & Doupe, 2002), and, in a fascinating study by Kao et al. (2005), to real-time changes in song production in adult songbirds—both tasks that would entail encoding temporal sequence.

The tolerance and even appetite that people show for relistening to the same music again and again is highly suggestive about the nature of its mental representation, the pleasure associated with it, and the neural mechanisms that might be involved. The final chapters take up these questions in more detail.

# 6

# In Performance

Since this book is concerned with the psychology of musical repetition, it has spent the majority of its time looking at empirical studies of listener behavior and the theories that might emerge from these data. But there is a very practical, real-world domain in which these issues must be grappled with in a more-than-theoretical way: music performance. Performers encounter the challenge of musical repetition every day: playing the same piece at the matinee and the evening performance, taking the same song set on a twenty-city tour, practicing a piece thousands of times in preparation for a concert, reencountering the same tune six times in a single rondo. And although they may devote time to speculation regarding the theoretical position of the many repetitions they encounter, there's a more pressing demand at hand: what will they *do*? What performance decisions will they make in relation to the repetition with which they're confronted? Their choices represent a huge body of data from which inferences can be drawn about repetition, music, and the mind.

Scores, seen from this perspective, present problems of repetition to performers: here's the same piece, how are you going to play it this time? Or: here's the same theme, will you play it similarly or add contrast? Western notation might seem to fix pitch and rhythm precisely, but in fact both these parameters admit interpretative variation. A violinist can raise a note slightly if it is serving as a leading tone or lower it slightly if it is about to resolve down. Since Carl Seashore's (1938) initial study on the subject, instrumentalists have repeatedly been shown to lack the capacity to play in precisely the whole number ratios depicted by a score (for a review, see Palmer, 1997). Moreover, if a computer is programmed to do what a human cannot, i.e., play in these exact whole number ratios, with a half note lasting precisely twice as long as a quarter note, and so on, the result is distinctively amusical.

Elements that invite expressive variation include microtiming, pitch inflection, dynamics, and articulation (Shaffer, 1995). This variability means that performers are regularly given an instance of notated repetition and implicitly called upon to decide whether their acoustic version should repeat as many of these expressive elements as possible, vary as many of them as possible, or somewhere in between; should they, in other words, realize notated repetition as acoustic repetition, or should notated repetition be considered an invitation to introduce expressive variation that resists the similarity apparent in the score?

If expressive variation in performance is going to be taken as an index of responses to various kinds of repetition, an important preliminary question is the degree to which performers are actually able to replicate subtle changes in microtiming, dynamics, articulation, and other nonfixed parameters across performances. What percentage of these inflections represent actual artistic intent and what percentage represent accidents that would not be replicable on demand? At one extreme, performers may be able to control expressive timing to the millisecond, repeating (if asked) a 26-millisecond-early entrance of a theme at precisely that interval each time it recurred; at another, performers may have very little control over this kind of timing, repeating (if asked) a 26-millisecond-early entrance of a theme sometimes 150 milliseconds early, sometimes 375 milliseconds early, and so forth, simply because they lacked the necessary degree of precision in motor control or the necessary degree of precision in the mental representation of the interval's timing.

Figure 6.1 shows fascinating data in qualified favor of a situation nearer the first extreme. The top and bottom graphs outline performances of the opening of the Mozart A Major Piano Sonata, K. 331, one of the most analyzed pieces in the classical repertoire, by two separate pianists, Pianist A and Pianist D. The Y-axis charts the percentage deviation in timing from the amount implied by the rhythmic duration of the current note in the score. Points along the 0-line represent notes that were held as long as the notation suggested; points above the 0-line represent notes that were lengthened in comparison to the notation; and points below it represent notes that were shortened.

The charts reveal broad differences between Pianist A and D. Pianist A is more liberal with timing in general, lengthening some notes almost 40 percent longer than notated, and hurrying some by 30 percent, where Pianist D restricts herself to a range between 25 percent longer than notated and 10 percent shorter. They have also chosen to expressively highlight some different events; Pianist A's most hurried note (represented by the lowest point on the graph) is midway through m. 2, but Pianist D's is in m. 3. There are also interesting similarities; they both slow down toward the end of phrases in measures 4 and 8, for example, represented by the general upward trend on the graph at those spots.

But the truly interesting thing about these data is the relationship between the solid and dotted line on each graph. These represent performances of the theme by the same pianist on its first statement and on its later repetition. Although the performers were not specifically asked to play the two iterations

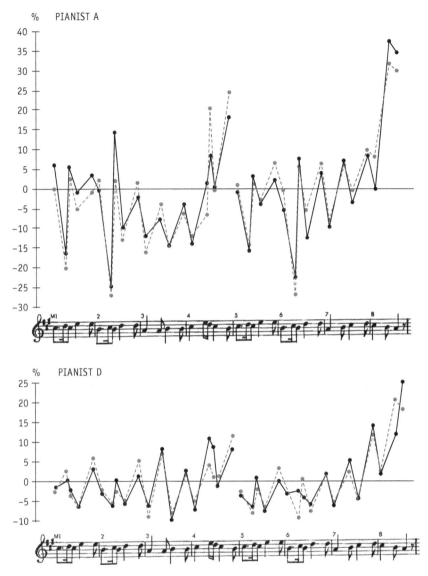

*Figure 6.1* Deviations from notated durations in the performance of the theme from Mozart's Piano Sonata in A major K. 331 on its first statement and on its repetition (indicated by solid and dotted lines) by two different pianists, Pianist A and Pianist D. Reproduced with permission from Gabrielsson, 1987.

of the theme as similarly as possible, they independently chose to interpret the movement in a way that expressively underscored the repetition. From the first to the second statement of the theme, both Pianist A and Pianist D replicated their unique expressive timing profiles to a stunning degree. The microtiming of Pianist A in response to the theme's first statement was much closer to the microtiming of Pianist A in response to the theme's second statement than it was close to anything produced by Pianist D. Timing at this fine a resolution is not normally expressly conceptualized or accessible to introspection by a performer (when asked to describe their expressive variations, musicians are often surprisingly off track, thinking they were speeding up when they were slowing down and vice versa—for a review, see Sloboda, 2001), yet it is clearly represented in some way and available for controlled execution and re-execution. Although this study uses timing as a proxy for expressive variation and doesn't provide data on other parameters, it's reasonable to imagine that dynamics, articulation, and other subtleties might be reproducible with this amount of exactitude.

In a series of papers (Shaffer, 1980; 1981; Shaffer, Clarke & Todd, 1985), Shaffer demonstrated that a similar degree of expressive fidelity tended to hold not only between within-piece repetitions of an individual theme, as in the Gabrielsson study, but also between successive repetitions of an entire piece. In Shaffer (1984), the expressive timing of a pianist's performance of the first of Chopin's *Trois Nouvelles Études* was recorded on one occasion, and then again during two performances a full year later. The pianist was permitted to rehearse the piece a bit at the start of the session, just before each performance, but otherwise did not play the piece over the course of the intervening year.

Both the expressive timing and the relationship between the left and right hand were replicated to a startling degree in performances separated by twelve full months. This similarity seems to suggest that the performer had a particular interpretation of the piece that she sought to communicate in each performance, and didn't specially seek to introduce expressive variation. It is possible, however, that had she kept the piece in her repertoire, practicing and performing it regularly throughout the year, the extent of the repetitiveness might have pushed her to seek additional differentiation over time, yielding, in this hypothetical paired study, a larger expressive variance between the first performance and the one recorded a year later. Contrary to this intuition, however, in unpublished work mentioned in Lehmann (2007), Ashley (2004) showed levels of expressive stability in performances by Paul McCartney separated by even longer stretches of time, spans during which the song remained a fixture on his set list.

These studies show that performers *can* replicate acoustically what's repeated notationally, but do they always *want* to? Although Shaffer's work illustrates that certain expressive decisions about how to perform a particular piece are stored with impressive precision and remain executable even across significant temporal gaps, what about repetitions within a piece? When a notationally equivalent A section crops up again and again in a rondo, for example, does the performer seek to vary her renderings from iteration to iteration, or replicate them as closely as possible? What implicit knowledge or folk psychology about what audience members want or what is aesthetically desirable might this imply?

Repp (1992) conducted an elaborate study analyzing the expressive timing in twenty-eight professional recordings of Schumann's *Träumerei*, a slow and sensitive nineteenth-century piece that would seem particularly amenable to interpretive manipulation. The piece opens with an eight-measure phrase enclosed in repeat signs. All but two pianists took the repeat. For the remaining twenty-six pianists, Repp systematically compared the timing profiles (the patterns of successive beat lengthening and shortening) of the two iterations of the phrase, quantitatively addressing the question of how similarly they were performed. Correlations between the repetitions ranged from .510 to .953. There aren't enough data to generalize with confidence, but it is tempting to note that some of the mainstays of the American concert stage and record bins during the end of the twentieth century, Vladimir Ashkenazy and Alfred Brendel, turned in some of the highest correlations, and some of the performers who were more influential earlier in the century, such as Artur Schnabel and Alfred Cortot, turned in some of the lowest. If that trend proved nonspurious, it would be consistent with the idea that the general interpretive freedom that might have characterized performances before the advent of the era of recordings extended to performances of repetition: earlier in the century, performers might have been more comfortable seeking expressive variation even within the confines of notated repetition. Repp has a more pointed perspective, observing that the performances of the pianists with the low correlations struck him as "mannered. It seems that these pianists deliberately tried to play differently from the norm, but were not willing or able to do so consistently. Perhaps they tended to convey an improvisatory quality" (Repp, 1992, p. 2567). Of the pianists in this low correlation group, only Argerich occupies a prominent position in current concert life; the variability in her expressive choices from instance to instance clearly forms an important part of her enthusiastic reception by contemporary audiences. Yet across all performances, the correlation between the grand average timing pattern (calculated by computing the geometric mean of the note timings across all twenty-eight recordings) for the first and second statement of mm. 1-8 was .987, a level of similarity so high that it led Repp to conclude that "any variations across repeats for individual pianists were either random or idiosyncratic" (p. 2552).

The Repp study also explicitly examined the extent of commonalities (shared expressive characteristics) and individualities (unique expressive characteristics) across all twenty-eight performances of the same piece. His data, although they stem from only one dimension of expressive inflection (timing), reflect the predictable interplay between these qualities; in some ways, all the performance choices have a lot in common with one another, but in other ways, each performance is unique. Repp poses an intriguing question about the nature of the boundary between musical convention and more idiosyncratic choices: can this boundary be understood in some systematic way, perhaps as a reflection of constraints on motor and perceptual behavior? By revisiting the data and examining timing patterns at different levels of the musical structure, Repp was able to determine that performance variability increased at lower structural levels and decreased at higher ones. Performers tended to follow the same basic expressive patterns over the larger scale—slowing down at phrase and section endings, for example—but tended to show different patterns of expressive lengthening at the very smallest, note-to-note and chord-to-chord levels. In a way, this apparent performance practice of retaining commonalities at higher structural levels while subtly diverging at lower ones mirrors, in actual production and action (performance choices), the tendency to shift attention to lower levels of the music that other chapters have theorized to characterize the *perception* of repetitive episodes. On the one hand, listeners might tend to direct more attention to the low-level, nuanced characteristics of sounding music when it's repetitive; on the other hand, performers, when confronted with a piece that's played frequently by other instrumentalists, might shift their *expressive* attention to the music's lower-level elements, introducing more personal and variant inflections.

## Repetition and Performance Practice

Historical performance practice traditions can shed light on these questions. For example, in the Baroque period, it was customary to add ornamentation when repeating a section in a binary dance movement, or when repeating the A section in a da capo aria. Although some composers (notably J. S. Bach) wrote out these elaborations, they were left most of the time to the discretion of the performer, for whom the score provided only a repeat sign. This practice represents a more dramatic divergence between notated repetition and acoustic output than discussed above; performers changed not just the microtiming and articulatory characteristics of the passage in question, but actually added notes and flourishes and new rhythms. In Figure 6.2, for example, the Sarabande is first notated "straight," and then in a version full of suggested ornamentation. The more elaborate version adopts the same structural skeleton but hangs strings of trills and sixteenth notes on top of it.

In *Playing Bach on the Keyboard: A Practical Guide* (2003), Troeger advises that "it was expected of the eighteenth-century performer that he or she would, to some extent, ornament and embellish a movement upon repetition" (p. 200). Specific suggestions put by Troeger to the aspiring keyboardist about the performance of these repeated movements include changing the dynamics (or registration, if playing on the harpsichord), emphasizing the accents and contrasts more vigorously (Troeger links this advice to the metaphor of oration so pervasive during the Baroque era: forcefulness should increase over the course of a persuasive speech), adding decorative embellishments, or playing a full double—an ornately decorated version of the movement, as shown in Figure 6.2, where florid sixteenth-note runs have been introduced into what had been a largely eighth-note texture.

It's hard to speculate about how eighteenth-century composers and performers might have expected their repetitive practices to affect listeners, but treatises of the time framed discussions of musical repetition in terms of rhetoric, the oral art of persuasion. This theoretical emphasis on reception makes it relatively easy to believe that composers and performers sustained a practical emphasis on intended listener effects. For example, the second A section in a da capo aria was explicitly spoken of in terms of the possibility it afforded for demonstration of the vocalist's virtuosity. But if the only goal was to demonstrate virtuosity, why would the performer not add ornamentation straightaway from the beginning? The assumption behind the practice of reserving the decorative embellishment for the second iteration might have been that presenting the musical structure in a plain and simple form first allowed the listener to follow the flourishes and displacements of the ornate repetition without getting confused and disoriented. A similar kind of relationship seems to hold between jazz standards and their extravagant and syncopated renditions in performance, or between a theme and its myriad different versions within a set of variations; knowledge of a simpler version makes it easier to grasp the twists and turns of more complex settings. But these are all unambiguous cases of variation rather than repetition; what's interesting about Baroque performance practice is the way that notated repetition actually served as a tacit invitation for performed variation.

Semiologist Omar Calabrese identifies what he terms a "neo-Baroque" tendency in contemporary cultural practice, noting that when mass communication is the norm, if "all has already been said and already been written... as in the Kabuki theater, it may then be the most miniscule variant that will produce pleasure in the text, or that form of explicit listening which is already known" (Calabrese, 1992). In an age of music dominated by recording technology, it seems likely that both types exist—pleasure in the replay of a favorite track or album, exactly identical from iteration to iteration, and pleasure in live performances that subtly vary an established and overlearned canon, stretching a resolution in a particular place, or delaying an arrival. When planning their embellishments in the repeat, eighteenth-century performers could count on their listeners having had exactly one exposure to the passage—the exposure within the first part of their own performance; contemporary performers can often count on their listeners having had dozens of prior exposures. The

*Figure 6.2*   Bach English Suite No. 2 in A Minor, Sarabande and notated ornaments.

Figure 6.2 (*Continued*)

overlearning that recording technology makes available, and in some circles prevalent, can set up a background within which very subtle changes might not only be newly detectable but also newly valued. In an age where recordings of a Beethoven Sonata by any of the past fifty years' most celebrated pianists are readily available, some pressure, in fact, might exist for live performances to produce readings that are unique and differentiated, justifying the time and expense of attending an actual concert. Indeed, Repp (1995) showed that student performances of a particular work shared more expressive characteristics with each other than did professional performances of the same work; this difference is consistent with the notion that the younger pianists, the students, having grown up in the age of recorded music, might have a narrower notion of what is stylistically appropriate than artists raised in an era when more diverse and local approaches to performance thrived.

Paradoxically, then, recording technology both produces a pressure toward conformity and a pressure toward individuality. The repeatability of specific recordings across time and across space can serve to narrow experience, exposing many people to the same standard, and reducing the diversity of people's "listening biographies." This can result in a kind of standardization (Philip, 2004; Clarke, 2007); for example, the ubiquity of note-perfect recordings has reduced tolerance for performance mistakes and created a kind of "clean-ness" in contemporary playing that some criticize as bland and mechanical. The spread of recordings has also contributed to making vibrato and tuning practices more uniform. Standards came to be defined not in relation to a *geographically* local community but rather to an extended *culturally* local community, defined by a shared body of listening experience made possible by the fact that recorded sound can pass from one corner of the world to another in seconds (see Katz, 2004). Similar concerns have been lodged about the effect of globalization on the reduction of linguistic diversity (Crystal, 2000).

But even as these forces conspire to promote musical conformity, a reactionary upswell emerges to foster diversification. For example, concert promoters tasked with justifying live concerts by specific performers have to highlight the distinction between their event and the litany of readily available, top-notch recordings of the same work. Often, they capitalize on the stylistic novelty the performer brings to the interpretation. One of the classical performers most reliably capable of selling out a hall and creating hysterical excitement among aficionados is Martha Argerich. Although the reception history of star performers (as a parallel to the more traditionally practiced reception history of canonic works) is a complex subject worthy of its own dedicated volume, it seems apparent that the spontaneity, uniqueness, and unpredictability of her performances plays an important role. One stamp of Argerich's genius, as popularly received, is the difference between what she performs and the versions of the pieces available on recording, but another is the technical flawlessness, whose note-perfect-ness matches recordings closely enough for the expressive inflections to be well received. In this one artist, both the conforming and individualizing pressures of recording culture are well represented.

Notated repeats in music written after the eighteenth century rarely represent a call for embellishment at the level of rhythm and pitch; however, it is possible that performers generally interpret notated repeats as an opportunity for additional freedom in expressive parameters such as dynamics and articulation. Just as Shaffer (1984) compared expressive inflections in multiple performances of the same piece, a comparison of expressive inflections across multiple iterations of the same passage or section within a single performance could yield fascinating insight into performers' implicit ideas about musical repetition. Are the differences in microtiming and dynamics of a similar magnitude to those represented by different performances of the same piece? If the differences in expressive choices from the initial performance of a passage to its repetition later in the piece were larger than the differences from performance to performance, it might indicate a desire to engage listeners by working *against* notated repetition; conversely, if the differences were smaller, it might indicate a desire to engage listeners by working *with* the notated repetition. Are repetitions of the theme in a rondo, for example, expressively cumulative, such that later iterations assume a memory not only for the theme, but also for its performance the first time around? Do performers reference their first rendition by, for example, stretching a key moment more the second time around? Or do they try to realize the most expressive manifestation of the notation and play it the same way each time? Does this aspect of performance practice vary from style to style, or composer to composer? Corpus analyses of existing recordings could provide much insight into these sorts of questions, and behavioral studies could provide insight into the effect of these practices on listeners.

In a study currently in progress in my lab, participants are listening to commercially available performances of classical rondos in two different forms: the original version, or one modified so that the musician's first performance of the theme (the A section) has been spliced in to replace all subsequent performances of the A material throughout the piece. Listeners are thus hearing performances featuring expressive variation each time the A section returns or performances featuring verbatim repetition each time the A section comes back. Without knowledge of this manipulation, listeners in separate groups are being asked to rate the performances along various aesthetic dimensions (interest, enjoyment), to rate the degree of repetitiveness in the piece, to rate various parameters (tension, interest) continuously as the piece progresses, and to perform a recognition memory task at the end of the session comparing passages from performances they heard to the same passages in performances they did not hear. The goal of this study is to understand more about the effect on listeners of the relationship between repetition and performance variation.

## Repetition and the Performance of Form

"Repetition is the simplest and most pervasive agent by which musical forms are generated; without it, coherent musical form is virtually inconceivable" (Smyth, 1993). Form, in the perceptual sense, refers to how listeners apprehend a relationship among the different parts of a piece of music. Repetition, in many cases, defines these constituent parts—when something is treated as a unit compositionally by being extracted and reinserted, it is treated as a unit perceptually; the start and endpoints are made clear. More significantly, perhaps, repetition can define a character or structure in relation to surrounding entities; by recurring, it establishes its identity and allows for contrast with the other elements of the piece (cf. Hatten, 1994). Repetition defines a unit, then, not only in the sense of segmentation, but also in the sense of narrative—a structure that, while inherent to the piece, is implicitly re-created by the listener as the piece progresses. Livingstone, Palmer & Schubert (2012) asked listeners to continuously rate valence and arousal—indices of emotional response—during recordings of orchestral pieces including one segment played twice, one paired with a similar variation, and one paired with a contrasting segment. In addition to showing the expected consistency in a listener's emotional response to repeated segments— as compared to a varied response to contrasting segments—the study also reinforces how phrase boundaries can be defined implicitly by a listener's response.

Smyth's quotation about the role of repetition in form is couched within a defense of the practice of performing repeats—something he is careful to specify as more than "an external matter which, at best, may serve to impress a section more strongly upon the hearer's memory" (Smyth, 1993, p. 78-79). Instead, argues Smyth, repeats serve to create the proper balance within the form. He is particularly concerned with the way structural events, as identified by Schenkerian analysis, might occur purposefully at a piece's midpoint, for example, and the ways that omitting the repeats might obliterate these calculated effects.

Historically, as a discipline, music theory has been heavily invested in notions and values such as balance and unity (cf. Cohn & Dempster, 1996; Morgan, 2003; Kramer, 2004). Particular musical structures have traditionally been isolated and made to serve as subjects of discussion because they advanced one or the other of these aesthetic aims. Yet although experimental psychology has supported many of music theory's perceptual claims, the issue of unity and balance has marked a real point of divergence. In 1987, Nicholas Cook launched the first salvo, a study purporting to show that listeners were incapable of perceiving tonal closure. Specifically, his data suggested that listeners didn't mind whether or not a piece ended in the key with which it had begun. Although the methodology of this study has subsequently been identified as problematic (see Gjerdingen, 1999 for a nice summary), additional, better-controlled experiments have since accumulated (cf. Marvin & Brinkman, 1999) to support the claim that local relationships are more salient to most listeners than the kind of long-range connections privileged by music theorists for their role in advancing impressions of unity. The fact that theorists have been inclined to view musical processes and structures through the lens of balance and unity means that their ideas about repetition have tended to relate to the way it serves or fails to serve these aesthetic desiderata; if performers take only one thing from their experience in a typical theory class as a conservatory undergraduate, it's likely to be the idea that unity and cohesion are things to strive for. But how might repetition be marshaled in support of these aims? Consensus seems to suggest that its efficacy is enhanced when its operation is covert—when it influences perception obliquely, without drawing attention to itself.

Richard Taruskin, for example, criticizes Roger Norrington's recording of the *Prelude* and *Liebestod* from Wagner's *Tristan and Isolde* because its fast tempi "greatly cheapen the music by calling unwanted attention to its glaring overreliance on melodic sequences" (Taruskin, 1996, p. 127). The assumption behind this statement is that speeding the music up compresses the individual repeating units that comprise the sequential structure into a small enough time span that the general listener, formerly blissfully ignorant of the underlying structure, can now recognize the degree of repetitiveness. In Taruskin's reading, the revelation of the repetitiveness amounts to an exposure of the trick behind the magic, and ruins the effect.

As other chapters have suggested, people can harbor mistrust about repetition, finding it distasteful and embarrassing. It is not unreasonable to presume, therefore, that the more listeners become aware that repetition is being wielded as an affective tool, the more they might warily disengage from the experience. Performers would then have a mandate to use the repetitive structure available to them while not making it obvious—they want to make the repetition work, without letting listeners know what they're up to. To hide the repetitive underbelly of the piece at hand, a performer might adjust the tempo, as in the case just described, but also might modify the expressive dimensions of the performance of the repeated section with each iteration. For example, some performances of Schubert's Moment Musical Op. 94/3 emphasize the middle voice during one repetition, the top in another, the bottom in a third, and play one of the repetitions much more quietly than the surrounding ones. This strategy amounts to shifting the domain of aesthetic interest away from the notes and rhythms and towards subtle aspects of the voicing and dynamics, setting up contrast in these domains even while repetition dominates in the other. But performers do not always vary their expressive decisions so dramatically; more often the changes are quite subtle. For example, a performer might choose to let a certain iteration move a bit faster because it's at a particularly exposed place in the structure. This quickening in tempo tacitly acknowledges something like "I know you know this already; just tagging it and getting on with things." Or a performer might subtly alter expressive dimensions depending on the way the repeating section was approached. For instance, in mm. 93-100 of Beethoven's Sonata Op.2/1, the retransition to the opening them plays teasingly with the theme's initial motive, potentially leading the performer to humorously emphasize or exaggerate it on repeat. But if the theme had entered unprepared at a surprising juncture, it might be played unobtrusively, with no special emphasis, to play up its incognito status.

Edward Cone frames the issue concisely with respect to Chopin's Polonaise in A major:

> This is a piece notable for the six-fold statement of its opening period, each time literally repeated: AABABA Trio, ABA—thus six A's in all. But the second A is already different from the first. The first was preceded by silence and followed by its repetition; the second is preceded by the first and followed by B. The third is now preceded and followed by B, and the fourth is preceded by B but followed by the Trio, and so on. My contention is that each statement is influenced by its position, by what precedes and what follows it, so that each is, in important respects, different from all others (Cone, 1968, p. 46).

From a performer's perspective, the question is whether these interrelationships and contextual reconfigurations are best highlighted by neutral, exact replications that, without extra inflection, allow new readings to emerge in the listener's mind, or whether subtly different expressive choices might better emphasize these recontextualizations. Slight context-based adjustments might seem inevitable or natural, compelling a performer to modify interpretive elements without any explicit consideration of the likely effect on the listener.

Figure 6.4 shows waveform visualizations of each recurrence of the main theme (A) in a performance by Grigory Sokolov of Chopin's Polonaise Op. 40/1 in A major. Between the first iteration of the theme (mm. 1-8, shown in Figure 6.3) and its second, immediate restatement, several changes are just noticeable on the visualization. The arrival of the melodic peaks on the downbeats in m. 2 and m. 4 receive agogic emphasis through slightly delayed onsets and dynamic accent; but on the next iteration (marked A2 in Figure 6.3), Sokolov moves through the peaks in a fairly straight manner, without added delay or accent. Perhaps the

*Figure 6.3*  From Chopin, Polonaise in A major, Op. 40/1.

initial run-through's emphasis was sufficiently strong to make additional demar-
cation on the second iteration extraneous; continued accents could have seemed
heavy-handed or redundant. This expressive distinction can be understood to
communicate respect toward the listener; it assumes that the listener absorbed
the expressive contour on the first hearing, and that a fuss needn't be made of it
every time.

Yet on the sixth iteration of the theme (A6), Sokolov unleashes even more
power, adding octaves in the bass and exaggerating the emphasis on the melodic
peaks. At this point in the piece, the theme bears the weight of all the bombast
that has led up to it, and by moving smoothly through several of the previous
repetitions, Sokolov has left himself room to release maximum volume on its
final statement. Had he emphasized the accents as much on previous iterations,
it might have started to sound overly aggressive. Despite being composed of
lots of thick chords, the theme benefits from a sense of horizontal progression,
where the chords increase and decrease in loudness to create a sense of movement toward and away from various goals. Similarly, the entire piece, despite
being composed of lots of repetitions of individual themes, benefits from a sense
of horizontal progression. This impression can be achieved in part by changes in

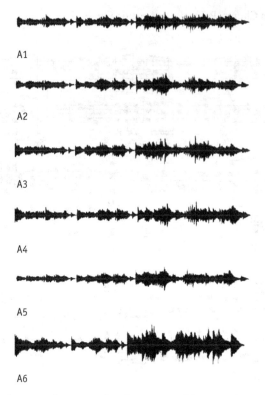

A1

A2

A3

A4

A5

A6

*Figure 6.4*  Waveform visualizations of performances of the main theme on each of its occurrences during Grigory Sokolov's performance of Chopin's Polonaise in A major, Op. 40/1.

the performance of the individual repetitions, such that the final iteration can serve as the culmination of a goal-directed process. Harrison (2002) articulates a view commonly held among performers: "musical repetition of any kind may be experienced as flat and mechanical unless brought to life by sensitive performance; changes in volume and tone colour are one way, for example, in which a good organist avoids monotony in accompanying a hymn" (p. 9). Skilled performance can transform cyclical structure at one level, such as a series of repetitions of a particular theme, into process-based structure at another. Sokolov, for example, layers a large-scale dynamic trajectory across the course of the superficially identical repetitions.

This intuition reflects an interesting distinction between within-piece and between-piece repetition (examined more fully in Chapter 5). When repetitions occur within an individual piece, there is a pressure toward the kind of expressive variation that will allow for a sense of musical development and progress; yet when repetitions occur between pieces (as in multiple performances of the same work), near-exact repetition or untransformed repetition may be more acceptable. This divide can exist even though the length constituting a piece in one case might be equivalent to the length constituting a section repeat in another case. Listeners can be understood to parcel time into a special category, describable as narrative time or aesthetic time, as a piece progresses (Kramer, 2010). Within this special span, they listen for musical directedness. But once a piece ends, ordinary time reasserts itself, and another performance of the same piece, when it starts again, marks a new period of narrative time. Highly compartmentalized pieces, in which individual sections might sometimes be extracted and performed on their own, represent a special case in between these two extremes. Repeating sections in such pieces might be performed with higher expressive fidelity, especially if the piece intentionally alludes to the experience of rehearing a complete work.

A place in which the performer has an even more dramatic role in the rendering of repetitive material is the formal repeat, notated by repeat signs enclosing a section, such as the exposition or the development-recapitulation in a sonata. Here the question is not how similarly to play the repetition to the original version, but whether to play the repetition at all. Performance practice related to these kinds of repeats changes with time and fashion. It is currently customary to ignore the repeat sign at the end of the exposition in a sonata. In an incisive article on the subject, Jonathan Dunsby observes that even highly meticulous musical thinkers tend to "throw up their hands" with regard to the question of formal repeats, quoting the influential Charles Rosen, who in *The Classical Style* averred that "there is no rule: some repeats are dispensable, others are necessary" (quoted in Dunsby, 1987, p. 196-197).

The kind of repetition embodied by the formal repeat is read by some as inorganic, a convention that is imposed on the musical structure without regard to its content; yet others, especially theorists in the Schenkerian tradition (like Smyth in the passages quoted above), have argued that formal repeats contribute essentially to the balance or proportion of a movement, such that the music is left lopsided or off balance if they are skipped. The argument against part repetition is unsurprising given the history of intellectual skepticism regarding the practice of musical repetition. The argument in favor of it is intriguing in what it omits. Rather than defend the formal repeat on the basis of pleasure, or—if not pleasure—some more immediate and sensory kind of percept, theorists have tended to defend it on the basis of its contribution to relatively high-level and distant estimations of "balance." What repetition is meant to serve, these arguments claim, has to do with the proportions between relatively long stretches of musical time, the kind of relationships that might be best reflected on at some remove. It is only in special cases, such as when an ambiguous note or chord at a section's start is rendered unambiguous when repeated after the cadence of the section's end, that theorists tend to acknowledge a more local consequence for part repetition.

The da capo aria, a favorite element of Baroque opera, exemplifies the challenge musical repetition presents to extramusical notions of story and narrative. The aria's repeat of the A section poses a problem for plot advancement; the fact that events are changing comes into conflict with the fact that the music is staying the same. As a result, action tends to be relegated to recitative, the freer sections in between arias, where passages don't normally coalesce into repeated tunes. Arias are reserved for commentary that takes place outside narrative time; the events stop progressing, and a character takes advantage of the halted clock to explore a particular perspective or feeling. The magical temporal world of the aria allows a feeling to be sung about repeatedly without the pressure for plot to continue. (Although as early as the time of Mozart, composers were interested in developing set pieces that allowed the plot to advance even during the melodic bit.)

The artifice of the divide between plot-advancing recitative and stopped-time arias eventually burdened the genre enough that the practice fell away, but formal repeats persisted in music not governed by the demands of drama or language. How might composers in the late eighteenth century, the time during which so many of these formal repeats were notated, have thought about how they should be performed? Dunsby looks to Daniel Türk's 1789 *Klavierschule* for clues. In that volume, Türk advises teachers to instruct their students to execute notated formal repeats immediately, without pause, in service of continuity. Not only does he give no indication that notated repeats are optional, he actually suggests that pianists should occasionally replay individual sections even when the notation doesn't imply it. At its peak, then, performance practice convention may have made formal repetition even more common than notation suggests.

Figure 6.5 shows the results of Broyles's (1980) survey of formal repeats in the first movements of more than three hundred instrumental works. His survey indicates that the notation of formal repeats declined rapidly across the turn of the century, with almost all pieces surveyed from before 1780 including them but the majority of pieces from the first part of the nineteenth century avoiding them entirely.

What caused such a rapid and dramatic decline in the use of the formal repeat? Broyles points to sentiments expressed in public on the subject about a decade after it had started to fall from favor. In 1789, André-Ernest Modeste Grétry lodged the complaint documented in Chapter 1 comparing formal repeats to the socially outlandish repetition of an entire conversation half. And in 1791, Johann Friedrich Reichardt described the formerly customary repetition of the second half of a form as "unnatural and senseless," a reflection, according to Broyles, of the growing influence of metaphors of organicism drawn from the new sciences of biology. But the quotations above are equally readable as applications of metaphors drawn from drama and language—both Reichardt's use of

| | Pieces Examined With Repeats | | Without Repeats | |
|---|---|---|---|---|
| | No. | Percentage | No. | Percentage |
| Before 1780 | 128 | 98.5% | 2 | 1.5% |
| 1780-89 | 58 | 79.5% | 15 | 20.5% |
| 1790-99 | 35 | 37.0% | ·59 | 63.0% |
| 1800-10 | 6 | 12.0% | 44 | 88.0% |

*While this essay is not a statistical study per se, it is felt that enough works were investigated to verify the existence of a general trend away from repeating the second half in the late eighteenth and early nineteenth centuries.*

*Figure 6.5* Incidence of first movement formal repeats by period of composition. Reproduced with permission from Broyles, 1980.

the term "senseless" and Grétry's practice of drawing his negative examples from spoken discourse suggest that the aspiration to find quasi-linguistic *meaning* in music might have influenced practices as well.

Indeed, in an exchange in *The New York Review of Books* regarding the merits and demerits of repeating the exposition when performing any of Schubert's three last piano sonatas, Neal Zaslaw identifies a shift in theoretic conceptualizations of sonata form related to the influence of such metaphors:

> There has been another shift of emphasis since the time of the Viennese classics, from music conceptualized in more purely formal terms to music considered as if it were narrative. This shift, which is not an either/or proposition, but a matter of degree, goes along with a redefinition of sonata-form movements to stress their ternary rather than binary aspects. If such movements are two-part "architecture," repeats clarify the form; if they are three-part "narrative," repeats are redundant, as they seem to represent backtracking in the "plot" (Zaslaw, 1989).

Both of these conceptualizations bear the burden of metaphor, judging repetition's merits by whether a sonata might be more fruitfully construed as an edifice or a story. But there could be some border, a border particularly exemplified by the musico-cultural universal of repetitiveness, beyond which metaphors fail, and music must be viewed as distinctly musical. Such a conception, however, was glaringly unavailable to the participants in the historical exchange just chronicled; to justify attention and resources, music had to be thought about as a special case of a more established domain, a domain both more serious and more elevated. More than perhaps any other factor, this top-down limitation sty-mied discourse on the subject of musical repetitiveness.

## Repetition in Study and Practice

In his defense of concatenationism (more thoroughly discussed in Chapter 7), Levinson examines what it takes for a piece to make sense to a listener—for a listener to have a sense that he or she "gets it." He proposes that to have this impression, a listener must be able to feel and inhabit the musical progression, to embody it to some extent: evidence, Levinson claims, for the primacy of moment-to-moment experiences in musical listening. What might constitute proof that a listener had grasped the music in this way? "One of the clearest indi-cations that one has understood a piece of music at a basic level is one's ability to *reproduce* parts of it in some manner—by playing, singing, humming, or whis-tling it" (Levinson, 1997). Since this kind of understanding not only doesn't rely on conscious articulation but is also potentially not even susceptible to it, the ability to *repeat* the musical progression becomes the best proving ground for communication and shared sensibility.

In a study of training habits among professional popular musicians, Green (2002) found that almost all of them had begun by trying to copy their favor-ite recordings by ear. Suzuki students the world over are taught to listen and repeat the sounds on a CD sent home with the parents. And how many music lessons involve some variation on this scenario? The student plays a passage. "No, like *this*," says the teacher, performing it subtly differently—with some difficult-to-articulate but perceptually distinct adjustment to pace, voicing, and articulation. The student replays the passage, trying to match the teacher's style, and looks up quizzically. "Almost, but more like *this*," says the teacher, playing it again, perhaps with a bit of additional emphasis on the dimension the student's performance continues to lack. "Oh, like *this*," replies the student, successfully echoing the essence of the teacher's performance. "Yes!" says the teacher excit-edly, even before the passage is complete, once the expressive match is clear.

Episodes like this, played out from studio to studio and conservatory to conservatory all over the world, demonstrate that the ability to repeat another person's musical utterance lies at the heart of what we understand as musical communication. There's no more endearing image, perhaps, of a truly effective episode of musical communication than a person playing full-throttled air guitar. A short-lived reality TV show on VH1 called *Motormouth* chronicled particu-larly egregious instances of that other signature index of positive musical experi-ences: the in-car radio sing-along. Successful musical communication feels like a scooping up of the listener into the music, a process of bringing the listener along. This can take the form of imagined co-participation, in which the listener follows the musical logic so intensely that it comes to feel as if he's executing it. But it can also take the form of overt participation: singing along, or carefully reproducing the demonstration of a teacher, providing evidence that the student understood the teacher's point even though no words were exchanged.

It's ironic, perhaps, that I entered music cognition in frustration with precisely this kind of incident. As a pianist studying at the Peabody Conservatory of Music, I encountered so many situations in which repetition of this sort constituted the primary pedagogical technique that I became convinced the enterprise of music simply didn't understand itself. Taking the resistance to verbal articulation of principles as a discipline-wide failure to apply intellect to the domain of music performance, I started (against the advice of my teacher, which added a motivating layer of illicitness) taking the bus up to the Homewood Campus of Johns Hopkins University for a class in cognitive science.

At that time, the discipline was still very much in the thralls of the prospect of artificial intelligence, and it seemed plausible that things we didn't seem to understand at all, like music performance, might yield to some kind of computational account. This was precisely the time when psychologists had begun to record performances on specially equipped pianos that kept a precise trace of the timing and acceleration of every key press, allowing for new insight into the relationship between structural features of music, such as cadences, and expressive choices by performers.

Over the past decade of thinking about these questions, however, I've become convinced that the failure lies not in the practice of communicating musical insights through repetition, but in the refusal to accept this kind of exchange as a form of human communication with similar value to a verbal one. The failure, in other words, lay in my own perspective! But I believe this personal trajectory is representative of a larger one within cognitive science, a trajectory from viewing the brain as a sort of abstract computational device, with a certain account of language serving as the canonic domain of thought and communication, to viewing the brain as inextricably embodied, with more implicit, intuitive behaviors serving as more representative of its essential capacities (Gibbs, Jr., 2005). Along with this shift has come a recasting of language as a very different, and more music-like, phenomenon than previously postulated (Brandt, Gebrian & Slevc, 2012; Mithen, 2006). Seen through this lens, the communicative act of musical repetition simply underscores the social, participatory nature of human cognition.

Performers not only experience repetition as a central practice in pedagogical contexts, they also experience it on a relentless basis in the process of learning and perfecting a piece. Piano students love to play "the coin game." They put a stack of five coins on the left side of the music stand, and play through a tough passage. Every time they get it exactly right, they take one coin off the existing stack and move it over to a new stack on the right side of the music stand. If they make even one mistake, however, they have to move everything back to the left side and start again. The object is to play the passage five times in a row without an error—a feat represented in the end by the successful transfer of the entire stack of coins.

In addition to being fun, the coin game is effective because almost no child has the patience or dedication to repeat a passage the number of times necessary to achieve real improvement. Even if the student knows intellectually the particular notes involved in a challenging leap, if she hasn't created the appropriate motor routine, the performance won't be clean. Sometimes a student will be sufficiently ambitious to repeat the passage a few times, but usually only every other repetition is actually correct. Even more typically, a student will try a passage once, get it wrong, try it again, get it wrong again, and when she eventually gets it right, feel great and move on. But this kind of session, rife with repetition, has in effect drilled the erroneous version into her fingers.

The coin game helps students make sure they are working until they have repeated the *correct* version enough times to train *it* into their muscles. The critical notion here is that it takes consistent repetition to train the motor sequences necessary for executing skilled performance. Since, except in rare circumstances (computer music, etc.), producing music requires executing motor sequences, intense repetition is an important component of building a successful performance. Repetition lurks behind every recital, and expressive moments, no matter how spontaneous, depend on the accumulation of hours of practice room repetition.

In the same way that years and years of flowing water ultimately carved out the permanent-appearing landscape of the Grand Canyon, hours and hours of repetitive practice carve out a stable pattern of movements that are inextricably linked together, such that the whole sequence can unfold without much executive oversight. This process represents an actual physical instantiation of what repetitive listening only mirrors—an overlearned sequence in which individual time-slices are bound tightly, one to the next. Just as a performer can easily inadvertently learn an error by repeating it too often in practice, a listener can inadvertently learn an error by hearing it too many times on recording. Mark Katz (2004) recalls how obsessive relistening to a Heifitz recording that contained an accidental pluck of the open E string yielded persistent expectations for that "wrong note" despite knowledge of its status as an error. In other words, despite knowing intellectually that the sound was inadvertent, he continued to *feel* an expectation for it. The E had been tightly woven into the learned sequence of notes such that its sounding was implied by the sequence, even when he knew it shouldn't be. This tight coupling from one sound to the next, so fundamental to the experience of music listening, is even more fundamental to the act of music performance, which harnesses repetition to train motor sequences into muscles such that a pianist might find his mind wandering to the evening's dinner plans while midway through the development in a Chopin Sonata. Repetition works to automatize, both a boon and a danger for the instrumentalist and the morning commuter. Their responses to this phenomenon shed an interestingly different, and as yet insufficiently explored light on the cognitive science of musical repetition.

# 7

# Overt Participation, Implied Participation

"Feels like teen spirit: Thousands of young people flock annually to a Christian camp in rural France. What is drawing them there?" asked a headline in *The Independent* on August 20, 2011 (Williams, 2011). In an age of general decline in religious engagement, something has managed to spark fervor in teenagers and young adults from many different countries and many different denominations of Christianity, inspiring them to develop Taizé services at their own church in their home country or make pilgrimages to the Communauté de Taizé, an ecumenical community founded in 1940 and currently inhabited by a hundred monks dedicated to a life of simplicity. What is it about the culture of Taizé that has galvanized a subset of young people globally?

One of the most distinctive elements of Taizé worship is its emphasis on repetitive song. In a sequence characteristic of Taizé practice, a short musical phrase is repeated in its entirety by the whole congregation an open-ended number of times, leading into an extended period of collective silence, on the order of ten or fifteen minutes. Brother Roger, the Taizé community's founder, describes it in this way:

> When common prayer gives a foretaste of the joy of heaven on earth, people come running from everywhere to discover what they had been unconsciously lacking. Nothing contributes more to communion with the living God than a common prayer that is both meditative and accessible to old and young alike. The high point of this prayer is the singing which never ends and which continues afterwards in the silence of the heart when we are alone again (Brother Roger, quoted in Harrison, 2002).

He attributes the movement's popularity to the "joy" transmuted by its habits of prayer, and doesn't shy away from acknowledging the role of the musical repetitiveness. Jointly participating in repetitive music making, the Taizé monks affirm, is pleasant, even joyful, and contributes to the movement's allure. The repetitiveness also makes the tradition uniquely welcoming; newcomers needn't be familiar with a particular hymnbook in advance because the music teaches how to participate as it goes along. Even people new to the worship style can corporally enact the essential practice of the community by singing with the group—something that must create a thrilling sense of belonging, especially for adolescents (a large percentage of Taizé pilgrims each year) who may be in search of a clearer social identity.

Brother Roger locates the prayer's climax in the silence that follows the singing. The notion of "the singing that never ends" traces the song's path from the sounding, external world of the co-participating community across the silence into "the heart." The song's presence in the interior, subjective, felt world of the individual when he is "alone again" is described as the most powerful part of the experience. Why might repetitive music in particular have the ability to pull something experienced externally into such vivid internal reenactment?

Previous chapters have traced the affinity between the repetitive looping of imagined music—i.e., earworms—and the looping indulged in by highly repetitive musical styles, with both phenomena harnessing the motor system to mimic processes of kinesthetic learning. This connection that can exist between sounding music in the external world and imagined music in the internal one has been hypothesized to set up the conditions whereby a person can experience a highly pleasurable sense of extended subjectivity, or a perceived merging with the music. The successful and even galvanizing practice of Taizé seems to capitalize on the power of this connection, taking advantage of the way shared, participatory repetition can extend to the internal, imagined soundscape when silence is allowed to fall over the congregation.

Silent periods experienced in a public setting can often awkwardly highlight the ways an individual might fail to blend into the crowd, overexposing every shuffle, sniff, and neurotic thought. But after an extensive period of joint and repetitive singing, it is almost impossible not to continue to experience the sound of the looped phrases, as well as the tactile sense of the muscle movements involved in producing those phrases. Each individual in the silent gathering persists in having a sense of "being sung," even as no one moves or makes a sound. It's easy to imagine how this private, internal experience, and the knowledge that it is being shared by dozens of near-strangers who come from all over the world, even as you stand together silently, overtly sharing nothing, might have a stunning and ecstatic bonding effect.

Harrison explains how this can be experienced as a kind of intimacy, setting the Taizé practice in stark opposition to what she views as the impersonal nature of contemporary society. Astutely, Harrison observes that an intimate spiritual encounter has always been the longed-for goal of mystical experience. The post-repetitive silence in Taizé prayer takes the internal, subjective experience of embodied repetitive singing and casts it throughout a diverse populace, such that a sense of felt intimacy can arise in the absence of any discourse or exchange of thoughts and ideas—it is an intimacy that is lived rather than arrived at in conversation, a particular asset for a movement that seeks to transcend denominations, nationalities, languages, and generations.

Harrison draws a link between the repetition found in the music of the Taizé and the kind of repetitive restatement of simple utterances that characterize some intimate relationships. People who know each other very well sometimes use overfamiliar phrases not to exchange new information, but rather to point to all the unsaid qualities surrounding the edges of the words. This kind of repetition shifts the focus away from what is straightforwardly denoted by the conversation and toward aspects of the shared present experience that transcend verbal report. It exposes the limitations of what the words are capable of capturing. Similarly, by repeating simple songs like the one shown in Figure 7.1, participants in a Taizé service can create the sensation that what is meant by words like soul, spirit, yearning, and eternal waiting goes beyond what these words themselves are able to convey.

Although charismatic liturgies and Taizé services seem very different on the surface, with one involving dancing and shouting and one involving stillness and silence, Harrison draws a telling connection between the two (see James, 1902 for a fascinating chronicle of the commonalities underlying diverse religious experiences). In charismatic services, she notes, repetitive singing, accompanied by much physical gesturing,

> sometimes functions as a way of leading into 'singing in the Spirit'; the reiterations of one phrase, expressing adoration, are gradually stilled and a single chord is sustained as voices and instruments improvise in rapturous praise. This is not a dissimilar process from the way in which a Taizé chant can lead into a particularly intense silence (Harrison, 2002, p. 42).

Although in the case of charismatic worship, repetition creates an opportunity for a rapturous episode of *actual* participation, repetition in Taizé creates instead a special kind of silence that is filled with a rapturous sense of *virtual* participation.

This sense of virtual participation, I would argue, can arise even in cases not preceded by any actual participation. Consider two progressively more virtual and less actual examples of this phenomenon. On the one hand, take a pop song based on extensive vamping, such as Stevie Wonder's *Superstition*. Simplified

*Figure 7.1* "Iedere Nacht Verlang Ik" Text, English translation and music by the Taizé Community. Copyright © 2011, Ateliers et Presses de Taizé, Taizé Community, France. GIA Publications, Inc., exclusive North American agent. 7404 S. Mason Ave., Chicago, IL 60638; www.giamusic.com; 800.442.1358. All rights reserved. Used by permission.

SONG OF REFLECTION:  Iedere nacht verlang ik (My soul yearns for you)
*repeat as led by cantors*

arrangements of this piece start with a repeat-sign-enclosed measure accompanied by the directive "repeat til ready"—an allusion to the origin of vamping: a practice that permitted the band or accompanist to fill an indefinite period of time while the vocalist drank a glass of water, consulted a lyric sheet, or otherwise got their act together for the next song.

But that repeated bass line makes it almost impossible not to move with some degree of overtness, at least foot tapping or head nodding if not full-fledged dancing. A listener compelled to move by this repeated bass line isn't participating in the sense of playing an instrument or contributing to the actual production of the music's sound, but is participating in the sense that the music has physically taken hold of parts of her body. This kind of foot-tapping doesn't feel like independent movement distally triggered by sounding music, but rather like a result of the music having acted upon you proximally, lifting and moving you of its own volition. Furtive swaying and tapping is often easy to spot even among listeners who aren't aware they've moved at all.

Pop concerts expect and allow for this kind of engagement, but the typical classical concert doesn't permit the bodily involvement of audience members; even subtle one-finger conducting or thumb tapping is frowned upon. Much classical music nonetheless harnesses the movement-inciting tendency of repetition to choreograph experiences of subjectivity and identification in listening. In *The Rite of Spring*, for instance, Stravinsky habitually introduces ostinatos and then disrupts them, encouraging listeners to develop a sense of virtual participation by repeating short fragments and then pulling out the rug from underneath with a sudden interruption, creating a sense of violence (for a deep exploration of repetitive processes in Stravinsky, see Horlacher, 2011). Another example is the third movement of Brahms's Violin Concerto in D major, Op. 77, a hyper-repetitive opening evocative of the Hungarian style, where part of the theme's oft-observed exuberance comes from the way it seems to involve the audience motorically even as they sit motionless. The sort of virtual participation fostered by the Stravinsky and Brahms passages are even more virtual than that exemplified by the Stevie Wonder eample; not only is the typical audience member not playing the music, she's also not moving whatsoever. Repetition can serve as a practical aid to participatory involvement in collaborative musics like that used in Taizé services, allowing even the neophyte to successfully join the music making, but it can also serve as an expressive aid to *virtual* participatory involvement in presentational musics where there is a clear divide between the active performers and the passive listeners.

As discussed in Chapter 2, Richard Middleton (2006) draws a distinction between the repetition of short motivic units, which he terms musematic, and the repetition of longer musical entities such as phrases, which he terms discursive. He views discursive repetition as a contributor to structured discourse, and musematic repetition as more visceral and groove-inducing. But even repetition that is very far at the discursive end of the spectrum, such as repetition of a chorus within a song, or the repeated sounding of a particular track, can provide the scaffolding for a participatory experience. Once a listener "knows how it goes," he is free to sing along, or indulge in some air guitar, or tap out the rhythms. Prior to this affordance to move along with the music is an affordance to *think* along with the music. And it is the extended subjectivity of this thinking-along-with, wherein the music seems to emerge both out of the world and out of your own imagination, that marks the distinctive pleasure of musical repetition. This pleasure can apply equally whether the repetition is musematic or discursive.

Leydon (2002) examines perceptions of musical subjectivity related to repetition in the works of minimalist composers. She starts with Cumming's (2001) account of generalized experiences of musical subjectivity, which specifies three possible sources for the phenomenon: timbre, which engages the listener in a sense of virtual vocality as he imaginatively embodies the kind of voice that might produce that sound; gesture, which engages the listener in a sense of virtual kinesthetic as he imaginatively embodies the kind of movement that might trace that path; and syntax, in which he imaginatively embodies the kind of intention or drama that might produce that sequence. Leydon asks what kinds of subjectivity might arise in the absence of this last feature, when pervasive low-level repetition breaks down a sense of syntax or teleology.

The tropes Leydon identifies are maternal, kinetic, mantric, totalitarian, motoric, and aphasic. Figure 7.2 presents a brief explanation of each type, with accompanying examples. Included on this list are all the attributes and phenomena with which repetition has been popularly associated: regression, insanity, mass production and reproduction, movement, and transcendence. They are

*maternal*

repetition evokes a 'holding environment', or regression to an imagined state of prelinguistic origins (Raymond Scott's *Soothing Sounds for Baby*)

*mantric*

repetition portrays a state of mystical transcendence (Arvo Pärt's "liturgical minimalism"; John Adams's *Shaker Loops*)

*kinetic*

repetition depicts (or incites) a collectivity of dancing bodies (Spring Heel Jack; various electronica)

*totalitarian*

repetition evokes an involuntary state of unfreedom (Rzewski's *Coming Together*, Andriessen's *De Staat*)

*motoric*

repetition evokes an indifferent mechanized process (Nyman's *Musique à Grande Vitesse*, Adams's *Short Ride in a Fast Machine*)

*aphasic*

repetition conveys notions of cognitive impairment, madness, or logical absurdity (Nyman's *The Man Who Mistook His Wife for a Hat*, Satie's *Vexations*)

*Figure 7.2* Six repetition tropes with some representative works; reproduced from Leydon, 2002. Used by permission of R. Leydon.

presented as a list of topics in the sense that the term "topics" has been used in music theory (Mirka, forthcoming): nonmusical entities that can be evoked or alluded to by musical means through convention or association. Yet in addition to all the expressive uses chronicled by Leydon, I would argue that there's a more fundamental process at work with repetition, one on par with the kind of subjectivities outlined by Cumming. Even as timbre can provide a locus for extended vocality, gesture for extended kinesthetics, and syntax for extended intentionality, repetition can function underneath to heighten all of these experiences, to systematically erode the distinction between the exterior and the interior, and to draw the listener into the world of the music. Repetition, in other words, can not only serve as a means for topical allusion in the way chronicled by Leydon, but also as a basic engineer of extended subjectivity, preliminary to any particular topical resonance.

Leydon engages with Middleton's distinction between musematic and discursive modes of repetitiveness to build an argument about the role of hierarchy in the sense of subjectivity communicated by repetition. She argues that musematic repetition, by flattening out hierarchies, can evoke a lack of volition, but discursive repetition, by building larger-scale structures, more frequently imbues the music with a sense of will or intent. This book's perspective on repetition's role in attentional shifts offers a possible mechanism for the difference Leydon observes. Music dominated by musematic repetition doesn't generally offer much in the way of larger-scale structuring; across repeated hearings, listeners will tend to burrow into the music's "grain," its nuances of timing, timbre, and articulation, where there is more communicative richness. When a listener is pulled into close connection with these attributes, it feels more like entering into a kind of sympathy with the music than like responding to an argument or appeal the music is making. But music characterized by discursive repetition is often hierarchically structured, allowing for the gradual orientation across repeated listenings to larger-scale musical relationships. When these elements are the object of attention, the listener can feel much more as though the music were willfully communicating via syntax and design.

David Huron provides the useful overview of musical repetition types shown in Figure 7.3. The y-axis plots a continuum of perceived segment variety, from verbatim repetition to an entirely through-composed style, and the x-axis plots the length of segment repetition from short to long. Metronome ticks, featuring the verbatim repetition of short (single click) segments occupy the lower left corner of the chart, and encores, featuring the verbatim repetition of long (entire piece or movement) segments occupy the lower right corner. A rondo, which features a good deal of moderate-length repetitions of a single section, sits near the middle of the chart, somewhat lower than the vertical midpoint due to the high degree of repetition (and associatedly low level of segment variety), and somewhat right of the horizontal midpoint due to the relatively long length of the repeating section. Middleton's musematic-discursive opposition would map nicely onto the x-axis of Hurons's chart. And the chart's general linear trend, though weak, supports another of Middleton's ideas—namely, that verbatim, groove-inducing kinds of repetition happen more frequently with short musematic segments, but that more discourse-establishing segment variety tends to be mixed in with the discursive repetition of longer units. If the chart's y-axis were slightly reconceptualized to indicate depth of hierarchy, from flat to complex, although the listed genres might shift around to a certain degree (with sonata-allegro moving higher, for example, and program music lower), the position on the graph could be understood to predict the attentional effect of repetition in these genres. Repetition in musics occupying a higher spot would be predicted to encourage shifts to broader temporal spans, and repetition in musics occupying lower spots would be predicted to push attention down into nuance attributes.

This chart, plotting genres irrespective of composer or style, is necessarily crude, unable to capture the ways different genres might be wielded differently

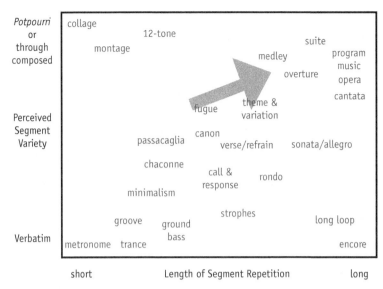

*Figure 7.3*  David Huron's survey of the landscape of different kinds of repetition found in musical works, reproduced with permission from his video "Musical Form: A Psychological Perspective," uploaded to vimeo.com on January 30, 2012.

by different composers. Schubert, as described in Chapter 3, has regularly been accused of some kind of deficiency with regard to large forms on account of his "tendency to repeat extended stretches of music in development sections or second-theme groups... precisely the stations in the musical process where it would be more normative to avoid such repetition " (Burnham, 2005, p. 31).

Yet Burnham follows Adorno in laying out a careful defense of this repetition as communicative of a particular aesthetic, rather than indicative of some kind of compositional inadequacy. He focuses on the G major quartet as a canonic example of this sort of usage:

Repetition is like a holographic presence in this quartet; it is there at all levels, heard from every angle. Such repetition is not the makeshift device of a composer incapable of controlling large forms; it is rather the very condition of his expression, the very condition of a subjectivity staking everything on the surface materiality of the musical medium. In the quivering repetitions of Schubert's later instrumental music, we do not hear the progress of an idealistic World Soul filling the void left by Kant's transcendental analytic; we hear the gathering of subjectivity facing that void with the solitary truth of its inwardness... [This repetition] recognizes subjectivity as all there is... and also as the only knowable truth. And this truth bears repeating, in the double sense that it can be repeated and it must be repeated. The repetition of Schubert's illusory landscapes can thus be understood as an existential act (Burnham, 2005, p. 37).

For Adorno and Burnham, Schubert's themes are "truth characters" that appear or are "invoked"; they invite no formal procedures or development, but rather represent a kind of "ritual." To me personally, repetition in Schubert always seems to point and repoint to the music as a kind of edge, or liminal entity. The refusal to modify and develop serves to reiterate the implication that the repeated passage is the furthest music can go toward the inexpressible thing it's butting up against; there can be no progress or advancement because the border has been reached. Each time the music repeats, it casts my ear more and more in the direction of the unsayable thing beyond the notes. It's a kind of interpretative equivalent of the shift to higher temporal spans sustained by some listeners in relation to repetition (see Margulis, 2012), but instead of shifting attention to a different aspect of the musical stimulus itself, it shifts attention increasingly to some barely grasped semantic associate.

This is what Burnham seems to mean by repetition as "the very condition of his expression, the very condition of a subjectivity staking everything on the surface materiality of the musical medium." Everything is staked on this surface materiality because it is stretched across something more than musical, revealing by way of relief, by the shape that something pushes into the musical fabric, what lies beyond it. Development asks us to follow a narrative set up by the music; repetition asks us to embody it. Development asks us to watch a story that's out there in the world; repetition asks us to enter a particular subjectivity.

In a participatory music like the Taizé song discussed above, repetition encourages a subjective identification arrived at through physically joining in, but in a presentational music like the Schubert quartet just considered, repetition encourages a subjective identification arrived at through a virtual and sympathetic extension of a listener's sensibilities. The mechanism underpinning these two processes is not dissimilar; it relates essentially to the knowability repetition makes possible, and further to the tight coupling between musical sound and percepts of motor movement. Knowability creates a link between the sounds as they are occurring in the world and as they can be imagined internally in the mental soundscape. The music-movement coupling brings about a virtual sense of sound production, as if the person hearing the music were in some way actually producing it.

The kinds of experiences repetition can make possible vary depending on their position on the spectrum from musematic to discursive (in Middleton's terminology) or short to long length of repeating unit (in Huron's). The participatory example considered above, the music of the Taizé, entails repetition of relatively longer phrase- and section-length entities, and expressly seeks to include the entire congregation in overt performance. The presentational example of Stevie Wonder's *Superstition* features repetition of short measure-long segments, and encourages overt participation from the audience—not *performance* in the sense of playing an instrument or singing, but *participation* in the sense of tapping, rocking, nodding, dancing—an experience halfway between the classically participatory and classically presentational. Everyone is moving, but only Stevie Wonder and the band are *playing*. The fully presentational examples discussed above, such as the classical rondo, largely feature distal, nonadjacent repetitions of larger segments—discursive repetitions, in Middleton's terminology. But the way these repetitions make certain passages available for sympathetic, imagined participation doesn't differ essentially from the functions of repetition in the participatory styles. When a passage is repeated several times across the course of the piece, the listener gains an enhanced ability to *think through* that passage, to match an internal auditory image with the external sound increasingly well and with an intensified orientation toward the future across the course of each iteration. This process weaves the listener more and more into a sense of virtual participation across the course of the piece.

A forthcoming documentary film called *Alive Inside* chronicles Alzheimer's and dementia patients whose condition has deteriorated to a state of unresponsiveness and near catatonia, yet who nevertheless wake up, becoming alert and engaged, when presented with familiar music from their youth. A particularly moving excerpt from the film can be viewed at http://www.ximotionmedia.com. In this clip, a gentleman called Henry is shown to go from a near catatonic state in which his eyes are downcast and he's unable to answer simple questions or recognize family members, to a fully alert condition in which his eyes not only open wide, but he starts to sway enthusiastically and sing along joyfully and with expression.

Neurologist and writer Oliver Sacks, who sensitively documents this kind of response in *Musicophilia: Tales of Music and the Brain* (2007), offers on-screen perspective in the film. He recalls Kant's characterization of music as "the quickening art" and observes how directly the music in the clip can be seen to "quicken" its listener. With astonishing swiftness, the music seems to lift Henry's arms, open his eyes, and actually *move* him. But the music serving as the agent of these transformations is not just any music; it's music that's familiar to Henry from his youth. Repetition has allowed him not only to have heard it, but also to have thought it, felt it, and lived it. Henry must be experiencing something like time travel—the sudden, Proust-madeleine-like transportation to what it felt like to be Henry decades before—because of the match between the external, sounding music and the internal, predictive engagement that years of familiarity must have made possible. The music doesn't initially connect Henry to the outside world, although this is a wonderful eventual outcome. At first, it connects Henry to himself—to what it felt like to be Henry in the past listening to Cab Calloway. It felt (in the past) like the music sounds (in the present), an instant conduit not just to a past experience, but to an entire past state of being. It felt like the music sounds because repetition gradually causes music to play us. Henry is being quickened not merely by music, but by the musical experience repetition affords.

It doesn't matter that Cab Calloway isn't a fully participatory music. The audience is not meant to jump on stage, grab a saxophone, and join in. Repetition nonetheless extends a latent, virtual invitation to participate. Henry is meant to walk around humming the tunes. He's meant to let this music play his mind, to participate as an imaginative act. And it's the habit of this virtual participation that permits the awakening seen decades later in the video. Other overt evidence of virtual participation can be glimpsed in the phenomenon of "air guitar," whereby an appropriate response to a familiar lick can be to pseudo-perform it on an invisible instrument. It can also be witnessed in the way repetitive music that accompanies video games—*Tetris* is a classic example—can, with the aid of other addictive nonmusical elements, seem to possess a player such that he sits in front of the screen, lost in the blocks and the synthesized tunes, oblivious to the voice in the background that may be shouting "Dinner!"

Stickgold et al. (2000) report, in fact, that the repetitive encounters with *Tetris* imagery in avid players of the game can result in a visual effect similar to the auditory earworm. Individuals suffering from this condition experience intrusive imagery from the game while they're trying to fall asleep. Three amnesic patients in the study experienced the same involuntary visual imagery despite being unable to explicitly recall playing the game. This represents an example from another modality where excessive repetition can trigger a breakdown of the internal/external divide, such that a person experiences a temporary sense of possession by the stimulus even when it is physically absent. However, for visual imagery such as *Tetris* blocks, these episodes seem to be largely restricted to the hypnagogic state—the transition from wakefulness into sleep, when the individual isn't fully conscious. So far as I am aware, the way music can hijack brain states even during unambiguously conscious periods is unique. The boundary between perception and imagined participation is thinner for music than for other associated domains.

## Repetition and the Interpersonal

Many of the examples of virtual participation explored thus far involve a single listener. But what about situations that involve groups of people listening together? What role might repetition play in this setting? Does the individual listener normally sustain an imagined participatory connection with the music itself, or might this listener also experience an imagined co-participation involving her fellow listeners? A useful starting point is the examination of listening that is overtly co-participatory—listening among social dancers improvising together. Jackson (2001) examines improvisation in African-American vernacular dancing using Friedland's (1995) taxonomy of processes of social commentary in this style of movement. These processes include *annotation,* allusion to cultural symbols, *imitation,* disturbingly precise replication, and *subversion,* the parodying of cultural symbols. Jackson's other principal framework comes from Murray's (1976) study of improvisation in black vernacular music. Just as Friedman identified three basic processes of social commentary in African American dance, Murray identifies three basic improvisational strategies in the accompanying music: *vamping,* an improvised introduction often consisting of the repetition of a particular progression, *riffing,* the repetition of a brief musical phrase across the course of a stanza, and the *break,* a cadenza-like improvisatory passage between two musical phrases separated by a gap or interruption. Jackson pulls these musical strategies together with Friedman's dance strategies because he views sound and movement as "inseparable" in this tradition.

According to Jackson, dancers adopt the strategies of vamping, riffing, and breaks with a goal both toward individuation and toward ritualization. On the one hand, dancers repeat to create intensity, and to erect a layer of continuity between actions and episodes, aiming to establish a unique identity within the group. On the other, dancers repeat to ritualize, to use movement to form a community. Improvised beginnings and endings, often involving repetition that builds up or tapers away, are understood as attempts to

> mask and blur one's entry into the social moment and to produce an ongoing, mutable experience. Key to this agenda is the positive value of repetition....John Chernoff observes that 'we are not yet prepared to understand how people can find beauty in repetition' (1979, 55) (p. 47).

Jackson offers the specific example of jockeying: "a vamp that includes improvised, alternating (moving side-to-side in place) weight-shifting" (p. 47), from the Lindy Hop of the 1920s and 1930s. This understated repetitive movement allows the dancers to attune themselves to the movements of their partners and to the rhythmic qualities of the music. Top-rocking in hip hop dancing is another example of a vamp with a similar purpose.

In Jackson's account, repetition is understood to be a fundamentally social mode of negotiating the space between the definition of the individual and the definition of the community. A group can simultaneously repeat to establish continuity and common purpose, and to highlight the micro-differences that emerge between one person's execution of the movements and those of another. These individuating differences are viewed by Jackson as an important driver of stylistic change, since movements that drive individuation in a single performer might come to drive ritualization as they begin to be imitated and adopted by the group. Repetition allows individuals the ground on which to contribute something that can be recognized and accepted as creative, as well as the means for the group to ratify and extend it.

Csikszentmihalyi (1997) makes a broader point about what he views as the fundamentally social nature of creativity. He argues that for something to be appropriately termed creative, the innovation must occur within an established domain, and be accepted for inclusion by the community that defines the domain. Creativity is thus "jointly constituted by the interaction among domain, field, and person" (p. 29). In the example put forth by Jackson, repetition constitutes both the process that establishes the rules and standards against which novelty can emerge, and the process that represents the acceptance and inclusion of these acts as creative. Garcia (2005) affirms the documentation of repetition's role in the relationship between individual and community in the work of Chernoff (1979), who saw repetition as a way for individual contributions to be accepted by a community, and in the work of Keil (Feld and Keil, 1994), who coined the term *participatory discrepancies* to capture the way that repetition enables individuals to contribute material that is personalized yet consistent with the collective process.

When the audience members are not overt co-participants with the musicians, as in many Western musical traditions, this kind of repetition-based exchange between novelty and acceptance cannot emerge directly; however, it may occur indirectly. Consider a jazz improvisation—the audience can signal their acceptance of a new element braiding its way through the texture by whistling, nodding, clapping, or growing silent and attentive. In this way, even the "perceivers" of the performance can influence the negotiation between novelty and replication. The cues that register acceptance or distaste, interest or bafflement, can be even subtler nonverbal signals the audience member may not even be aware he is sending—performers often speak of "feeling" the audience, and having quite distinct impressions of their pleasure or displeasure at particular moments, despite an inability to pinpoint the behaviors that gave rise to this perception. The audience might sometimes influence the course of a particular improvisation despite lacking an instrument or a voice.

For notated, nonimprovisatory musics, much of this interchange is made impossible. A performer can't replay an appreciated passage in response to general enthusiasm for it in the hall (although there is an established historical practice of repeating individual movements or pieces at the end of a concert after shouts of "encore"—play it again!). Even at this kind of concert, however, the audience can make itself heard. For example, the familiarity of certain passages is often loud and salient even within a hall silent except for the music. In productions of Shakespeare, when an actor gets to "Tomorrow, and tomorrow, and tomorrow" the audience silently but noticeably bristles, registering their recognition of the famous bit even as the actor passes through it without markedness or pause. Similarly, at the opening of live performances of the Mendelssohn E Minor or Bruch G Minor Violin Concertos, it is often impossible not to notice the forceful anticipation of the coming notes occupying the silent minds of rows and rows of listeners. The same holds for famous passages within chamber works, symphony, and operas. A good example is the beginning of Act III in *Die Walküre*, the second opera in Wagner's Ring. The audience, already a good four hours into the cycle by that point, always perks up noticeably at the Ride of the Valkyries (even as connoisseurs feign nonchalance), leaning forward in their seats and listening intently. The familiarity of this oft-repeated music—whether from exposure to Wagner or exposure to Looney Tunes—is incapable of being ignored. Fairly or not, Elmer Fudd, the air regiment in *Apocalypse Now*, and (much more disturbingly) German newsreels from World War II all inhabit the mental landscape of the audience during this scene. It would be naïve to claim that this resonance is not palpable in the hall despite the lack of an overt reaction. The familiarity and web of associations engendered by repetition causes a nonvocal audience, for once, to know what's going on in the heads of their neighbors: "That's that music from the cartoon!" Or, in the example of the concerto, "That's the Mendelssohn E Minor!" This shared recognition connects the audience as insiders; it's as if someone had just alluded to the highway from your hometown, and everyone had gotten the reference.

This culture of knowingness is also relevant to the development of the cult of the performer across the course of the nineteenth and twentieth centuries. Horowitz (1987) incisively documents the way the rise over this time of the practice of repeatedly programming a canon of "masterworks" from the past, rather than programming new and various music from contemporary composers, led to an investment in the individuation offered by the renditions of specific conductors and performers, whose names came to take top billing on albums and concert flyers (see Figure 7.4).

When what distinguished a piece of music and made it worthy of "market recognition" was that Josquin wrote it, composers began signing their works; when what distinguished a piece of music and made it worthy of market recognition was that Toscanini performed it, his name received priority of place. In line not only with the added familiarity provided by repeated programming of the same works but also with the added familiarity provided by new technology permitting repeated listenings to the same performances, listeners became less attuned

*Figure 7.4* Album covers that represent the trend of featuring the performer or conductor more prominently than the composer.

to compositional deviations and more attuned to performative ones. Large-scale repetition of musical works provided the backdrop against which performers could individuate themselves. These individuating acts, to revisit Jackson's terminology, were then ritualized by receptive behavior: the public's listenings and relistenings to recordings that became accepted as canonic. Thus, it came to be nearly impossible to play certain Scarlatti sonatas or Schumann character pieces without evoking the recordings of Vladimir Horowitz, or to play the Goldberg Variations without evoking the recordings of Glenn Gould. A performer might make consciously different choices than either of these pianists, but the resonance of these prior renderings exists as a layer within the referential texture of the performance. It is not possible to revert to the "purer" ears of a person who hasn't heard these works through the renderings of Horowitz and Gould. Their influence and repetition within the culture exists as residue on the original works. There might be listeners new to classical music who don't register this resonance, but it exists for a high enough percentage of listeners in the typical concert hall and a high enough percentage of pianists programming these pieces, that this resonance might be considered to inhabit the ambient environment, and color the experience of even the neophyte listener. A person new to classical concert-going, for example, might notice the murmur going around the hall when the performer breaks into one of these Scarlatti pieces as an encore, or register the knowing smiles more experienced listeners exchange as the opening notes of *Kinderszenen* sound.

It was precisely this nonverbal but relevant audience participation, unsusceptible to complete performer control, that Glenn Gould sought to avoid by giving up the concert hall to concentrate exclusively on recordings. He strived for a relationship with the listener more like the one books establish with their readers—a subject beautifully chronicled in fiction by Alan Bennett's *An Uncommon Reader*, which traces the dawning of bibliophilia in a fictional version of Queen Elizabeth II, who has happened upon a traveling library outside the halls of the palace. According to the delighted revelation, "books did not care who was reading them or whether one read them or not ... all readers were equal, herself included" (p. 30). There is a text, and the reader interacts with it, without any danger of this perception and experience feeding back into or influencing the book itself. A page in *Macbeth* carries the print "Tomorrow, and tomorrow, and tomorrow" just the same whether the reader knows the monologue or not; in a live performance of *Macbeth*, the general familiarity with this episode is present in and alters the texture of the moment. Yet despite Gould's aspirations and the advent of incredible technology, music has not shed its performativity. Except in exceptional cases, books are not encountered as recorded traces of a live reading. Contrastingly, music, except in exceptional cases, *is* experienced as a record of an actual performance, to the extent that heavy editing has proved controversial in classical recordings (Hamilton, 2003), and record companies have based ad campaigns around the fidelity to original live sounds represented by their technology. Even when performativity is merely implied, as in music consumed through iPod earbuds, it colors the experience.

Although these examples are drawn from cases where listeners are aware of the repetitions, situations where listeners are unaware are perhaps even more common. Clarke (2011) uses these moments as an example of a larger deficiency in our vocabulary for talking about what it's like to listen to music.

> Many listeners may not be consciously aware during a long symphonic movement that a melody has been repeated with a different harmonization, or they may lack the language to describe such an event; but may nonetheless experience a strong response to it, perhaps through a sense of the familiarity of the material, without being able to pin down where that familiarity comes from (p. 197).

Repetition normally matters in this more implicit, felt way—as do the processes of individuation that drive subtle changes within the microtiming or dynamics of a repeated element.

Levinson (1997) scrutinizes what the role of familiarity might be within what he terms a concatenationist account of musical listening—one convinced that segment-to-segment progressions, rather than large-scale structures, serve as the basis for musical understanding, enjoyment, and valuation. For the concatenationist, form arises primarily out of the apprehension of moment-to-moment continuity between section edges, not out of the reflective comparison of large stretches of material. Levinson echoes Clarke's point in an analysis of the finale of Beethoven's Piano Sonata, Op. 110, where the final measures transmit an unmistakable sense of exquisite release. On the surface, it would seem that this example challenges the concatenationist account, since this effect appears to be dependent on this section's relationship with material from much earlier in the piece, outside the segment-to-segment window privileged by concatenationism.

But Levinson argues that each segment-to-segment span is imbued with the influence of the span that preceded it, resulting in an accrual of enrichment and significance across the course of even a very long piece, without the necessary accompaniment of explicit memory or intellectual grappling with the form. This accrual is enough, he claims, to achieve the sense of release commonly experienced in these measures. Repetition and inter-piece allusion work to gradually bind segment to segment, causing impressions to deepen as the sonata progresses such that the appreciation of the ending phrase, although still segment-to-segment, bit-to-bit, reflects the added but inarticulable weight of the bit-to-bit spans that have led to it.

In a way, repetition offers evidence for the oblique, under-the-radar workings of musical context. It's hard to explicitly identify repeating elements in music as it progresses (Margulis, 2012). Yet despite how challenging repetitions are to identify in real time, they affect a listener's experience. The simple introduction of repetition caused listeners in Margulis (2013) to report increased enjoyment, interest, and impressions of artistic intent in contemporary pieces of music.

A similar dissociation between the explicit and implicit became apparent during a music theory class on small forms. We were looking at the Finale from Haydn's Piano Sonata No. 51, shown in Figure 7.5. The students were having a hard time identifying mm. 21-28 as a modified return of mm. 1-8, although really all that had changed was a textural thinning in the left hand from octaves to single notes, a rhythmic displacement in the opening two measures, and an intensification in the fifth and sixth measures (mm. 25-26) consisting of rhythmic elaboration, melodic reduction, and a new articulation pattern.

Yet despite their initial inability to identify the relationship of the last two phrases to the first two, once it was pointed out to them, they nodded with recognition. They had not been able to verbalize the relationship, but once it had been verbalized *for* them, they were able to match that characterization with an experience they'd already been having. They didn't react as if they now heard something different in the music, but rather as if they now had a way of talking about something they had *already* heard. In other words, they accepted the theoretical language espousing an equivalency relation between mm. 1-8 and mm. 21-28 as *descriptive* of an experience they'd been having, rather than *prescriptive* of some new way they should be listening to the music.

Not only are listeners typically rather bad at identifying repetitions, whether they are modified repetitions as in this example or exact repetitions as in

*Figure 7.5* From Haydn Piano Sonata No. 51 Hob. XVI: 38 in E♭ Major, Finale.

Margulis (2012), but they are also simply rather loath to think explicitly about these kinds of relationships in music. Yet despite these two facts, repetitions affect even the highest-level impressions of music—responses like enjoyment and interest—suggesting that their work is largely done implicitly, outside conscious awareness.

Even in presentational musics, repetition can generate a tacit sense of participation and involvement that draws a listener into the material without the listener necessarily being aware of how this process is taking place. The subtle workings of musical repetitiveness lie in stark contrast to the marked, salient quality of linguistic repetitiveness. Such repetition in speech can be quite effective—think of Martin Luther King Jr.'s 1963 "I have a dream" speech—but its effectiveness is predicated on the audience's conscious marking of these repetitions. With each repeated utterance, the audience can grow more enthusiastic about the message, more swept up in the avowal and affirmation implied by the restatements. Since musical repetition is so much less salient, the effect can be more mysterious—a person leaves the theater humming a tune, for example, without being aware that she's heard it fifteen times across the course of the musical.

Marketing professionals are well aware of this difference. A jingle can be repeated several times across the course of a thirty-second commercial without rising to the level of egregiousness, as would the spoken repetition of the same message. Huron (1989) lays out the many ways this characteristic can be harnessed by advertisers. In a particularly telling example, he analyzes a 1983 radio advertisement for McDonald's, the beginning of which is accompanied by a rhythm that later gets incorporated into a jingle with the text "Sausage McMuffin and Sausage McMuffin with Egg." By repeating and involving listeners in this sticky rhythm, and then later grafting the take-home message to it, the corporation has cleverly hijacked the human propensity for musical earworms to leave the names of two of their sandwiches in the heads of unsuspecting radio listeners. Merely repeating the words "Sausage McMuffin and Sausage McMuffin with Egg" would not have had the same effect on memorability. Moreover, as Huron points out, people are much more willing to accept schlocky, sentimental, or manipulative language when it is sung than when it is spoken. Consider, by way of proof, the video clips at http://idolator.com/5771261/top-5-dramatic-readings-of-pop-songs-from-baby-to-poker-face, which feature Jude Law reading the lyrics from Lady Gaga's *Poker Face*, William Shatner reading the lyrics from Rihanna's *Umbrella*, and James Earl Jones reading the lyrics from Justin Bieber's *Baby* (Bain, 2011). Whatever you think of the merits of the original songs, the text sounds nowhere near as ludicrous when sung rather than read. Advertisers can set a message we'd reject if spoken to a tune, and let the relative innocuousness of its musical repetition burrow into our minds, enhancing message receptivity and retention to sometimes disturbing effect.

Despite the diversity of styles, traditions, and contexts within which musical repetition occurs, certain qualities of the practice remain relatively invariant. Repetition almost always carries an actual or virtual invitation to participate, whether overtly or subjectively. Moreover, repetition almost always exploits the ease with which kinesthetic and implicit knowledge can outstrip conceptual, explicit knowledge about a piece of music. The final chapter explores these distinctively musical functions of repetition.

# 8

# Repetition, Music, and Mind

When my children were young enough to be learning to speak new words every day, I found that I could increase their desire to repeat a word by speaking it to them with an exaggerated, quasi-musical contour. If I said "zebra," for example, clearly inviting them to repeat the word in response, they'd stare at me for a second and then look back down at their toy train. But if I said "ZEEEEEE-bra," with a dramatic prosodic curve, sliding high in pitch and then hyperbolically low, they'd drop the train and start playing repeat-the-funny-word. The factor galvanizing their involvement may simply have been the novelty of such strange pronunciations, but it seemed to me at the time that these "musicalized" pronunciations activated a very different response system than ordinary pronunciations. Their whole stance turned imitative—eyes studiously locked on my face, watching me form the sounds—and they'd respond in time, copying the contour and rhythm as closely as they were able. I remember marveling that by simply accentuating the musical aspects of speech I was able to elicit (1) motor engagement, (2) an urge to repeat, and (3) faster vocabulary learning. Observations about this connection have led, perhaps inevitably, to commercial exploitation in forms such as "Earworms Musical Brain Trainer: Your Personal Audio Language Trainer" (http://www.earwormslearning.com), where repetitions of particular rhythmic and prosodic pronunciations of foreign words are (hilariously) set to an underlying beat. Without condoning the particulars of this effort, I raise the example to illustrate that the tight coupling between music and imitation has not gone generally unnoticed.

Richman (2000) in fact views "collective, real-time repetitions of formulaic sequences" as the shared evolutionary origin of both music and language (p. 300).

> This is a fierce biological drive that ensures that human beings become and stay involved in speech and in interaction with others. This drive to repeat throws people into language and into vocal interactions with

each other. It also ensures that their interactions will be in rhythmic synchrony with each other as their repetitions create an interactive rhythm. Such interactive rhythmic synchrony is crucial for people being able to predict and understand the communicative moves and movements of others. Finally, it ensures that people constantly show and demonstrate their agreement and acceptance of language terms by repeating them (Richman, 2000, p. 305).

According to this account, it is the urge to repeat that drew people into dialogue with one another; this appetite and capacity for mimicry can be understood to have conferred an adaptive advantage insofar as it drove communication. Richman observes that although this drive to repeat is fundamentally musical, it would have been impossible for certain aspects of language, such as the development of a large repertoire of formulaic phrases (e.g., "how are you?"), to arise without it. Richman, in other words, not only identifies a drive to repeat as a central musical impulse, but also places this *musical* impulse at the root of the origins of language. For him, music, or musical utterances, trigger a drive to repeat; this coupling between music and repetition is tight and biologically endowed. The development of language depended on its ability to piggyback on the repetitive impulse of musicality.

As modern-day evidence for his claims about the prehistoric world, Richman points to the drive to repeat that is plainly evident in small children; a drive fundamental to their capacity to learn language. He speculates that in early prehistory this drive threw people into communication with one another, ultimately causing them to generate sound sequences that gained associations with particular things. In the initial stages of language's development, he argues, these formulaic musical sequences came to be remembered by individuals in the population and used holistically. Referential language emerged almost by accident, as a fortunate outcome of this constant vocal imitation: an account that diverges sharply from standard theories of language's earliest development.

## The Musicality of Linguistic Repetition

A two-part volume edited by Barbara Johnstone (1994) explores the role of repetition in discourse from a number of disciplinary and topical angles. In the introductory chapter, Johnstone intriguingly asks whether there are things "repetition always does" (p. 12); whether, that is, the individual cases of repetitiveness in language can usefully be considered as examples of a more general phenomenon; whether it is helpful to consider repetitiveness itself, apart from the many diverse guises in which it ordinarily appears.

> Does repetition serve universal cognitive or interactional functions? The function of repetition in general is to point, to direct a hearer back to something and say, "Pay attention to this again. This is still salient; this still has potential meaning; let's make use of it in some way." This accounts, for example, for the cognitive utility of repetition to learners, getting the learner's attention on a token of input for a second round in order to have something to work with. We can also call attention to the fact that we're getting one's attention, and we can take that one step further, when awareness of the ability to manipulate allows us to play with attention. Immediacy may be poetic. . . . Repetition is a mode of focusing attention. . . . Repetition focuses attention on the makeup of both the repeated discourse and the earlier discourse. Repetition puts the utterance in brackets, making it impossible to treat the language as if it were transparent, by forcing hearers to focus on the language itself. In that sense repetition is metalinguistic, even though it's not conscious talk about talk (p. 13).

To my knowledge, this is the best overarching summary of repetition's function in speech. The principal commonalities it identifies behind the various conversational uses of repetition are manipulation of attention, and an orientation toward the metalinguistic. When repetitive speech foregrounds this attentional manipulation, language can be pushed into the territory of play or poetry.

For example, on a recent night, my son picked a book of children's poetry to read to me before going to sleep. After perusing the first two lines of Roger McGough's *The Leader* (2004), "I wanna be the leader / I wanna be the leader," he turned to me with furrowed brows and asked why the line had been repeated. He was clearly skeptical, intimating it had been a mistake or he'd read it wrong. But when assured that it was a real part of the poem, he jumped fully into the character of a sing-songy child concerned with nothing else than being picked as "the leader"—a folly reinforced by a single final line after loads of repetition chronicling the child's desire and eventual selection as "leader"—"OK what shall we do?"

The repetition throughout this poem ("Yippee, I'm the leader / I'm the leader," etc.) doesn't confer extra information in an ordinary semantic sense; if examined from that perspective, it would seem redundant rather than playful and illuminating. Instead, as was soon apparent even to my four-year-old, the repetition conveyed information about the narrator that she wasn't consciously putting into the words themselves, information that escapes about her almost by accident: her eagerness, her physical antsiness (suggested by the "bounce" created by the rhythm of the repetitions), her lack of power in comparison to the person selecting the "leader" (suggested by the desperate insistence of the repetitions), and her simultaneous comfort level with this person (suggested by her willingness to speak so unreservedly). All of these disclosures are metalinguistic, in the sense that they involve information not present in the words themselves, in an ordinary, dictionary-lookup sense. Such metalinguistic information is present in all communication to a greater or lesser extent, but repetition draws particular attention to it; since the basic semantic content should already have been transmitted the first time around, the repetition draws attention to other dimensions of the utterance.

This shift, effected by repetition, away from what is directly captured by words and toward what is revealed by the structure, prosody, rhythm, and tempo of the *utterance* of the words, is essentially a shift toward a musical way of listening. The act of repetition highlights that there is more to be understood than what the words literally convey, drawing attention to these other qualities. It also engages, however covertly, the drive to repeat emphasized by Richman. Repetition by a speaker induces a participatory urge in the listener. It activates more than usual a tendency toward subvocalization, making prominent a sense of *what it would feel like to make the words sound that way*. It elicits a sort of sympathetic, internal utterance in the listener, placing her more in the position of a subject who imagines producing the words, rather than an object who simply hears them. Music works precisely via this elicitation of sympathetic, extended subjectivity. When language is being repetitive, in other words, language is being musical.

The most dramatic evidence for this claim comes from Diana Deutsch's speech-to-song illusion. This illusion uses an extreme exaggeration of ordinary repetitiveness to make a passage of speech actually sound as if it had been sung, but a subtler shift toward heightened musicality is still evident in more understated, realistic uses of repetitive speech. Rhetoric has long chronicled the conventional uses of repetition in oration and persuasive speech. Consider the following example of anaphora (repetition of a sentence's beginning):

> *We shall* go on to the end, *we shall fight* in France, *we shall fight* on the seas and oceans, *we shall fight* with growing confidence and growing strength in the air, *we shall* defend our Island, whatever the cost may be, *we shall fight* on the beaches, *we shall fight* on the landing grounds, *we shall fight* in the fields and in the streets, *we shall fight* in the hills; *we shall* never surrender (Winston Churchill, speech to the House of Commons, June 4, 1940).

and the following example of epiphora (repetition of a sentence's end):

> But whether white, black or brown, the hungry baby's belly turned inside out is the same color. Call it pain. Call it hurt. Call it agony. Most poor people are not on welfare.
> Some of them are illiterate and can't read the want-ad sections. And when they can, they can't find a job that matches their address. *They work hard every day*, I know. I'm one of them.
> I know *they work*. I'm a witness. They catch the early bus. *They work every day*. They raise other people's children. *They work every day*. They clean the streets. *They work every day*. They drive dangerous cabs. *They work every day*. They change the beds you slept in those hotels last night and can't get a union contract. *They work every day* (Jesse Jackson, address to the Democratic National Convention, July 19, 1988).

Barack Obama's famous acceptance speech in New Hampshire on January 8, 2008, used the same rhetorical strategy, repeatedly invoking the phrase "Yes we can."

It's no coincidence that the repeated utterances in these three examples ("We shall fight"; "They work hard every day"; and "Yes we can") provide an opportunity for shared subjectivity—the first and last explicitly with a "we" and the second via a "they" that, in designating a shared other, carves out an implicit "we." The repetition works to draw the listener into the subject position, increasing affiliation with the speaker and (they hope) with their social and political ideals.

Like other cases of repetition in speech, these oratorical ones pull attention away from the ordinary semantic meaning of the words and into a metalinguistic attitude toward them, asking us in turn to contemplate what it really might mean to "work every day"—to *feel* the strength and perseverance required—or to rally to the notion of a resolution to fight, as if it were a rousing chant at a football game, or to insist resolutely on an optimistic stance, even in the face of a setback. In each of these examples, the effect is greater than would be the case for the straightforward linguistic expression of any of these ideas, since the point is felt rather than objectively captured. This sense of co-experiencing rather than receiving information, so integral to music, increases sympathy between the speaker and listener in ways that can also be critical for persuasive speech.

Sherzer's chapter in Johnstone's volume (1994) explores the way postmodern writers use repetition in order to drive readers' attention away from plot and toward the language itself, and Ehrlich's chapter (1994) looks at the way that repetition of a narrative event can signal a shift in point of view. A classic example is Julian Barnes's 1991 novel *Talking It Over,* in which several characters recount the same events from their own contradictory perspectives. The repeating language, used so variously by the different narrators, makes the reader particularly suspicious of any one individual's account. Sherzer's and Ehrlich's contributions illustrate the capacity of repeated language one the one hand to shift attention down toward the component elements of the language itself and on the other to shift attention up toward issues of context and intent.

Knox's chapter (1994) attributes these shifts to the way repetition interfaces with Grice's conversational maxims—the unspoken assumptions that are thought to govern ordinary communication (Grice, 1991). According to Grice, people tacitly assume that each other's contributions are intended to be maximally relevant—an intuition that Sperber and Wilson (2004) extended into a more fleshed-out account referred to as relevance theory. Taken on the surface, repetition would seem to violate the maxim of optimal relevance. Accordingly, people don't take repetition on the surface. To preserve their assumption of maximal relevance, they assume the repetition points to some deeper, different meaning than the utterance would have had if stated only once. That different meaning might be found at a lower level of organization, for example in some aspect of the language or sounds themselves, or at a higher level, for example in the background context or intent. "When ideas are complex or words are insufficient, speakers may repeat their utterances in order to engage their hearers in interpretive efforts to make more of what is said" (Knox, 1994, p. 197).

It is telling that Knox identifies moments when "words are insufficient" as the ones during which repetition becomes a compelling alternative. People often talk about music as a communicative domain able to reach expressive territory beyond the borders of language. There are innumerable famous quotations to this effect, including Hans Christian Andersen's "Where words fail, music speaks," Victor Hugo's "Music expresses that which cannot be put into words and cannot remain silent," and Aldous Huxley's "After silence, that which comes nearest to expressing the inexpressible is music." The elusive entity referred to in these quotations, I argue, often consists of a sense of shared subjectivity—precisely the effect repetition can begin to construct even when used linguistically.

Actors harness the power of repetition with Meisner technique's centerpiece (see Meisner and Longwell,1987), a drill that capitalizes on precisely this affordance. Two actors face one another, repeating an honest observation about their partner, who then parrots it back from their own perspective, again and again until a new observation emerges, at which point they begin to exchange repetitions of that statement. For example:

You're smiling.
I'm smiling.
You're smiling.

I'm smiling.
You're smiling.
I'm smiling.
You're smiling.
I'm smiling.
You're embarrassed.
I'm embarrassed.
You're embarrassed.
I'm embarrassed.
...

The exercise aims to develop the capacity to read subtext and inflection in a part-ner, making it easier to connect at a spontaneous, emotional level. Repetition, in other words, allows actors to learn to attend to and understand one another in an unmediated, honest fashion, to create the kind of shared expressive space that allows for effective theatrical collaboration. Actors training this way are really borrowing a musical strategy—repetition—to improve their ability to sympa-thetically extend subjectivity. While music itself has been examined as a tool to facilitate entrainment and social cohesion, the musical strategy of repetition might be understood to accomplish similar effects, even when its constituent materials are comprised of words rather than notes.

## Repetition and the Implicit

Chapter 5 explored the distinction between implicit and explicit learning, with an emphasis on the notion that an essential distinguishing factor between the two types is whether or not the person doing the learning intended it or was even aware it happened. Implicit learning, the sort that can happen even when a person isn't trying to learn and might in fact expressly disavow that any learning had taken place, characterizes many domains. But implicit learning in music (for reviews, see Ettlinger, Margulis & Wong, 2011, and Rohrmeier & Rebuschat, 2012) is especially interesting because the idea that special training is required to "know" anything about music is so dominant within contemporary Western culture (Pitts, 2005). "Music?" people will say, dislodging the earbud through which a constant stream of sound has played. "I don't know anything about music!" Perhaps nowhere else is the gap between what people actually know and what they *think* they know so wide as in music.

Beyond the statistical learning literature surveyed in Chapter 5, there is a recent and growing body of research highlighting the existence of widespread musicality, unrestricted to specialists or individuals with special training. Almost twenty-five years ago, Sloboda (1991) made an argument for the universality of musicality, followed in a similar vein by Smith (1997). But as recently as 2000, when Koelsch, Gunter, Friederici & Schröger (2000) used ERP to find that people without formal musical training were sensitive to the degree to which unexpected chords violate a previously established musical context, the discovery was surprising enough to warrant the subtitle "Nonmusicians are musical." Since then, more and more studies have accrued to support this conclusion. The methodology of ERP has been particularly conducive to this line of research, since activity can be recorded that reflects sophisticated processing in the absence not only of conscious knowledge, but sometimes even of conscious attention.

Behavioral methodologies can also contribute, as well chronicled by Emmanuel Bigand's 2003 article *More About the Musical Expertise of Musically Untrained Listeners*. This title reflects an emergent (and still ongoing) shift in the literature from the term "nonmusician" to the term "listener without formal training." Although the term nonmusician is more concise, it carries a connotation (however unintended) that reifies cultural assumptions relegating musicality to the domain of specialists. The more research that emerges illustrating the amazing implicit knowledge possessed by listeners who have not undergone any special formal musical training, the clearer it becomes that the word nonmusician is misleading. Bigand and Poulin-Charronnat (2006) provide a list of the musical abilities known to be independent of specialized training. Indeed, the capacity to be moved by a series of sounds, or tap along to their beat, or be compelled enough by them to voluntarily place them on looped replay itself reveals the existence of a fundamental musicality. Many of these abilities are cognitively impressive. Henkjan Honing and colleagues (Desain and Honing, 1999), for example, famously demonstrated in the early 1990s (by hooking a shoe up to a computer program that had been trained to find the beat in national anthems) that even the ability to tap along to beat-dominated music required a sophisticated level of tonal processing that was considered, at the time, implausible in a person without special training. Yet despite the fact that the program needed to know all sorts of things about parallelism and tonal structure to successfully tap a shoe along with the patriotic songs, people in stadiums the world over, many of whom have never had a music lesson, can be seen to nod, clap, and tap along with no special effort at all. Excluding the descriptive "musical" from these people reflects a conceptualization of musicality that is biased toward the productive capacity—the ability to produce music by playing an instrument or singing—and away from the perceptive capacity, the ability to listen expertly and behave appropriately in response.

Among the tasks demonstrated by Bigand to elicit similar performances from people with and without musical training were (1) distinguishing melodies that had been written using the same compositional system as melodies presented in a training phase from foils that had been written using a different system; (2) distinguishing melodies presented in a training phase from new melodies regardless of whether the melodies had initially been presented in a structurally coherent or incoherent sequence (suggesting that large-scale structure doesn't preferentially aid learning in people with formal training); and (3) identifying the consonance of tuned or slightly mistuned chords when the chords were expected or surprising given the preceding context. This last test, the harmonic priming task, provocatively suggests that listeners with and without formal training generate similar syntactic expectations.

Oechslin, Läge & Vitouch (2012) detail a problem with the demands posed by tasks used in some music perception experiments. When participants must evidence an ability by providing a verbal report, existence of the underlying capacity in someone who hasn't learned the relevant vocabulary might get overlooked.

> Declarative knowledge and specialist vocabulary is a prerequisite for reliable descriptions of what has been heard, and reproduction demands specific motor skills. Musical novices possess little of these. To quantify listening performance, we ideally should assess listeners' responses in a way that is independent of their expertise level (Oechslin, Läge & Vitouch, 2012, p. 1).

For example, Oechslin et al. note, if we're interested in interval recognition abilities, we might not get very far by asking people without special training to identify major sixths, but asking them to identify the *My Way* interval can reveal surprising adeptness with this task. Listeners are often able to categorize and process in the absence of conventional labels. If experimental tests depend on specialized terminology, these abilities may go unnoticed.

Marvin and Newport (in press) demonstrate how tasks designed to be independent of specialized labeling can reveal surprising skills in everyday listeners. Absolute pitch has typically been conceptualized as the ability to remember and identify pitches when presented in isolation, a skill that depends on the possession of knowledge of verbal labels acquired through training ("G," "C# "). But Marvin and Newport used a clever adaptation of the statistical learning tasks described in Chapter 5 to reveal enhanced pitch memory even in participants who lacked knowledge of these special labels. After exposing participants to streams of tones with varying transition probabilities, such that the stream was composed of specific three-note "words" despite no surface indication of segmentation (such as pauses or dynamics), they asked listeners to discriminate between pairs of three-note sequences that matched or did not match "words" in the initial stream's vocabulary. Crucially, some of these discriminations pit actual sequences against minor-third transpositions of them. Most listeners, reliant on relative rather than absolute pitch and more invested in the intervallic relationship between the notes than their actual pitch level, were not able to distinguish between the two. Some, however, could recognize the originals over their transpositions—indicating that their memory trace included absolute pitch information. The performance on this task by this subgroup of listeners unable to overtly label pitches was similar to the performance of people with absolute pitch as diagnosed by a more traditional labeling task (e.g., playing a note and asking the listener to name it). Several other studies have shown that listeners without special training or even the form of "incipient AP" chronicled by Marvin and Newport seem to store and reproduce familiar tunes within a semitone of the key in which they're typically performed (Levitin, 1994; Schellenberg & Trehub, 2003). Henkjan Honing makes a beautiful appeal for the universality of important aspects of musicality in *The Illiterate Listener* (2011), and Brandt, Gebrian & Slevc (2012) argue that this universal musical capacity actually underlies the acquisition of speech.

What does this contrast between the sophistication of most people's implicit knowledge about music and the patchiness of their explicit knowledge about it mean for the way repetition tends to function within musical structure and as a type of musical behavior (the insistent revisiting of a single track, for example)? Across rehearings, a person's implicit knowledge increases much faster than his explicit knowledge. Thus, his sense of orientation within the piece, his felt understanding of it, increases but without the expected associated increase in conceptual understanding. The effect is reminiscent of the perceptual fluency hypothesis (discussed in Chapter 5) advocated by Jacoby (1983) and Bornstein (1992) as a way to understand the relationship between pleasure and repeated exposures. According to this classic account, increased exposures create additional mental competency with the stimulus. In the absence of conscious recognition of the repeated nature of the exposures, this gets pleasurably misinterpreted as elevated personal competence and acuity, an effect that wears off once the individual identifies the true source of the perceptual fluency. But the hypothesis put forward here is distinct from the classic perceptual fluency model because the pleasure it postulates is not dependent on a lack of awareness about the repetition. Instead, this hypothesis claims, listeners can be well aware they're rehearing a piece numerous times—they can put the iPod on repeat, or restart the track themselves—but nevertheless fervently believe that *they are not learning anything*.

Viewed from one perspective, they may be right. The amount of explicit knowledge they gain might be minimal, involving perhaps the memorization of the lyrics, the tune, and some of the more salient rhythmic elements. But the amount of implicit knowledge they're gaining might be significant. It might consist of an array of capacities including an increased sense of tonal orientation, a refined sense of the timbral "signature" of the work (Krumhansl, 2010), an intuitive sense of the piece's larger-scale formal trajectory (Margulis, 2012), and a progressively more internalized, embodied sense of how the piece goes. Instead of this implicit knowledge leading ultimately toward some simpler, explicit, conceptual information about the piece, it remains largely unverbalized and unconceptualized, retaining the richness and present-moment orientation of lived rather than catalogued experiences.

Musical experience's resistance to conceptualization has been chronicled by Raffman (1993), by Jankélévitch in Abbate's wonderful translation (2003), and by DeBellis (1995). As referenced previously, a recent study (Margulis, 2010) shows how listeners provided with conceptual frameworks for listening reported enjoying their experiences less than listeners who encountered the music in a less mediated way. Repeated listenings benefit from their ability to thwart the gradual construction of conceptual scaffolding that tends to accompany repetition in other domains. People can listen and listen and listen again without ever being able to condense and reduce the experience to a summary.

Yet this is not to say that interplay between repetition and conceptualization cannot occur in some situations. For example, a superfan devotee of a particular band or genre might take pleasure in amassing as many facts and details about individual recordings as possible across repeated listenings, and a professional performer or theorist might eagerly seek deeper explicit insights with each hearing. But I would still wager that for most listeners, the pace of the acquisition of implicit knowledge beats the pace of the acquisition of explicit knowledge across repeated listenings, and that this advantage for the implicit is one important driver of repetitive behavior in music listening.

One empirical prediction that comes out of this hypothesis is that people who approach a piece of music with the goal of increasing conceptual understanding—people who study a piece analytically, for example—might ultimately find themselves motivated to pursue fewer total repeated hearings in connection with it than with another piece that was matched in terms of the listener's initial enthusiasm and musical complexity. The narrowing of the gap between explicit and implicit knowledge acquisition across repeated hearings in such listeners should diminish the pleasure boost effected by the customary differential between the rapid acquisition of implicit knowledge and the slow acquisition of explicit knowledge in typical listeners.

## Repetitive Language, Musical Language

The speech-to-song illusion, detailed in earlier chapters, exploits an atypical occurrence—the regularly spaced, exact repetition of an utterance across a full minute's time—to reveal that repetition can take an acoustic stimulus originally processed as speech and instigate a profound phenomenological shift whereby that same stimulus comes to be experienced as music. Although this illusion demonstrates the powerful connection between repetition and musical attending, it does not represent a typical, everyday usage of repeated language. What functions does repetition usually play in language, and might some of these functions be rewardingly viewed as quasi-musical? Might we come to understand something about repetition in music by looking to common instances of repetition in speech?

Here, it's worthwhile once more to turn to Barbara Johnstone's two-volume set *Repetition in Discourse* (1994). Her opening chapter *Repetition in Discourse: A Dialogue* lays out the set's principal theoretical thrusts, and offers a tour through the varieties of repetition typically found in dialogue. To illustrate the role of culture in what gets recognized as an instance of repetition, she puts forth the example of a physicist fielding reporters at a press conference with the pronouncement "Read my lips: no new forces." If a listener lacked familiarity with the 1988 American presidential election, Johnstone observes, the intertextual repetition represented by the first five words would go unnoticed.

Repetition of this sort, in fact, can go a ways toward *constructing* a culture. The physicist's one-liner embraces the audience as members of a knowing community. Who are "we"? We are the people who get the reference. The physicist's allusion allows her to flatter the audience's cultural literacy indirectly, nonovertly—by assuming the audience will get it, the physicist is able to tacitly include them in her world, plausibly overcoming some of the potential cultural divide between a person working in a science often construed as difficult to understand and receptive members of the public. Repetition in the form of allusion erects a sense of shared knowing or membership.

Many musical allusions work this way, delineating a group of insiders defined by those who get the reference. For example, when Leperello groans during the last act of Mozart's *Don Giovanni* about the tune he's being subjected to at dinner, members of contemporary audiences who recognize the lilt of Mozart's own aria "Non più andrai" from *The Marriage of Figaro* often laugh with particular theatricality, as if to signal to other concertgoers that they're in on the joke. This sort of knowingness is a crucial element of many P. D. Q. Bach and Victor Borge performance experiences; the laughter sometimes serves as more of an audible marker of having gotten the reference than an expression of heartfelt sentiment.

Once an occurrence has been identified as a repetition, the potential for meaningful upheaval emerges. If the allusion is recognized, for example, "Read my lips: no new forces" entails a special twist at the word "forces." Musical repetition often serves precisely to make such disruption possible. Consider m. 21 of the Waldstein Sonata, reproduced in Figure 8.1. Heard in relation to this passage, the diatonic ii chord represents no special instance of wit or surprise. But heard

*Figure 8.1* From Beethoven, Sonata Op. 53, first movement, mm. 17–25.

in relation to the parallel moment in the sonata's opening, m. 5 in Figure 8.2, m. 21 represents a good deal of both. Except for the sixteenth note figuration and chromatically intensified grace note at the beginning of m. 20, the opening four measures of the passage in Figure 8.1 (mm. 17–20) exactly replicate the opening four measures of the piece, shown in Figure 8.2. Thus, although a listener encountering either of these passages in the abstract might expect the continuation to the diatonic harmony in m. 21 more than to the chromatic harmony in m. 5, by starting with the chromatic continuation—placing it first, and letting it function as a referent in the listener's mind—the more normative continuation in m. 21 has been made to seem surprising (see the discussion of this excerpt in Margulis, 2007b). The moment of the d-minor harmony in m. 21 is similar to the moment when the word "forces" comes into the physicist's statement; it follows four measures that have alluded to the piece's opening, just as the previous words had alluded to a political promise, and introduces a continuation that is only funny if you get the reference. By conditioning us to perceiving wit in the stylistically normative chord, Beethoven has made us insiders in this piece. He's made all of us *knowing*, a brilliantly inclusive gesture that folds us into the logic of

*Figure 8.2* From Beethoven Sonata Op. 53, first movement, mm. 1–13.

the work. Again, the repetition builds a sense of "us" via allusion—who are we? We are the people who get that this d-minor chord is funny.

Although this type of repetitive gambit can characterize both speech and music to similar effect, it is arguably more powerful in music because it is less marked. Repetitive and allusive speech is uncommon, making occurrences more marked and noticeable. Although the strategy of constructing a "we" by the technique of allusion rather than by some explicit appeal is already rather subtle, in music it is even more so because the fact that a repetition or allusion is happening may be less available to conscious awareness. People immersed in the allusions and inter-references of a particular musical style are very much a part of a constructed "we," but may entirely lack recognition of the way that tacitly acknowledged repetitions worked to construct this sense of shared identity (for more on musical identities, see MacDonald, Hargreaves & Miell 2002).

This allusional capacity can be exploited to create a sense of play, one of repetition's primary functions within discourse (Johnstone, 1994). In music, the kind of play made possible by repetition can range from the pleasure of virtual participation described elsewhere in this book to full-blown humor. Huron (2004) tagged 629 instances of audience laughter during live recordings of music by Peter Shickele, better known as P. D. Q. Bach, and categorized the musical devices that seemed to elicit the outbursts. In addition to other expectation-violating gambits such as incongruous sounds, metric disruptions and implausible delays, Huron identifies excessive repetition as a common trigger—the repetition of a passage beyond the number of times that would be typical. By way of example, Huron cites an instance from the first movement of Schickele's Concerto for Horn and Hardart where a single eight-note passage is repeated twelve times in a row. He notes that audible laughter can be heard starting at the fourth repetition, consistent with Johnstone's estimate that repetitions beyond three veer into the comic.

Consider this children's classic:

Knock knock.
Who's there?
Banana.
Banana who?
Knock knock.
Who's there?
Banana.
Banana who?
Knock knock.
Who's there?
Banana.

Banana who?
Knock knock.
Who's there?
Orange.
Orange who?
Orange you glad I didn't say banana?

Most people think this is funny (or at minimum exasperating) by the third
banana. Johnstone points out the paradox inherent in the fact that increased
familiarity over the course of multiple repetitions actually serves to *defamiliarize*,
as attention is pushed to some other level of the discourse structure. There can
be an uncanniness to this process, whereby something completely ordinary that
normally escapes notice is suddenly made to seem strange. In a monograph on
the uncanny, Royle (2003) identifies its deep connection to laughter and humor
(a similar thesis is explored in LeDrew, 2006). This nonlinear relationship
between repetition and familiarity, according to which a certain number of repetitions increase familiarity but an excessive number actually works to defamiliarize or make strange, intriguingly parallels the nonlinear relationship identified
between repeated exposure and numerous other percepts, such as preference.

Another fascinating paradox raised by percepts of repetition is best illustrated
by Johnstone's linguistic examples. As she explains, repetition in conversation
can signal two utterly opposite relational stances. On the one hand, repetition
can signal agreement, successful learning, a message received. Parent: "Take the
trash out." Child: "Take the trash out." This exchange makes us believe that the
child gets it, and that the bin will be curbside by evening. But repetition can also
signal disagreement.

> If you take a position and I repeat your position, one function of my
> repetition is to preface that I am getting ready to disagree with you, or
> perhaps the repetition itself constitutes the disagreement with you. The
> closer the repetition is to identical, the closer it often is to direct dis-
> agreement (Johnstone, 1994, p. 8).

This kind of conversational gambit takes advantage of the fact that repetition
pushes attention away from the typical meaning of an utterance and drives attention to metalinguistic questions about the language and its current use. When
a conversation partner repeats a statement, he is already introducing a degree
of subversion into the exchange. The act of repetition itself moves the statement's significance away from its literal meaning and into some more dynamic,
relational realm.

According to Johnstone, then, repetition serves two basic functions in discourse: generally, it serves to manipulate attention. More particularly, it tends to drive attention toward consciousness about elements that were previously transparent. This constitutes a kind of pushing at the edge of discourse, a struggle to say things that are unsayable at the level of the literal, a restlessness with what's typically available in language, a challenge to highlight the relationship between the utterance and the listener and to explicitly involve the listener in the material essence of what's being communicated. Meaning under such circumstances becomes less of a fixed, established entity and more of a construction built creatively in the moment of reception—a listener cannot simply passively accept the content that has been encoded for him, but must rather actively and unboundedly constitute it.

All of these receptive strategies, brought into play especially by linguistic repetition, edge up against the ordinary mechanisms of music listening. Music's meaning lies much more clearly in the relationship between the listener and the sound, in a confrontation with the unsayable, in an unrestricted movement out from what is literally present in the acoustic signal. All of these forms of listening, which might be thought of as quintessentially musical, can be elicited by repetition even in domains outside of music, such as language. Thus, even when linguistic repetition does not, as in the speech-to-song illusion, effect a stark perceptual shift that makes the words literally sound as if they'd been sung, it can effect a subtler shift that elicits more musical modes of attending, more musical ways of making sense of a soundscape.

Brandt, Gebrian & Slevc (2012) view these musical modes of attending as developmentally prior to linguistic ones, positing that "spoken language is introduced to the child as a vocal performance, and children attend to its musical features first" (p. 1). They observe that although adults show a different pattern of hemispheric dominance for apprehending music (right dominant) and language (left dominant) (Schön et al., 2010), there is also broad overlap between the two involving a bilateral frontal-temporal network (Griffiths et al., 1999). Brandt, Gebrian & Slevc speculate that infants employ generalized listening strategies, which then become increasingly specialized over the course of development, such that a music system can be looked at independently of a language system. Consistent with this viewpoint, Kotilahti et al. (2010) found overlapping activation in newborns when they process infant-directed speech on the one hand and instrumental music on the other. Infants acquire the ability to understand the musical elements of speech (stress patterns and prosody) before they acquire the ability to understand its more strictly linguistic elements (vocabulary and syntax). They prefer speech in which these elements are exaggerated and vocalized with particular prominence. This preference is so obvious in the way babies respond to speech that has been modified in this manner (see the mesmerized

*Figure 8.3*  Babies entranced by infant-directed speech. Reproduced with permission from Trehub, 2003.

faces in Figure 8.3) that even the most baby-talk-averse adult, seeking these glorious stares, often finds himself quasi-singing repeated phrases after a few minutes of interaction.

## Similarity and Variation

In this book, I have tried to keep variation and similarity out of the picture, maintaining a focus on a more literal sort of repetition in an effort to answer some of the foundational questions raised by this practice. Musical variation has a long and venerable history of scholarship; its ubiquity, however, can obscure the cultural universal of musical repetition, which is in many ways a stranger phenomenon. But after a book's worth of grappling with repetition *qua* repetition, it's worth stepping back and looking at what this work might suggest about similarity and variation.

Viewed from the standpoint of this book, similar passages are those in which some, but not all, characteristics repeat. Variations avail themselves simultaneously of repetition and of difference. It has been a claim throughout this volume that repetition pushes attention to different levels and aspects of the stimulus: down toward more nuanced, subtle aspects or up toward more large-scale, structural aspects. Variation, in a way, mimics this subjective perceptual process.

It takes the shifting qualities that a listener normally imposes on the music and repositions them within the music itself.

Variation elevates the parameter along which the changes are occurring to a more prominent role within the musical discourse. If things are repeating but timbre is changing, timbral contrast becomes something the piece is "about"— Ravel's *Bolero* is a good example. If notes and rhythms are repeating but the texture is changing, texture becomes highly marked and expressively relevant— Beethoven's 32 Variations in C Minor, WoO 80 is a good example. Listeners involve themselves with these changing dimensions in a process similar to the way they involve themselves with newly perceived dimensions of a literally repeating passage.

Zbikowski (2002) adopts a cognitive perspective to examine, among other things, the ways that similarity feeds into categorization. Deliège (2007) has extensively explored the mechanisms of similarity perception in music, emphasizing in particular the implicit role similarity plays in segmentation, the process by which the musical surface is chunked into groups or units. She has established that listeners repeatedly exposed to a particular theme are capable of recognizing it in variation. Conversely, acquaintance with a body of varied instances can cause a listener to abstract a thematic category that might not literally match any particular statement, but rather involve a set of characteristics—for example: large leap in the melody, tremolo in the lower register, and movement from major to minor—such that new passages could be accurately classified as either belonging to the thematic family or not.

One important factor in this categorization process is salience—highly noticeable features are by definition more available for similarity assessment—but another important factor is repetition. The elements that remain invariant from iteration to iteration come to seem essential and category defining. Repetition in this way connects fundamentally to basic processes of pattern matching and sense making, extending far beyond the special cases considered here.

## Repetition, Memory, and Communication

Both Johnstone (1994) and Merritt (1994) draw attention to the ways repetition can enhance information storage and processing. A conventional professorial maneuver is to pace around the front of the classroom slowly and meaningfully repeating an essential point: "Energy equals mass times the speed of light squared. Energy…equals…mass…times the speed of light…squared." Not only does repetition aid memory in a straightforward and widely acknowledged way, but also repetition of this sort gives students a longer span of time over which to absorb the individual piece of information than if it had been merely stated once; it also provides students who hadn't been paying attention an opportunity to tune in (Merritt, 1994).

Language is constrained not only by a robust semantics (specific word denotations capable of being looked up in a dictionary), which music largely lacks (see Swain, 1997), but also by an arguably more elaborate set of syntactic rules (see Swain, 1995). These characteristics might be viewed to provide firmer scaffolding for linguistic structures, obviating to some extent repetition's necessity as a memory and learning aid. Music, on the other hand, may depend more on the structure-building capacity of repetition.

Neuhaus, Knösche & Friederici (2009) start from Hugo Riemann's term *Beziehendes Denken* (1916), a phrase they translate as "structural hearing" but that might be more literally construed as "connection-making thinking." It refers to the act of "'setting parts of the whole in relation to each other'...seeking coherence between adjacent or nonadjacent sections" (Neuhaus, Knösche & Friederici, 2009, p. 485): the act of perceiving a form. As discussed in Chapter 5, they used ERP to investigate brain responses to form perception in listeners without formal training, finding an anterior negativity (N300) at the recognition of the repetition of the A section both in forms where the repetition was adjacent (AABB) and where it was nonadjacent (ABAB). Although Margulis (2012) suggested that it's difficult for listeners to explicitly identify longer repetitions, especially on first exposure, this ERP study shows that there may nevertheless be implicit recognition that helps listeners navigate through the structure.

Although music can adopt schemas (Leman, 1995) and standard forms (Caplin, 1998) to constrain compositional possibilities and listener expectations, most pieces to some extent teach the listener how to listen to them as they go along. Repetition is a critical element in this process. While a number of constraints govern the composition of musical ideas (Gestalt perceptual tendencies like those reflected in gap-fill melodies, stylistic conventions, performance feasibility, and so on), these constraints do not result in a vocabulary of "words" like those employed in language. In the absence of such a vocabulary, each individual piece is comparatively more dependent on repetition to establish the identity of the basic units with which the music will play. In improvisational music, repetition can serve to communicate acceptance of and agreement on the basic units of the improvisation—one player knows she has successfully transmitted the intended unit when it has been adopted and manipulated by another performer in the group.

According to Merritt (1994),

> Familiar items can function much like concrete items in building the foundation for comprehending abstract messages. Cognitive accessibility (ease of learning) of an item, can, in fact, perhaps be conceptualized

in terms of something like degree of experiential reachability—with concrete items as 100% experientially reachable. This may be why abstract messages are so often repeated, since through repetition they become more familiar, and through familiarity they become more experientially reachable (p. 33).

The more abstract a message, the more repetition is required to make it tractable and concrete—for a person to feel they understand it in an embodied, sensory way. Since music typically traffics in the abstract and nondenotive more than everyday speech, this viewpoint makes it particularly understandable that repetition is employed as a common tool. Indeed, as previous chapters have explored, repetition often allows a listener to make a passage experientially concrete in that he can ultimately "think" the phrase using auditory imagery, even in the absence of external stimuli. This can be interpreted as a kind of concretization that facilitates engagement with a communicative medium lacking as many denotive capabilities as language. The auditory image of a musical idea feels very real and concrete, despite the utter absence of either a tangible object or an articulable concept. Since music represents an expressive act taken by another person or other people, the acquisition of this variety of knowledge—invisibly felt rather than physically held or intellectually grasped—carries with it a sense of intimacy that can be profound. It is unsurprising that adolescents, still seeking proof that they can satisfyingly connect to other people and especially to their peers, often exhibit a special voracity for music, resulting in a lifelong preference for music first encountered during this period (Holbrook & Schindler, 1989).

## Repetition and the Musical

Musical repetition, then, far from a topic that should embarrass music scholars, constitutes an essential core practice in performance and listening that is illuminative of what is special about this fundamentally human mode of attending. Art music in the twentieth century can be understood as having followed two divergent paths in reaction to discomfort with repetition as a communicative strategy; one path, best represented by composers labeled as minimalist, entailed the stubborn placement of repetition at the very center of stylistic practice, and the other, best represented by serialism and some aleatoric musics, entailed the equally stubborn, at-all-costs avoidance of repetition. It's hard not to speculate about what the course of musical history might have looked like for the past hundred years had repetition not been such a flashpoint.

Embracing characteristics that are particular to music, such as repetition, can also help us derive new insights into other domains, such as language, which have tended primarily to contribute models to music scholars rather than to receive ideas and frameworks from them. An example of the gradually changing tide on this issue is the Brandt, Gebrian & Slevc (2012) paper that recasts language as dependent on music-like processing of auditory input in infancy. However, influence needn't entail the repositioning of music as somehow prior or more central to another domain, but might simply help draw attention to some process or mechanism that previously fell to the side of conventional models.

What's happening in music is indeed sometimes language-like or dance-like—but sometimes what's happening in music is simply music-like. Repetition seems to me such an element. Although repetition can characterize other relevant domains, it is most essentially connected with the functions and practice of music. Musical repetition cannot be understood simply as an artifact of domain-independent hedonism; if I like a particular dish, I might return to a restaurant again and again to order it. However, beyond a gradual assimilation of this practice into my daily life, the potential acquisition of a sort of nostalgia for the experience in between visits, and a possible improvement in my ability to identify subtle changes in the preparation from evening to evening, these repeated encounters are unlikely to materially transform what it is essentially like to eat this dish. But repeated encounters with a particular music can alter what it is to listen to that piece, choreographing a different sense of subjectivity, facilitating an engagement with structural features at a different level than those initially apprehended, and assimilating the external sounds into a broadened sense of self. Repetition draws us into music, and repetition draws music into us. It represents a starting point for confronting some of music's most elusive and defining qualities. Since human beings are fundamentally musical, when we understand more about the musical capacity, we understand more about ourselves. In this way, something as simple as putting a track on repeat can serve as a window into who we are.

# References

Abbate, C. (2004). Music: Drastic or gnostic? *Critical Inquiry, 30,* 505–536.

Adorno, T. W. (2009). *Night music: Essays on music 1928–1962* (W. Hoban, Trans.). London: Seagull Books. (Original work published 2003).

Agawu, V. K. (1991). *Playing with signs: A semiotic interpretation of classic music.* Princeton, NJ: Princeton University Press.

Arewa, O. B. (2006). From J.C. Bach to hip hop: Musical borrowing, copyright and cultural context. *North Carolina Law Review, 84,* 547–645.

Ashley, R. (2004). *All his yesterdays: Expressive vocal techniques in Paul McCartney's recordings.* Unpublished manuscript.

Attali, J., Massumi, B., Jameson, F., & McClary, S. (1985). *Noise: The political economy of music.* Minneapolis, MN: University of Minnesota Press.

Auner, J. (2003). "Sing it for me": Posthuman ventriloquism in recent popular music. *Journal of the Royal Musical Association, 128,* 98–122.

Bailes, F. (2007). The prevalence and nature of imagined music in the everyday lives of music students. *Psychology of Music, 35,* 555–570.

Bain, B. (2011). Top 5 dramatic readings of pop songs, from "Baby" to "Poker Face." Retrieved from http://idolator.com/5771261/top-5-dramatic-readings-of-pop-songs-from-baby-to-poker-face.

Barnes, S. J., Hua, J. M., Pinel, J. P. J., Takahashi, A., & Wig, G. S. (2005). Conditioned effects of kindling three different sites in the hippocampal complex of the rat. *Behavioral Neuroscience, 119,* 1572–1579.

Beaman, C. P., & Williams, T. I. (2010). Earworms ("stuck song syndrome"): Towards a natural history of intrusive thoughts. *British Journal of Psychology, 101,* 637–653.

Beauvois, M. W. (2007). Quantifying aesthetic preference and perceived complexity for fractal melodies. *Music Perception, 24,* 247–264.

Becker, J. (2004). *Deep listeners: Music, emotion, and trancing.* Bloomington: Indiana University Press.

Bennett, A. (2007). *The uncommon reader: A novella.* New York: Farrar, Straus, and Giroux.

Bennett, S. (2002). *Musical Imagery Repetition (MIR).* (M. Phil. dissertation). University of Cambridge, Cambridge, UK.

Berliner, P. (1994). *Thinking in jazz: The infinite art of improvisation.* Chicago, IL: University of Chicago Press.

Berlyne, D. E. (1971). *Aesthetics and psychobiology.* New York, NY: Appleton-Century-Crofts.

Berlyne, D. E. (1974). *Studies in the new experimental aesthetics.* Washington, DC: Hemisphere.

Bharucha, J. J. (1987). Music cognition and perceptual facilitation: A connectionist framework. *Music Perception, 5,* 1–30.

Bigand, E. (2003). More about the musical expertise of musically untrained listeners. In G. Avanzini, C. Faienza, D. Minciacchi, L. Lopez & M. Majno (Eds.), *The neurosciences and music* (pp. 304–312). New York, NY: New York Academy of Sciences.

Bigand, E., & Poulin-Charronnat, B. (2006). Are we "experienced listeners"? A review of the musical capacities that do not depend on formal musical training. *Cognition, 100,* 100–130.

Boecker, H., Dagher, A., Ceballos-Baumann, A. O., Passingham, R. E., Samuel, M., Friston, K. J., Poline, J.-B., Dettmers, C., Conrad, B., & Brooks, D. J. (1998). Role of the human rostral supplementary motor area and the basal ganglia in motor sequence control: Investigations with $H_2$ $^{15}O$ PET. *Journal of Neurophysiology, 79,* 1070–1080.

Borges, J. L. (1962). *Ficciones* (A. Kerrigan, Trans.). New York, NY: Grove Press.

Bornstein, R. F. (1989). Exposure and affect: Overview and meta-analysis of research, 1968–1987. *Psychological Bulletin, 106,* 265–289.

Bornstein, R. F. (1992). Subliminal mere exposure effects. In R. F. Bornstein & T. S. Pittman (Eds.), *Perception without awareness: Cognitive, clinical, and social perspectives* (pp. 191–210). New York, NY: Guilford Press.

Bornstein, R. F., & D'Agostino, P. R. (1994). The attribution and discounting of perceptual fluency: Preliminary tests of a perceptual fluency/attributional model of the mere exposure effect. *Social Cognition, 12,* 103–128.

Bornstein, R. F., & D'Agostino, P. R. (1992). Stimulus recognition and the mere exposure effect. *Journal of Personality and Social Psychology, 63,* 545-552

Boulez, P.. (1984, 28 June). On new music. *The New York Review of Books,* pp. 14–15.

Boyer, P., & Liénard, P. (2006). Why ritualized behavior? Precaution systems and action parsing in developmental, pathological and cultural rituals. *Behavioral and Brain Sciences, 29,* 595–613.

Brainard, M. S., & Doupe, A. J. (2002). What songbirds teach us about learning. *Nature, 417*(6886), 351–358.

Brainerd, C. J., & Kingma, J. (1984). Do children have to remember to reason? A fuzzy-trace theory of transitivity development. *Developmental Review, 4,* 311–377.

Brainerd, C. J., & Reyna, V. F. (1996). Mere memory testing creates false memories in children. *Developmental Psychology, 32,* 467–478.

Brandt, A. K., Gebrian, M., & Slevc, R. (2012). Music and early language acquisition. *Frontiers in Psychology, 3,* 327.

Bregman, A. S. (1994). *Auditory scene analysis: The perceptual organization of sound.* Cambridge, MA: MIT Press.

Brown, S. (2006). The perpetual music track: The phenomenon of constant musical imagery. *Journal of Consciousness Studies, 13*(6), 43–62.

Brown, S., Martinez, M. J., Hodges, D. A., Fox, P. T., & Parsons, L. M. (2004). The song system of the human brain. *Cognitive Brain Research, 20,* 363–375.

Broyles, M. (1980). Organic form and the binary repeat. *The Musical Quarterly, 66,* 339–360.

Burkholder, J. P. Borrowing. *Grove Music Online.* (Accessed November 10, 2011). http://www.grovemusic.com.

Burnham, S. G. (1995). *Beethoven Hero.* Princeton: Princeton University Press.

Burnham, S. G. (2005). Landscape as music, landscape as truth: Schubert and the burden of repetition. *19th-Century Music, 29,* 31–41.

Cabib, S. (1993). Neurobiological basis of stereotypies. In A. B. Lawrence & J. Rushen (Eds.), *Stereotypic animal behavior: Fundamentals and applications to welfare* (pp. 119–145). Wallingford, UK: CAB International.

Calabrese, O. (1992). *Neo-baroque: A sign of the times* (C. Lambert, Trans.). Princeton, NJ: Princeton University Press.

Calvert, S. L. (1991). *Impact of singing on students' verbatim recall and learning.* Paper presented at the Annual Meeting of the American Psychological Association, San Francisco, CA.

Calvert, S. L. (2001). Impact of televised songs on children's and young adults' memory of educational content. *Media Psychology, 3,* 325–342.

Calvert, S. L., & Tart, M. (1993). Song versus verbal forms for very-long-term, long-term, and short-term verbatim recall. *Journal of Applied Developmental Psychology, 14,* 245–260.

Calvo-Merino, B., Glaser, D. E., Grèzes, J., Passingham, R. E., & Haggard, P. (2005). Action observation and acquired motor skills: An fMRI study with expert dancers. *Cerebral Cortex, 15,* 1243–1249.

Cambouropoulos, E. (2006). Musical parallelism and melodic segmentation: A computational approach. *Music Perception, 23,* 249–267.

Caplin, W. E. (1998). *Classical Form: A Theory of Formal Functions for the Instrumental Music of Haydn, Mozart, and Beethoven.* New York, NY: Oxford University Press.

Chen, J. L., Penhune, V. B., & Zatorre, R. J. (2008). Moving on time: Brain network for auditory-motor synchronization is modulated by rhythm complexity and musical training. *Journal of Cognitive Neuroscience, 20,* 226–239.

Chernoff, J. (1979). *African rhythm and African sensibility: Aesthetics and social action in African musical idioms.* Chicago: University of Chicago Press.

Clarke, E. F. (2011). Music perception and musical consciousness. In D. Clarke & E. Clarke (Eds.), *Music and Consciousness: Philosophical, Psychological, and Cultural Perspectives* (pp. 193–213). New York, NY: Oxford University Press.

Clarke, E.F. (2007). The impact of recording on listening. *Twentieth-Century Music, 4,* 47-70.

Clarke, E. F. (2005). Creativity in performance. *Musicae Scientiae, 19,* 157–182.

Clayton, M., Sager, R., & Will, U. (2004). In time with the music: The concept of entrainment and its significance for ethnomusicology. *ESEM Counterpoint, 1,* 1–45.

Cohn, R., & Dempster, D. (1996). Hierarchical unity, plural unities: Toward a reconciliation. In K. Bergeron & P. V. Bohlman (Eds.), *Disciplining music: Musicology and its canons* (pp. 156–181). Chicago, IL: University of Chicago Press.

Cole, M. (1969). The vogue of the instrumental rondo in the late eighteenth century. *Journal of the American Musicological Society, 22,* 425–455.

Cone, E. T. (1968). *Musical form and musical performance.* New York, NY: W.W. Norton & Company.

Cone, E. T. (1977). Three ways of reading a detective story—or a Brahms intermezzo. *Georgia Review, 31,* 554–574.

Conklin, K., & Schmitt, N. (2008). Formulaic sequences: Are they processed more quickly than nonformulaic language by native and nonnative speakers? *Applied Linguistics, 29,* 72–89.

Cook, N. (1987). The perception of large-scale tonal closure. *Music Perception, 5,* 197–206.

Cooke, M. (2008). *A History of Film Music.* Cambridge, UK: Cambridge University Press.

Cooper, S. J., & Dourish, C. T. (1990). *Neurobiology of Stereotyped Behaviour.* New York, NY: Clarendon Press/Oxford University Press.

Cox, Arnie. (2011). Embodying music: Principles of the mimetic hypothesis. *Music Theory Online, 17*(2). Retrieved from http://www.mtosmt.org/issues/mto.11.17.2/mto.11.17.2.cox.html.

Crawley, A. M., Anderson, D. R., Wilder, A., Williams, M., & Santomero, A. (1999). Effects of repeated exposures to a single episode of the television program *Blue's Clues* on the viewing behaviors and comprehension of preschool children. *Journal of Educational Psychology, 91,* 630–637.

Creel, S. C., & Tumlin, M. A. (2012). Online recognition of music is influenced by relative and absolute pitch information. *Cognitive Science, 36,* 224–260.

Cross, I. (1999). Is music the most important thing we ever did? Music, development, and evolution. In S.W. Yi (Ed.), *Music, Mind, and Science* (pp. 10–39). Seoul, Korea: Seoul National University Press.

Cross, I. (2003). Music, cognition, culture, and evolution. In I. Peretz & R. Zatorre (Eds.), *The Cognitive Neuroscience of Music* (pp. 42–56). New York, NY: Oxford University Press.

Cross, I. (2008). Musicality and the human capacity for culture. *Musicæ Scientiæ, Special Issue: Narrative in music and interaction,* 147–167.

Cross, I. (2009). The nature of music and its evolution. In S. Hallam, I. Cross, & M. Thaut (Eds.), *The Oxford Handbook of Music Psychology* (pp. 3–13). New York, NY: Oxford University Press.

Cross, I. (2012). Music and biocultural evolution. In M. Clayton, T. Herbert, & R. Middleton (Eds.), *The Cultural Study of Music: A Critical Introduction* (pp. 17–27). London, UK: Routledge.

Crystal, D. (2000). *Language death*. Cambridge, UK: Cambridge University Press.

Csikszentmihalyi, M. (1997). *Creativity: Flow and the psychology of discovery andinvention*. New York, NY: HarperCollins Publishers.

Cumming, N. (2001). *The sonic self: Musical subjectivity and signification*. Bloomington, IN: Indiana University Press.

DeBellis, M. (1995). *Music and conceptualization*. Cambridge, UK: Cambridge University Press.

Deleuze, G. (1988). *Le Plio*. Paris: Editions de Minuit.

Deleuze, G. (2004). *Difference and repetition* (P. Patton, Trans.). New York, NY: Columbia University Press.

Deliège, I. (1989). A perceptual approach to contemporary musical forms. *Contemporary Music Review, 4*, 213–230.

Deliège, I. (2007). Similarity relations in listening to music: How do they come into play? *Musicae Scientiae, 11*(1 suppl), 9–37.

DeNora, T. (2000). *Music in everyday life*. Cambridge, UK: Cambridge University Press.

Desain, P., & Honing, H. (1999). Computational models of beat induction: The rule-based approach. *Journal of New Music Research, 28*, 29–42.

Deutsch, D. (2003). *Phantom words and other curiosities*. San Diego, CA: Philomel Records.

Deutsch, D. (2006). The enigma of absolute pitch. *Acoustics Today, 2*, 11–19.

Deutsch, D., Henthorn, T., & Lapidis, R. (2011). Illusory transformation from speech to song. *Journal of the Acoustical Society of America, 129*, 2245–2252.

Deutsch, D., Lapidis, R., & Henthorn, T. (2008). The speech-to-song illusion. *Journal of the Acoustical Society of America, 124*, 2471.

DeVoto, M. (2004). *Debussy and the veil of tonality: Essays on his music*. Hillsdale, NY: Pendragon Press.

Dewey, J. (1895). The theory of emotion. *Psychological Review, 2*, 13–32.

Diaz, F. M. (2011). Mindfulness, attention, and flow during music listening: An empirical investigation. *Psychology of Music*. doi: 10.1177/0305735611415144.

Dissanayake, E. (2006). Ritual and ritualization: Musical means of conveying and shaping emotion in humans and other animals. In S. Brown & U. Volgsten (Eds.), *Music and manipulation: On the social uses and social control of music* (pp. 31–56). New York, NY: Berghahn Books.

Dowling, W. J., & Harwood, D. L. (1986). *Music Cognition*. Orlando, FL: Academic Press.

Dowling, W. J., Tillmann, B., & Ayers, D. F. (2001). Memory and the experience of hearing music. *Music Perception, 19*, 249–276.

Dunsby, J. M. (1987). The formal repeat. *Journal of the Royal Musical Association, 112*, 196–207.

Ehrlich, S. (1994). Repetition and point of view in represented speech and thought. In B. Jonstone (Ed.), *Repetition in discourse: Interdisciplinary perspectives* (Vol. 1, pp. 86–97). Norwood, NJ: Ablex Publishing Corporation.

Eilam, D., Zor, R., Szechtman, H., & Hermesh, H. (2006). Rituals, stereotypy and compulsive behavior in animals and humans. *Neuroscience and Biobehavioral Reviews, 30*, 456–471.

Eliot, T. S. (1968). *Four Quartets*. New York: Mariner.

Endress, A. D., Dehaene-Lambertz, G., & Mehler, J. (2007). Perceptual constraints and the learnability of simple grammars. *Cognition, 105*, 577–614.

Ettlinger, M., Margulis, E. H., & Wong, P. C. M. (2011). Implicit memory in music and language. *Frontiers in Psychology, 2*, 211.

Evans, D. W., Leckman, J. F., Carter, A., & Reznick, J. S. (1997). Ritual, habit, and perfectionism: The prevalence and development of compulsive-like behavior in normal young children. *Child Development, 68*, 58–68.

Evans, D. W., & Maliken, A. (2011). Cortical activity and children's rituals, habits and other repetitive behavior: A visual P300 study. *Behavioural Brain Research, 224*, 174–179.

Feld, M. (2005). *Temporal orientation in sonata-form first groups: With special reference to the work of A. B. Marx*. (Ph.D. dissertation). Columbia University, New York, NY.

Feld, S., & Keil, C. (1994). *Music Grooves: Essays and Dialogues*. Chicago, IL: University of Chicago Press.

Fernald, A., & Morikawa, H. (1993). Common themes and cultural variations in Japanese and American mothers' speech to infants. *Child Development, 64*, 637–656.

Fernald, A., & O'Neill, D. K. (1993). Peekaboo across cultures: How mothers and infants play with voices, faces, and expectations. In K. MacDonald (Ed.), *Parent–child play: Descriptions and implications* (pp. 259–285). Albany, NY: State University of New York Press.

Fernald, A., & Simon, T. (1984). Expanded intonation contours in mothers' speech to newborns. *Developmental Psychology, 20*, 104–113.

Field, J. (2004). Verbatim recall. In J. Field, *Psycholinguistics: The Key Concepts* (pp. 318–320). New York: Routledge.

Fink, R. (2005). *Repeating ourselves: American minimal music as cultural practice.* Berkeley, CA: University of California Press.

Finney, S. A., & Palmer, C. (2003). Auditory feedback and memory for music performance: Sound evidence for an encoding effect. *Memory & Cognition, 3*, 51–64.

Fitch, W. T. (2006). The biology and evolution of music: A comparative perspective. *Cognition, 100*, 173–215.

Freeman, W. J. (1995). *Societies of brains: A study in the neuroscience of love and hate.* Mahwah, NJ: Lawrence Erlbaum.

Friedland, L. (1995). Social commentary in African American movement performance. In B. Farnell (Ed.), *Human action signs in cultural context* (pp. 136–157). Metuchen, NJ: Scarecrow Press, Inc.

Friedson, S. M. (1996). *Dancing prophets: Musical experience in Tumbuka healing.* Chicago, IL: University of Chicago Press.

Fujii, N., & Graybiel, A. M. (2003). Representation of action sequence boundaries by macaque prefrontal cortical neurons. *Science, 301*(5637), 1246–1249.

Fujii, N., & Graybiel, A. M. (2005). Time-varying covariance of neural activities recorded in striatum and frontal cortex as monkeys perform sequential-saccade tasks. *Proceedings of the National Academy of Sciences, 102*(25), 9032–9037.

Gabrielsson, A. (1987). *Once again: The theme from Mozart's Piano Sonata in A Major (K. 331), a comparison of five performances.* Paper presented at Action and Perception in Rhythm and Music, Stockholm, Sweden.

Gabrielsson, A. (2011). *Strong experiences with music: Music is much more than just music* (R. Bradbury, Trans.). New York, NY: Oxford University Press.

Gabrielsson, A., & Wik, S. L. (2003). Strong experiences related to music: A descriptive system. *Musicae Scientiae, 7*, 157–217.

Gallope, M., & Kane, B. (2012). Colloquy: Vladimir Jankélévitch's philosophy of music. *Journal of the American Musicological Society, 65*, 215–256, 299.

Garcia, L.-M. (2005). On and on: Repetition as process and pleasure in electronic dance music. *Music Theory Online, 11*(4). Retrieved from http://www.mtosmt.org/issues/mto.05.11.4/mto.05.11.4.garcia.html.

Garner, J. P., Meehan, C. L., & Mench, J. A. (2003). Stereotypies in caged parrots, schizophrenia and autism: Evidence for a common mechanism. *Behavioral Brain Research, 145*, 125–134.

Gernsbacher, M. A. (1985). Surface information loss in comprehension. *Cognitive Psychology, 17*, 324–363.

Gjerdingen, R. O. (1999). An experimental music theory? In N. Cook & M. Everest (Eds.), *Rethinking Music* (pp. 161–170). New York, NY: Oxford University Press.

Gjerdingen, R. O. (2007). *Music in the Galant style.* New York, NY: Oxford University Press.

Goehr, L. (2007). *The imaginary museum of musical works: An essay in the philosophy of mkusic.* New York, NY: Oxford University Press.

Gould, G. (1966). The prospects of recording. *High Fidelity, 16*, 46–63.

Grahn, J. A., & Brett, M. (2007). Rhythm and beat perception in motor areas of the brain. *Journal of Cognitive Neuroscience, 19*, 893–906.

Grahn, J. A., & Brett, M. (2009). Impairment of beat-based rhythm discrimination in Parkinson's disease. *Cortex, 45*, 54–61.

Grahn, J. A., Henry, M. J., & McAuley, J. D. (2011). FMRI investigation of cross-modal inter-actions in beat perception: Audition primes vision, but not vice versa. *Neuroimage, 54,* 1231–1243.

Grahn, J. A., & Rowe, J. (2013). Finding and feeling the musical beat: Striatial dissociations between detection and prediction of regularity. *Cerebral Cortex, 23,* 913–921.

Graybiel, A. M. (2008). Habits, rituals, and the evaluative brain. *Annual Review of Neuroscience, 31,* 359–387.

Graybiel, A. M., & Rauch, S. L. (2000). Toward a neurobiology of obsessive-compulsive disorder. *Neuron, 28,* 343–347.

Green, D. M. (1979). *Form in tonal music: An introduction to analysis* (2nd ed.). New York: Holt, Rinehart and Winston.

Green, L. (2002). *How popular musicians learn: A way ahead for music education.* London: Ashgate.

Greenberg, S., Marsh, J. T., Brown, W. S., & Smith, J. C. (1987). Neural temporal coding of low pitch. I. Human frequency-following responses to complex tones. *Hearing Research, 25*(2-3), 91–114.

Gretry, A.-E. M. (1789). *Mémoires, ou essais sur la musique.* Paris.

Grice, P. (1991). *Studies in the Way of Words.* Cambridge, MA: Harvard University Press.

Griffiths, T. D., Johnsrude, I., Dean, J. L., & Green, G. G. R. (1999). A common neural substrate for the analysis of pitch and duration pattern in segmented sound? *NeuroReport, 10*(18), 3825–3830.

Guck, M. (1996). Music loving, or the relationship with the piece. *Music Theory Online, 2*(2). Retrieved from http://www.mtosmt.org/issues/mto.96.2.2/mto.96.2.2.guck.html.

Guinee, L. N., & Payne, K. B. (1988). Rhyme-like repetitions in songs of humpback whales. *Ethology, 79*(4), 295–306.

Halpern, A. R. (1988). Perceived and imagined tempos of familiar songs. *Music Perception, 6,* 193–202.

Halpern, A. R., & Bartlett, J. C. (2011). The persistence of musical memories: A descriptive study of earworms. *Music Perception, 28,* 425–431.

Halpern, A. R., & Zatorre, R. J. (1999). When that tune runs through your head: A PET investiga-tion of auditory imagery for familiar melodies. *Cerebral Cortex, 9,* 697–704.

Hamilton, A. (2003). The art of recording and the aesthetics of perfection. *British Journal of Aesthetics, 43,* 345–362.

Hanninen, D. A. (2003). A theory of recontextualization in music: Analyzing phenomenal trans-formations of repetition. *Music Theory Spectrum, 25,* 59–97.

Hansen, J., & Wänke, M. (2009). Liking what's familiar: The importance of unconscious familiar-ity in the mere-exposure effect. *Social Cognition, 27,* 161–182.

Harnad, S. (1987). *Categorical Perception: The Groundwork of Cognition.* Cambridge, UK: Cambridge University Press.

Harrison, A. (2002). *"The singing which never ends"—An investigation into the popularity of repeti-tive chants and their contribution to the renewal of Christian worship.* (M.A. thesis). Leeds, UK: University of Leeds.

Hasty, C. F. (1997). *Meter as Rhythm.* New York: Oxford University Press.

Hatten, R.S. (2004). *Interpreting musical gestures, topics, and tropes: Mozart, Beethoven, Schubert.* Bloomington, IN: Indiana University Press.

Hatten, R. (1994). *Musical meaning in Beethoven: Markedness, correlation, and interpretation.* Bloomington and Indianapolis, IN: Indiana University Press.

Haueisen, J., & Knösche, T. R. (2001). Involuntary motor activity in pianists evoked by music perception. *Journal of Cognitive Neuroscience, 13,* 786–792.

Hayes, D. S., Chemelski, B. E., & Palmer, M. (1982). Nursery rhymes and prose pas-sages: Preschoolers' liking and short-term retention of story events. *Developmental Psychology, 18,* 49–56.

Hepokoski, J. A., & Darcy, W. (2006). *Elements of sonata theory: Norms, types, and deformations in the late–eighteenth-century sonata.* New York, NY: Oxford University Press.

Herbert, R. (2011). An empirical study of normative dissociation in musical and non-musical everyday life experiences. *Psychology of Music*. doi: 10.1177/0305735611430080.

Holbrook, M. B., & Schindler, R. M. (1989). Some exploratory findings on the development of musical tastes. *Journal of Consumer Research, 16*, 119–124.

Honing, H. (2011). *The Illiterate Listener: On Music Cognition, Musicality and Methodology*. Amsterdam, Netherlands: Amsterdam University Press.

Horlacher, G. (2011). *Building blocks: Repetition and continuity in the music of Stravinsky*. New York, NY: Oxford University Press.

Horowtiz, J. (1987). *Understanding Toscanini*. New York, NY: Knopf.

Horst, J. S., Parsons, K. L., & Bryan, N. M. (2011). Get the story straight: Contextual repetition promotes word learning from storybooks. *Frontiers in Psychology, 2*, 17. doi: 10.3389/fpsyg.2011.00017.

Hove, M. J., & Risen, J. L. (2009). It's all in the timing: Interpersonal synchrony increases affiliation. *Social Cognition, 27*, 949–961.

Hunter, I. M. L. (1984). Lengthy verbatim recall (LVR) and the mythical gift of tape-recorder memory. In M. J. L. Kirsti & N. Pekka (Eds.), *Advances in Psychology* (Vol. 18, pp. 425–440). Amsterdam, Netherlands: North-Holland Publishing Company.

Hunter, P. G., & Schellenberg, E. G. (2010). Music and emotion. In M. R. Jones, R. R. Fay & A. N. Popper (Eds.), *Music Perception*. (Vol. 36, pp. 129–164). New York, NY: Springer.

Hunter, P. G., & Schellenberg, E. G. (2011). Interactive effects of personality and frequency of exposure on liking for music. Personality and Individual Differences, *50*, 175–179.

Huron, D. (1989). Music in advertising: An analytic paradigm. *The Musical Quarterly, 73*, 557–574.

Huron, D. (2004). *Music-engendered laughter: An analysis of humor devices in PDQ Bach*. Paper presented at the 8th International Conference on Music Perception and Cognition, Evanston, IL.

Huron, D. (2006). *Sweet Anticipation: Music and the Psychology of Expectation*. Cambridge, MA: MIT Press.

Huron, D. (2007). *Paper presented at the Music Cognition Colloquium*, University of Arkansas, Fayetteville, AR.

Huron, D., & Margulis, E. H. (2010). Musical expectancy and thrills. In P. N. Juslin & J. A. Sloboda (Eds.), *Handbook of Music and Emotion: Theory, Research, Applications* (pp. 575–604). New York, NY: Oxford University Press.

Jackson, J. D. (2001). Improvisation in African-American vernacular dancing. *Dance Research Journal, 33*, 40–53.

Jacoby, L. L. (1983). Perceptual enhancement: Persistent effects of an experience. *Journal of Experimental Psychology: Learning, Memory, and Cognition, 9*, 21–38.

Jaffe, J., Beebe, B., Feldstein, S., Crown, C. L., Jasnow, M. D., Rochat, P., & Stern, D. N. (2001). Rhythms of dialogue in infancy: Coordinated timing in development. *Monographs of the Society for Research in Child Development, 66*, 1–149.

Jakobovits, L. A. (1966). Studies of fads: I. The "Hit Parade." *Psychological Reports, 18*, 443–450.

James, W. (1902). *The varieties of religious experience: A study in human nature. Being the Clifford Lectures on Natural Religion delivered at Edinburgh in 1901–1902*. London & Bombay: Longmans, Green, & Co.

Janata, P. (2009). The neural architecture of music-evoked autobiographical memories. *Cerebral Cortex, 19*(11), 2579–2594.

Janata, P., & Grafton, S. T. (2003). Swinging in the brain: Shared neural substrates for behaviors related to sequencing and music. *Nature Neuroscience, 6*, 682–687.

Janata, P., Tomic, S. T., & Haberman, J. (2012). Sensorimotor coupling in music and the psychology of the groove. *Journal of Experimental Psychology: General, 141*, 54–75.

Janata, P., Tomic, S. T., & Rakowski, S. K. (2007). Characterization of music-evoked autobiographical memories. *Memory, 15*, 845–860.

Janik, V. M., & Slater, P. J. B. (1997). Vocal learning in mammals. *Advances in the Study of Behavior, 26*, 59–99.

Jankélévitch, V. (1961/2003). *Music and the ineffable* (C. Abbate, trans.). Princeton, NJ: Princeton University Press.

Jarvella, R. J. (1971). Syntactic processing of connected speech. *Journal of Verbal Learning & Verbal Behavior, 10*, 409–416.

John, O., P., Naumann, L. P., & Soto, C. J. (2008). Paradigm shift to the integrative big five trait taxonomy: History, measurement, and conceptual issues. In O. P. John, R. W. Robins & L. A. Pervin (Eds.), *Handbook of Personality: Theory and Research* (pp. 114–158). New York, NY: Guilford Press.

Johnson, J. L., & Hayes, D. S. (1987). Preschool children's retention of rhyming and nonrhyming text: Paraphrase and rote recitation measures. *Journal of Applied Developmental Psychology, 8*, 317–327.

Johnstone, B. (1987). Perspectives on repetition: An introduction. *Text, 7*, 205–214.

Johnstone, B. (Ed.). (1994). *Repetition in Discourse: Interdisciplinary Perspectives*. Norwood, NJ: Ablex Publishing Corporation.

Jolicoeur, P., & Kosslyn, S. M. (1985). Is time to scan visual images due to demand characteristics? *Memory & Cognition, 13*, 320–332.

Jones, M. R. (1976). Time, our lost dimension: Toward a new theory of perception, attention, and memory. *Psychological Review, 83*, 323–355.

Jones, M. R., & Boltz, M. (1989). Dynamic attending and responses to time. *Psychological Review, 96*, 459–491.

Jones, M. R., Moynihan, H., MacKenzie, N., & Puente, J. (2002). Temporal aspects of stimulus-driven attending in dynamic arrays. *Psychological Science, 13*, 313–319.

Juslin, P. N. (2001). Communicating emotion in music performance: A review and a theoretical framework. In P. N. Juslin & J. A. Sloboda (Eds.), *Music and Emotion: Theory and Research*. (pp. 309–337). New York, NY: Oxford University Press.

Kalanithi, P. S. A., Zheng, W., Kataoka, Y., DiFiglia, M., Grantz, H., Saper, C. B., Schwartz, M.L., Leckman, J.F., & Vaccarino, F. M. (2005). Altered parvalbumin-positive neuron distribution in basal ganglia of individuals with Tourette syndrome. *Proceedings of the National Academy of Sciences, 102*(37), 13307–13312.

Kao, M. H., Doupe, A. J., & Brainard, M. S. (2005). Contributions of an avian basal ganglia-forebrain circuit to real-time modulation of song. *Nature, 433*, 638–643.

Katz, M. (2004). *Capturing Sound: How Technology Has Changed Music*. Berkeley, CA: University of California Press.

Keenan, J. M., MacWhinney, B., & Mayhew, D. (1977). Pragmatics in memory: A study of natural conversion. *Journal of Verbal Learning & Verbal Behavior, 16*, 549–560.

Keil, C. (1987). Participatory discrepancies and the power of music. *Cultural Anthropology, 2*, 275–283.

Keil, C. (1995). The theory of participatory discrepancies: A progress report. *Ethnomusicology, 39*, 1–19.

Keil, C., & Feld, S. (1994). *Music Grooves: Essays and Dialogues*. Chicago, IL: University of Chicago Press.

Kellaris, J. J. (2001). *Identifying properties of tunes that get "stuck in your head": Toward a theory of cognitive itch*. Paper presented at the Society for Consumer Psychology Winter 2001 Conference, Scottsdale, AZ.

Keren, H., Boyer, P., Mort, J., & Eilam, D. (2010). Pragmatic and idiosyncratic acts in human everyday routines: The counterpart of compulsive rituals. *Behavioural Brain Research, 212*, 90–95.

Kessler, E. J., & Krumhansl, C. L. (1982). Tracing the dynamic changes in perceived spatial representation of musical keys. *Psychological Review, 89*, 334–368.

King, A. J. (2006). Auditory neuroscience: Activating the cortex without sound. *Current Biology, 16*(11), R410–R411.

Kivy, P. (1993). *The Fine Art of Repetition: Essays in the Philosophy of Music*. Cambridge, UK: Cambridge University Press.

Knox, L. (1994). Repetition and relevance: Self-repetition as a strategy for initiating cooperation in nonnative/native speaker conversations. In B. Johnstone (Ed.), *Repetition in Discourse: Interdisciplinary Perspectives* (Vol. 1, pp. 195–206). Norwood, NJ: Ablex Publishing Corporation.

Koelsch, S. (2010). Towards a neural basis of music-evoked emotions. *Trends in Cognitive Sciences, 14*, 131–137.

Koelsch, S., Gunter, T., Friederici, A. D., & Schröger, E. (2000). Brain indices of music processing: "Nonmusicians" are musical. *Journal of Cognitive Neuroscience, 12*, 520–541.

Kotilahti, K., Nissilä, I., Näsi, T., Lipiäinen, L., Noponen, T., Meriläinen, P., Huotilainen, M. & Fellman, V. (2010). Hemodynamic responses to speech and music in newborn infants. *Human Brain Mapping, 31*, 595–603.

Kraemer, D. J. M., Macrae, C. N., Green, A. E., & Kelley, W. M. (2005). Musical imagery: Sound of silence activates auditory cortex. *Nature, 434*(7030). 158.

Kramer, J. D. (2002). The nature and origins of musical postmodernism. In J. Lochhead & J. Auner (Eds.). *Postmodern Music/Postmodern Thought* (pp. 13–26). New York, NY: Routledge.

Kramer, J. D. (2004). The concept of disunity and musical analysis. *Music Analysis, 23*, 361–372.

Kramer, L. (2010). Interpreting music. Berkeley and Los Angeles, CA: University of California Press.

Krumhansl, C. L. (1990). *Cognitive foundations of musical pitch.* New York, NY: Oxford University Press.

Krumhansl, C. L. (1996). A perceptual analysis of Mozart's Piano Sonata K. 282: Segmentation, tension, and musical ideas. *Music Perception, 13*, 401–432.

Krumhansl, C. L. (2010). Plink: "Thin slices" of music. *Music Perception, 27*, 337–354.

Krumhansl, C. L., & Jusczyk, P. W. (1990). Infants' perception of phrase structure in music. *Psychological Science, 1*, 70–73.

Kunst-Wilson, W. R., & Zajonc, R. B. (1980). Affective discrimination of stimuli that cannot be recognized. *Science, 207*(4430), 557–558.

Lamont, A. (2011). University students' strong experiences of music: Pleasure, engagement and meaning. *Musicae Scientiae, 15*, 229–249.

Lamont, A. (2012). Emotion, engagement and meaning in strong experiences of music performance. *Psychology of Music, 40*, 574–594.

Lauter, J. L., Hersocvitch, P., Formby, C., & Raichle, M. E. (1985). Tonotopic organization in human auditory cortex revealed by positron emission tomography. *Hearing Research, 20*, 199–205.

Leaver, A. M., Van Lare, J., Zielinski, B., Halpern, A. R., & Rauschecker, J. P. (2009). Brain activation during anticipation of sound sequences. *Journal of Neuroscience, 29*, 2477–2485.

LeDrew, S. (2006). Jokes and their relation to the uncanny: The comic, the horrific, and pleasure in Audition and Romero's Dead films. *PsyArt.* Retrieved from http://www.psyartjournal.com/article/show/ledrew-jokes_and_their_relation_to_the_uncanny_.

Lehéricy, S., Benali, H., Van de Moortele, P.-F., Pélégrini-Issac, M., Waechter, T., Ugurbil, K., & Doyon, J. (2005). Distinct basal ganglia territories are engaged in early and advanced motor sequence learning. *Proceedings of the National Academy of Sciences, 102*(35), 12566–12571.

Lehmann, A. (2007). Expression and interpretation. In A. Lehmann (Ed.), *Psychology for Musicians: Understanding and Acquiring the Skills* (pp. 85-106). New York, NY: Oxford University Press.

Leman, M. (1995). *Music and Schema Theory: Cognitive Foundations of Systematic Musicology.* New York, NY: Springer.

Leonard, H. L., Goldberger, E. L., Rapoport, J. L., & Cheslow, D. L. (1990). Childhood rituals: Normal development or obsessive-compulsive symptoms? *Journal of the American Academy of Child & Adolescent Psychiatry, 29*(1), 17–23.

Lerdahl, F. (2001). The sounds of poetry viewed as music. *Proceedings of the National Academy of Sciences, 930*, 337–354.

Lerdahl, F., & Jackendoff, R. (1983). *A Generative Theory of Tonal Music.* Cambridge, MA: MIT Press.

Levinson, J. (1997). *Music in the Moment.* Ithaca, NY: Cornell University Press.

Levitin, D. J. (2006). *This is your brain on music: The science of a human obsession.* New York, NY: Dutton/Penguin Books.

Levitin, D. J., & Rogers, S. E. (2005). Absolute pitch: Perception, coding, and controversies. *Trends in Cognitive Sciences, 9*, 26–33.

Levitin, D. J. (1994) Absolute memory for musical pitch: Evidence from the production of learned melodies. *Perception & Psychophysics, 56*, 414-423.

Lewin, D. (1986). Music theory, phenomenology, and modes of perception. *Music Perception, 3*, 327, 53–108.

Leydon, R. (2002). Towards a typology of minimalist tropes. *Music theory online, 8*(4). Retrieved from http://www.mtosmt.org/issues/mto.02.8.4/mto.02.8.4.leydon.html.

Li, C. N., & Hombert, J.-M. (2002). On the evolutionary origin of language. In M. I. Stamenov & V. Gallese (Eds.), *Mirror Neurons and the Evolution of Brain and Language.* (pp. 175–205). Amsterdam, Netherlands: John Benjamins Publishing Company.

Lidov, D. (1979). Syntactical strata in music. In S. Chatman & U. Eco (Eds.), *A Semiotic Landscape* (pp. 1003–1010). The Hague, Netherlands: Mouton.

Lidov, D. (2004). *Is language a music? Writings on musical form and signification.* Bloomington, IN: Indiana University Press.

Liikkanen, L. A. (2008). *Music in everymind: Commonality of involuntary musical imagery.* Proceedings of the 10th International Conference on Music Perception and Cognition, Sapporo, Japan.

Liikkanen, L. A. (2012). Inducing involuntary musical imagery: An experimental study. *Musicae Scientiae, 16*, 217–234.

Lippman, E. A. (1994). *A History of Western Musical Aesthetics.* Lincoln, NE: University of Nebraska Press.

Livingstone, S. R., Palmer, C., & Schubert, E. (2012). Emotional response to musical repetition. *Emotion, 12*, 552–567.

Lomax, A. (1968). *Folk song style and culture: A staff report on cantometrics.* Washington, DC: American Association for the Advancement of Science.

Lorenz, K. (1966). *On Aggression.* New York: Harcourt, Brace & World.

MacDonald, R. R., Hargreaves, D. J., & Miell, D. (2002). *Musical identities.* New York, NY: Oxford University Press.

Mandler, G., Nakamura, Y., & Van Zandt, B. J. (1987). Nonspecific effects of exposure on stimuli that cannot be recognized. *Journal of Experimental Psychology: Learning, Memory, and Cognition, 13*, 646–648.

Margulis, E. H. (2007a). Moved by nothing: Listening to musical silence. *Journal of Music Theory, 51*, 245–276.

Margulis, E. H. (2007b). Surprise and listening ahead: Analytic engagements with musical tendencies. *Music Theory Spectrum, 29*, 197–217.

Margulis, E. H. (2010). When program notes don't help: Music descriptions and enjoyment. *Psychology of Music, 38*, 285–302.

Margulis, E. H. (2012). Musical repetition detection across multiple exposures. *Music Perception,29*, 377–385.

Margulis, E. H. (2013). Aesthetic responses to repetition in unfamiliar music. *Empirical Studies of the Arts, 30*, 45–57.

Margulis, E. H., Uppunda, A. K., Mlsna, L. M., Parrish, T. B., & Wong, P. C. M. (2009). Selective neurophysiologic responses to timbre in musicians with different listening biographies. *Human Brain Mapping, 30*, 267–275.

Margulis, E. H., & Beatty, A. P. (2008). Musical style, psychoaesthetics, and prospects for entropy as an analytic tool. *Computer Music Journal, 32*, 64–78.

Marvin, E. W., & Brinkman, A. (1999). The effect of modulation and formal manipulation on perception of tonic closure by expert listeners. *Music Perception, 16*, 389–408.

Marvin, E. W., & Newport, E. L. (In press). A statistical learning test of absolute pitch without labeling: Effects of musical training and tone language.

McAdams, S. (1989). Psychological constraints on form-bearing dimensions in music. *Contemporary Music Review, 4*, 181–198.

Meyer, L. (1973). *Explaining music: Essays and explorations*. Berkeley and Los Angeles, CA: University of California Press.

McDermott, J. H., Wrobleski, D., & Oxenham, A. J. (2011). Recovering sound sources from embedded repetition. *Proceedings of the National Academy of Sciences, 108*, 1188–1193.

McDermott, J. H. & Hauser, M. D. (2005). The origins of music: Innateness, uniqueness, and evolution. *Music Perception, 23*, 29–59.

McGarva, A. R., & Warner, R. M. (2003). Attraction and social coordination: Mutual entrainment of vocal activity rhythms. *Journal of Psycholinguistic Research, 32*, 335–354.

McGough, R. (2004). *The Kingfisher book of comic verse*. London: Kingfisher.

McGurk, H., & MacDonald, J. (1976). Hearing lips and seeing voices. *Nature, 264*, 746–748.

McNeill, W. H. (1995). *Keeping together in time: Dance and drill in human history*. Cambridge, MA: Harvard University Press.

McRoberts, G. W., McDonough, C., & Lakusta, L. (2009). The role of verbal repetition in the development of infant speech preferences from 4 to 14 months of age. *Infancy, 14*, 162–194.

Meisner, S., & Longwell, D. (1987). *Sanford Meisner on Acting*. New York: Vintage.

Merritt, M. (1994). Repetition in situated discourse—Exploring its forms and functions. In B. Johnstone (Ed.), *Repetition in Discourse: Interdisciplinary Perspectives* (Vol. 1, pp. 23–36). Norwood, NJ: Ablex Publishing Corporation.

Meyer, L. B. (1956). *Emotion and Meaning in Music*. Chicago, IL: University of Chicago Press.

Meyer, L. B. (1967). *Music, the Arts, and Ideas*. Chicago, IL: University of Chicago Press.

Middleton, R. (2006). In the groove or blowing your mind? The pleasures of musical repetition. In A. Bennett, B. Shank, & J. Toynbee (Eds.). *The Popular Music Studies Reader* (pp.15–20). New York, NY: Routledge.

Miller, E. K., & Cohen, J. D. (2001). An integrative theory of prefrontal cortex function. *Annual Review of Neuroscience, 24*, 167–202.

Miller, G. (2000). *The mating mind: How sexual choice shaped the evolution of human nature*. New York, NY: Doubleday & Co.

Mirka, D. (Ed.) (Forthcoming). *Oxford handbook of topic theory*. New York, NY: Oxford University Press.

Mithen, S. (2006). *The singing neanderthals: The origins of music, language, mind, and body*. Cambridge, MA: Harvard University Press.

Monaghan, P., & Rowson, C. (2008). The effect of repetition and similarity on sequence learning. *Memory & Cognition, 36*, 1509–1514.

Monahan, J. L., Murphy, S. T., & Zajonc, R. B. (2000). Subliminal mere exposure: Specific, general, and diffuse effects. *Psychological Science, 11*, 462–466.

Morgan, R. P. (2003). The concept of unity and musical analysis. *Music Analysis, 22*, 7–50.

Morris, D. (1957). "Typical intensity" and its relation to the problem of ritualization. *Behavior 11*, 1–12.

Murphy, G. L., & Shapiro, A. M. (1994). Forgetting of verbatim information in discourse. *Memory & Cognition, 22*, 85–94.

Murray, A. (1976). *Stomping on the Blues*. New York, NY: Da Capo Press.

Nakahara, H., Doya, K., & Hikosaka, O. (2001). Parallel cortico-basal ganglia mechanisms for acquisition and execution of visuomotor sequences: A computational approach. *Journal of Cognitive Neuroscience, 13*, 626–647.

Nakamura, J., & Csikszentmihalyi, M. (2002). The concept of flow. In C. R. Snyder & S. J. Lopez (Eds.), *Handbook of Positive Psychology* (pp. 89–105). New York, NY: Oxford University Press.

Narmour, E. (1990). *The analysis and cognition of basic melodic structures: The implication-realization model*. Chicago, IL: University of Chicago Press.

Narmour, E. (1992). *The analysis and cognition of melodic complexity: The implication-realization model*. Chicago, IL: University of Chicago Press.

Nettl, B. (1983). *The study of ethnomusicology: Twenty-nine issues and concepts*. Urbana, IL: University of Illinois Press.

Neuhaus, C., Knösche, T. R., & Friederici, A. D. (2009). Effects of musical expertise and boundary markers on phrase perception in music. *Journal of Cognitive Neuroscience, 18*, 472–493.

Nilsson, U. (2009). Soothing music can increase oxytocin levels during bed rest after open-heart surgery: A randomised control trial. *Journal of Clinical Nursing, 18*, 2153–2161.

Nisbett, R. E., Peng, K., Choi, I., & Norenzayan, A. (2001). Culture and systems of thought: Holistic versus analytic cognition. *Psychological Review, 108*, 291–310.

North, A. C., & Hargreaves, D. J. (1995). Subjective complexity, familiarity, and liking for popular music. *Psychomusicology, 14*, 77–93.

North, A. C., & Hargreaves, D. J. (1999). Music and adolescent identity. *Music Education Research, 1*, 75–92.

Norton, A., Zipse, L., & Schlaug, G. (2009). Melodic intonation therapy: Shared insights on how it is done and why it might help. *Annals of the New York Academy of Sciences, 1169*, 431–436.

Novis, S., & Wong, P. C. M. (2011). *The fractal divide—Where complexity matters: Affective and cognitive responses to music.* Paper presented at The Neurosciences and Music IV: Learning and Memory, Edinburgh, Scotland.

Ockleford, A. (2005). *Repetition in music: Theoretical and metatheoretical perspectives.* London: Ashgate.

Oechslin, M. S., Läge, D., & Vitouch, O. (2012). Training of tonal similarity ratings in non-musicians: a "rapid learning" approach. *Frontiers in Psychology, 3*, 142.

Ollen, J. & Huron, D. (2004). Listener preferences and early repetition in musical form. *Proceedings of the 8th International Conference on Music Perception and Cognition, Evnaston, IL*, 405-407.

Orr, M. G., & Ohlsson, S. (2001). The relationship between musical complexity and liking in jazz and bluegrass. *Psychology of Music, 29*, 108–127.

Palmer, C. (1997). Music performance. *Annual Review of Psychology, 48*, 115–138.

Patel, A. D. (2008). *Music, language, and the brain.* New York, NY: Oxford University Press.

Pawley, A., & Snyder, F. H. (1983). Two puzzles for linguistic theory: Nativelike selection and nativelike fluency. In J. C. Richards & R. W. Schmidt (Eds.), *Language and Communication* (pp. 191–226). New York: Longman.

Payne, R. S., & McVay, S. (1971). Songs of humpback whales. *Science, 173*, 585–597.

Pereira, C. S., Teixeira, J., Figueiredo, P., Xavier, J., Castro, S. L., & Brattico, E. (2011). Music and emotions in the brain: Familiarity matters. *PLoS ONE, 6*, e27241.

Philip, R. (2004). *Performing music in the age of recording.* New Haven, CT: Yale University Press.

Picker, J. M. (2001). The Victorian aura of the recorded voice. *New Literary History, 32*, 769–786.

Pilotti, M., Antrobus, J. S., & Duff, M. (1997). The effect of presemantic acoustic adaptation on semantic "satiation." *Memory & Cognition, 25*, 305–312.

Pinker, S. (1997). *How the mind works.* New York, NY: W. W. Norton & Company.

Pitman, R. K. (1989). Animal models of compulsive behavior. *Biological Psychiatry, 26*, 189–198.

Pitts, S. E. (2005). *Valuing Musical Participation.* Aldershot, UK: Ashgate Aldershot.

Praeger, F. (1882-83). On the fallacy of the repetition of parts in the classical form. *Proceedings of the Royal Musical Association, 9th Session*, 1–16.

Pressing, J. (2002). Black Atlantic rhythm: Its computational and transcultural foundations. *Music Perception, 19*, 285–310.

Raffman, D. (1993). *Language, music, and mind.* Cambridge, MA: MIT Press.

Rafii, Z., & Pardo, B. (2011). A simple music/voice separation system based on the extraction of the repeating musical structure. Poster presented at *The 36th International Conference on Acoustics, Speech and Signal Processing* in Prague, Czech Republic.

Rafii, Z., & Pardo, B. (2012). Music/voice separation using the similarity matrix. Paper presented at The 13th International Society for Music Information Retrieval, October 8–12, Porto, Portugal.

Rahn, J. (1993). Repetition. *Contemporary Music Review, 7*, 49–57.

Rappaport, R. A. (1999). *Ritual and religion in the making of humanity.* Cambridge, UK: Cambridge University Press.

Rauschecker, J. P. (2011). An expanded role for the dorsal auditory pathway in sensorimotor control and integration. *Hearing Research, 271,* 16–25.

Rauschecker, J. P., & Scott, S. K. (2009). Maps and streams in the auditory cortex: Nonhuman primates illuminate human speech processing. *Nature Neuroscience, 12,* 718–724.

Raymond W. Gibbs, J. (2005). *Embodiment and cognitive science.* Cambridge, UK: Cambridge University Press.

Rentfrow, P. J., & Gosling, S. D. (2003). The do re mi's of everyday life: The structure and personality correlates of music preferences. *Journal of Personality and Social Psychology, 84,* 1236–1256.

Rentfrow, P. J., & McDonald, J. A. (2010). Preference, personality, and emotion. In P. N. Juslin & J. A. Sloboda (Eds.), *Handbook of Music and Emotion: Theory, Research, Applications* (pp. 669–695). New York, NY: Oxford University Press.

Repp, B. (1992). Diversity and commonality in music performance: An analysis of timing microstructure in Schumann's "Traumerei." *Journal of the Acoustical Society of America, 92,* 2546–2568.

Repp, B. H. (1995). Expressive timing in Schumann's "Träumerei:" An analysis of performances by graduate student pianists. *Journal of the Acoustical Society of America, 98,* 2414–2427.

Reyna, V. F., & Brainerd, C. J. (1995). Fuzzy-trace theory: An interim synthesis. *Learning and Individual Differences, 7,* 1–75.

Richman, B. (2001). How music fixed "nonsense" into significant formulas: On rhythm, repetition, and meaning. In N. Wallin, B. Merker, & S. Brown (Eds.), *The Origins of Music* (pp. 301–314). Cambridge, MA: MIT Press.

Rohrmeier, M., & Rebuschat, P. (2012). Implicit learning and acquisition of music. *Topics in Cognitive Science, 4,* 525–553.

Rosen, C. (2005, November 3). Playing music: The lost freedom. *The New York Review of Books, 52*(17). Retrieved from http://www.nybooks.com/articles/archives/2005/nov/03/playing-music-the-lost-freedom/?pagination=false.

Rossano, M. J. (2012). The essential role of ritual in the transmission and reinforcement of social norms. *Psychological Bulletin, 138,* 529–549.

Rouget, G. (1980). *La musique et la transe: esquisse d'une théorie générale des relations de la musique et de la possession.* Paris: Gallimard Paris.

Royle, N. (2003). *The uncanny: An introduction.* New York: Routledge.

Ruwet, N. (1975). Théorie et méthodes dans les etudes musicales: Quelques remarques rétrospectives et préliminaires. *Musique en Jeu, 17,* 11–36.

Sachs, J. S. (1967). Recognition memory for syntactic and semantic aspects of connected discourse. *Perception and Psychophysics, 2,* 437–442.

Sacks, O. (2007). *Musicophilia: Tales of music and the brain.* New York: Knopf.

Saffran, J. R., Aslin, R. N., & Newport, E. L. (1996). Statistical learning by 8-month-old infants. *Science, 274*(5294), 1926–1928.

Saffran, J. R., & Griepentrog, G. J. (2001). Absolute pitch in infant auditory learning: Evidence for developmental reorganization. *Developmental Psychology, 37,* 74–85.

Saffran, J. R., Johnson, E. K., Aslin, R. N., & Newport, E. L. (1999). Statistical learning of tone sequences by human infants and adults. *Cognition, 70,* 27–52.

Schellenberg, E. G. (2008). The role of exposure in emotional responses to music. *Behavioral and Brain Sciences, 31,* 594–595.

Schellenberg, E. G., & Trehub, S. E. (2003). Good pitch memory is widespread. *Psychological Science, 14,* 262–266.

Schoenberg, A., Strang, G., & Stein, L. (1967). *Fundamentals of Musical Composition.* London: Faber & Faber London.

Schoenpflug, U. (2008). Pauses in elementary school children's verbatim and gist free recall of a story. *Cognitive Development, 23,* 385–394.

Schön, D., Gordon, R., Campagne, A., Magne, C., Astésano, C., Anton, J.-L., & Besson, M. (2010). Similar cerebral networks in language, music and song perception. *Neuroimage, 51,* 450–461.

Schuftan, C. (2007). *The Culture Club*. Sydney, Australia: ABC Books.

Schulkind, M. D., Hennis, L. K., & Rubin, D. C. (1999). Music, emotion, and autobiographical memory: They're playing your song. *Memory & Cognition, 27*, 948–955.

Searcy, W. A., Nowicki, S., & Peters, S. (1999). Song types as fundamental units in vocal repertoires. *Animal Behavior, 58*, 37–44.

Sears, L. L., Vest, C., Mohamed, S., Bailey, J., Ranson, B. J., & Piven, J. (1999). An MRI study of the basal ganglia in autism. *Progress in Neuro-Psychopharmacology & Biological Psychiatry, 23*, 613–624.

Seashore, C. (1938). *Psychology of Music*. New York: McGraw-Hill.

Severance, E., & Washburn, M. F. (1907). Minor studies from the psychological laboratory of Vassar College: The loss of associative power in words after long fixation. *The American Journal of Psychology, 18*, 182–186.

Shaffer, L. H. (1980). Analysing piano performance. In G. E. Stelmach & J. Requi (Eds.), *Tutorials in Motor Behavior* (pp. 443–455). Amsterdam: North-Holland.

Shaffer, L. H. (1981). Performances of Chopin, Bach and Bartok: Studies in motor programming. *Cognitive Psychology, 13*, 327–376.

Shaffer, L. H. (1984). Timing in solo and duet piano performances. *The Quarterly Journal of Experimental Psychology Section A: Human Experimental Psychology, 36*, 577–595.

Shaffer, L. H. (1995). Musical performance as interpretation. *Psychology of Music, 23*, 17–38.

Shaffer, L. H., Clarke, E. F., & Todd, T. D. (1985). Metre and rhythm in piano playing. *Cognition, 20*, 61–77.

Sheffi, N. (2000). *The ring of myths: The Israelis, Wagner and the Nazis*. Sussex: Sussex Academic Press.

Sherzer, J. (1994). Transcription, representation, and translation: Repetition and performance in Kuna discourse. In B. Johnstone (Ed.), *Repetition in Discourse: Interdisciplinary Perspectives* (pp. 37–52). Norwood, NJ: Ablex Publishing Corporation.

Shockley, K., Santana, M. V., & Fowler, C. A. (2003). Mutual interpersonal postural constraints are involved in cooperative conversation. *Journal of Experimental Psychology: Human Perception and Performance, 29*, 326–332.

Shore, B. (1998). *Culture in mind: Cognition, culture, and the problem of meaning*. New York, NY: Oxford University Press.

Silvia, P. J. (2006). *Exploring the psychology of interest*. New York, NY: Oxford University Press.

Simcock, G., & DeLoache, J. S. (2008). The effect of repetition on infants' imitation from picture books varying in iconicity. *Infancy, 13*, 687–697.

Sisman, E. R. (1993). *Haydn and the classical variation*. Cambridge, MA: Harvard University Press.

Sloboda, J. (1991). Musical expertise. In K. A. Ericsson & J. Smith (Eds.), *Toward a general theory of expertise: Prospects and limits* (pp. 153–171). New York, NY: Cambridge University Press.

Sloboda, J. A. (2001). *Generative processes in music: The psychology of performance, improvisation, and composition*. New York: Oxford University Press.

Smith, A. (1795/1982). Of the Nature of that Imitation which takes place in what are called The Imitative Arts. In W. P. D. Wightman & J. C. Bryce (Eds.), *Glasgow Edition of the Works and Correspondence of Adam Smith* (Vol. 3) (p. 192). Indianapolis, IN: Liberty Fund.

Smith, J. D. (1997). The place of musical novices in music science. *Music Perception, 14*, 227–262.

Smith, J. D., Wilson, M., & Reisberg, D. (1995). The role of subvocalization in auditory imagery. *Neuropsychologia, 33*, 1433–1454.

Smith, N. A., & Schmuckler, M. A. (2008). Dial A440 for absolute pitch: Absolute pitch memory by non-absolute pitch possessors. *Journal of the Acoustical Society of America, 123*(4), EL77–EL84.

Smyth, D. H. (1993). "Balanced interruption" and the formal repeat. *Music Theory Spectrum, 15*, 76.

Sperber, D., & Wilson, D. (2004). Relevance theory. In G. Ward & L. Horn (Eds.), *Handbook of Pragmatics* (pp. 607–632). Oxford, UK: Blackwell.

Stahl, B., Kotz, S. A., Henseler, I., Turner, R., & Geyer, S. (2011). Rhythm in disguise: Why singing may not hold the key to recovery from aphasia. *Brain, 134*, 3083–3093.

Stein, D. J., Christenson, G. A., & Hollander, E. (Eds.). (1999). *Trichotillomania*. Arlington, VA: American Psychiatric Press.

Stern, D. N., Spieker, S., Barnett, R. K., & MacKain, K. (1983). The prosody of maternal speech: Infant age and context related changes. *Journal of Child Language, 10*, 1–15.

Stickgold, R., Malia, A., Maguire, D., Roddenberry, D., & O'Connor, M. (2000). Replaying the game: Hypnagogic images in normals and amnesics. *Science, 290*(5490), 350–353.

Suzuki, R., Buck, J. R., & Tyack, P. L. (2006). Information entropy of humpback whale songs. *Journal of the Acoustical Society of America, 119*(3), 1849–1866.

Swain, J. P. (1995). The concept of musical syntax. *The Musical Quarterly, 79*, 281–308.

Swain, J. P. (1997). *Musical languages*. New York, NY: W.W. Norton & Company.

Szpunar, K. K., Schellenberg, E. G., & Pliner, P. (2004). Liking and memory for musical stimuli as a function of exposure. *Journal of Experimental Psychology: Learning, Memory, and Cognition, 30*, 370–381.

Tan, S.-L., Spackman, M., & Peaslee, C. (2006). The effects of repeated exposure on liking and judgments of musical unity of intact and patchwork compositions. *Music Perception, 23*, 407–421.

Tan, S.-L., Cohen, A., Lipscomb, S. & Kendall, R. A. (2013). *The Psychology of Music in Multimedia*. New York: Oxford University Press.

Tannen, D. (2007). *Talking Voices: Repetition, Dialogue, and Imagery in Conversational Discourse (2nd ed.)*. New York, NY: Cambridge University Press.

Taruskin, R. (1996, January 28). Recordings view: Dispelling Wagnerian mists and mystiques, *New York Times*.

Tillmann, B., & Dowling, W. J. (2007). Memory decreases for prose, but not for poetry. *Memory & Cognition, 35*, 628–639.

Todd, N. P. M. (1995). The kinematics of musical expression. *The Journal of the Acoustical Society of America, 97*, 1940–1949.

Torres, J. (2011). *We the Animals*. New York: Mariner Books.

Tovey, D. F. (1927). Franz Schubert (1797–1828). In H. J. Foss (Ed.) *The Heritage of Music*, Vol. 1 (pp. 82–122). Oxford, UK: Oxford University Press.

Trehub, S. (2003). The developmental origins of musicality. *Nature Neuroscience, 6*, 669–673.

Troeger, R. (2003). *Playing Bach on the keyboard: A practical guide*. Pompton Plains, NJ: Amadeus Press.

Turino, T. R. (2008). *Music as social life: The politics of participation*. Chicago, IL: University of Chicago Press.

Türk, D. G., & Jacobi, E. R. (1968). *Klavierschule*. Kassel, Germany: Bärenreiter.

Twain, M. A. (1876). A literary nightmare. *Atlantic Monthly, 37*, 167–170.

Tyack, P. L., & Sayigh, L. S. (1997). Vocal learning in cetaceans. In C. T. Snowdon & M. Hausberger (Eds.), *Social Influences on Vocal Development* (pp. 208–233). New York, NY: Cambridge University Press.

Unyk, A. M., Trehub, S. E., Trainor, L. J., & Schellenberg, E. G. (1992). Lullabies and simplicity: A cross-cultural perspective. *Psychology of Music, 20*, 15–28.

Vakil, E., Kahan, S., Huberman, M., & Osimani, A. (2000). Motor and non-motor sequence learning in patients with basal ganglia lesions: The case of serial reaction time (SRT). *Neuropsychologia, 38*, 1–10.

Van Lancker-Sidtis, D., & Rallon, G. (2004). Tracking the incidence of formulaic expressions in everyday speech: Methods for classification and verification. *Language & Communication, 24*, 207–240.

Vitz, P. C. (1966). Affect as a function of stimulus variation. *Journal of Experimental Psychology, 71*, 74–79.

Volk, A., & van Kranenburg, P. (2012). Melodic similarity among folk songs: An annotation study on similarity-based categorization in music. *Musicae Scientiae, 16*, 317–339.

Wallace, W. T. (1994). Memory for music: Effect of melody on recall of text. *Journal of Experimental Psychology: Learning, Memory, and Cognition, 20*, 1471–1485.

Warker, J. A., & Halpern, A. R. (2005). Musical stem completion: Humming that note. *The American Journal of Psychology, 118*, 567–585.

Weber, M., Martindale, D., Riedel, J., & Neuwirth, G. (1958). *The Rational and Social Foundations of Music.* Carbondale, IL: Southern Illinois University Press.

Wessinger, C. M., Buonocore, M. H., Kussmail, C. L., & Mangun, G. R. (1997). Tonotopy in human auditory cortex examined with functional magnetic resonance imaging. *Human Brain Mapping, 5*, 18–25.

Williams, H. (2011, August 20). Feels like teen spirit: Thousands of young people flock annually to a Christian camp in rural France. *The Independent.* Retrieved from: http://www.independent.co.uk/news/world/europe/feels-like-teen-spirit-thousands-of-young-people-flock-annually-to-a-christian-camp-in-rural-france-2339347.html

Williamson, V. J, Jilka, S. R., Fry, J., Finkel, S., Müllensiefen, D. & Stewart, L. (2012). How do "earworms" start? Classifying the everyday circumstances of Involuntary Musical Imagery. *Psychology of Music, 40*, 259–284.

Wiltermuth, S. S., & Heath, C. (2009). Synchrony and cooperation. *Psychological Science, 20*, 1–5.

Witmer, R. (1993). Stability in Blackfoot songs, 1909–1968. In S. Blum, P. V. Bohlman & D. M. Neuman (Eds.), *Ethnomusicology and Modern Music History* (pp. 251–253). Urbana, IL: University of Illinois Press.

Wong, P. C. M., Chan, A. H. D., & Margulis, E. H. (2012). Effects of mono- and bi-cultural experiences on auditory perception. *Annals of the New York Academy of Sciences, 1252*, 158–162.

Wong, P. C. M., Chan, A. H. D., Roy, A. K., & Margulis, E. H. (2011). The bimusical brain is not two monomusical brains in one: Evidence from musical affective processing. *Journal of Cognitive Neuroscience, 23*, 4082–4093.

Wong, P. C. M., & Margulis, E. H. (2008). The complex dynamics of repeated musical exposure. Paper presented at the *10th International Conference on Music Perception and Cognition, Sapporo, Japan.*

Wong, P. C. M., Roy, A. K., & Margulis, E. H. (2009). Bimusicalism: The implicit dual enculturation of cognitive and affective systems. *Music Perception, 27*, 81–88.

Wood, W., & Neal, D. T. (2007). A new look at habits and the habit-goal interface. *Psychological review, 114*, 843–863.

Woods, D. W., Miltenberger, R. G., & Flach, A. D. (1996). Habits, tics, and stuttering: Prevalence and relation to anxiety and somatic awareness. *Behavior Modification, 20*, 216–225.

Zacks, J. M., Tversky, B., & Iyer, G. (2001). Perceiving, remembering, and communicating structure in events. *Journal of Experimental Psychology: General, 130*, 29–58.

Zajonc, R. B. (1968). Attitudinal effects of mere exposure. *Journal of Personality and Social Psychology, 9*(2, Pt.2), 1–27.

Zalla, T., Verlut, I., Franck, N., Puzenat, D., & Sirigu, A. (2004). Perception of dynamic action in patients with schizophrenia. *Psychiatry Research, 128*, 39–51.

Zaslaw, N. (1989, April 27). Repeat performance. *The New York Review of Books.* Retrieved from: http://www.nybooks.com/articles/archives/1989/apr/27/repeat-performance/?pagination=false

Zatorre, R. J., Chen, J. L., & Penhune, V. B. (2007). When the brain plays music: auditory-motor interactions in music perception and production. *Nature Reviews Neuroscience, 8*, 547–558.

Zatorre, R. J., & Halpern, A. R. (2005). Mental concerts: Musical imagery and auditory cortex. *Neuron, 47*, 9–12.

Zbikowski, L. M. (2002). *Conceptualizing music: Cognitive structure, theory, and analysis.* New York, NY: Oxford University Press.

Zinoman, J. (2012, June 24). Repeating a repetition repeatedly once again, *New York Times*, p. C1.

Zuckerkandl, V. (1956). *Sound and symbol.* New York, NY: Pantheon Books.

# Index

*2001: A Space Odyssey*, 84
Aaliyah, 58
Abbate, Carolyn, 2, 15, 41, 169
absolute pitch. *See under* pitch perception
acting exercises, repetition in, 164–165
Adams, John, 145
Adorno, Theodor, 58, 147–148
aesthetic mode of attending, 13–15
Agawu, V. K., 30
aleatoric music, 5, 179
*Alive Inside*, 149–150
Alzheimer's disease, 149
anaphora, 162
Andersen, Hans Christian, 164
Andriessen, Louis, 145
animals: repetitive behavior among, 59–61;
    vocalization among, 19–20
anticipatory attending, 112
aphasia, 62–63
*Apocalypse Now*, 153
Arewa, O. B., 30
*Are You That Somebody* (Aaliyah), 58
Argerich, Martha, 121, 126–127
*L'Arlesienne Suite* (Bizet), 100–101
Ashkenazy, Vladimir, 121
Ashley, R., 120
Attali, Jacques, 77
auditory repetition. *See also* musical repetition:
    expectation function of, 22; learning
    function of, 22; McGurk effect and,
    33; segmentation function of, 22;
    telephone example and, 33
*Auld Lang Syne*, 6
Auner, J., 84

*Baby* (Bieber), 158
Bach, Johann Sebastian: *English Suite No. 2*, 122,
    124–125; *Goldberg Variations*, 32, 93, 154;
    ornamentation with musical repetition and,
    122, 124–125; *Prelude in F Minor*, 29–30
Bach, P.D.Q., 170, 173
Bailes, F., 81–82
Bain, B., 158

Barnes, S. J., 64
Barnes, Julian, 164
Baroque Era, 122–123, 134–135
basal ganglia, 61–66, 68, 71–72, 74, 115–116
Beaman, C.P., 76, 82
beat induction, 65
beat sensitivity, 72, 166
Beatty, Andy, 109
Beauvois, M. W., 99
Becker, Judith, 67–68
Beethoven, Ludwig van: *32 Variations in C Minor,
    WoO 80*, 177; audience reverence for, 113;
    *Fifth Symphony*, 13; musical borrowing
    by, 28; musical repetition and, 52; *Piano
    Sonata, Op. 110*, 156; *Piano Sonata Op.
    13*, 49; *Sonata Op.2/1*, 130; *Sonata Op. 53*
    (Waldstein Sonata) and, 170–172; *String
    Quartets*, 15, 69, 105
Bennett, Alan, 155
Berio, Luciano, 15–16
Berliner, P., 112
Berlyne, D. E., 96–97
Beziehendes Denken (structural hearing,
    Riemann), 178
Bharucha, J. J., 92
Bieber, Justin, 158
Bigand, Emmanuel, 166
Big Five Inventory (personality dimensions),
    98–99
birds. *See* songbirds
Bizet, Georges, 100–101
Blackfoot, 34
Boecker, H., 64
*Bolero* (Ravel), 177
Borge, Victor, 170
Borges, Jose Luis, 26–27, 32
Bornstein, R. F., 96, 113, 168
Boulez, Pierre, 81
*Bowls* (Caribou), 58
Boyer, P., 56, 59
Brahms, Johannes: *Second Symphony*, 27–29,
    75; *Violin Concerto in D major, Op. 77*,
    143–144

Brainard, M. S., 116
Brainerd, C. J., 85–86
Brandt, A. K., 137, 168, 175, 180
Bregman, A. S., 53
Brendel, Alfred, 121
Brother Roger (Taizé founder), 140–141
Brown, Steven, 20, 76, 83–84
Broyles, M., 48–49, 134–135
Bruch, Max, 153
Bruckner, Anton, 57
Buck, J., 19
Burkholder, J. P., 28
Burnham, Scott, 58, 113, 147–148

Cabib, S., 61
cadence, 23, 46
Cage, John, 5
Calabrese, Omar, 123
Calloway, Cab, 150
Calvert, S. L., 86
Calvo-Merino, B., 112
Cambouropoulos, E., 39
Caplin, William, 11, 39–41, 178
Caribou, 58
Carter, Elliott, 15–16
caudate nucleus, 61–62
cerebellum, 115
Cervantes, Miguel de, 26–27
Chernoff, John, 151–152
children: infant-directed speech and, 20–21,
    23–24, 175–176; musical competence
    among, 2; musicalized pronunciations and,
    159; repetitive behavior among, 5, 70–71,
    86, 160; verbatim memory and, 86
Chopin, Frédéric, 120, 130–132
Churchill, Winston, 162
Clapping Music (Reich), 79
Clarke, E.F., 12, 34, 120, 126, 155
The Classical Style (Rosen), 133
Clayton, M., 111
cognitive science: animal subjects and, 63–64;
    brain anatomy and, 61–66, 68, 71–72, 74,
    115, 175; language and, 1–3, 19; motor
    functions and, 64, 66, 115–116; music and,
    1–4, 12–13, 19, 30, 53, 61, 65–66, 68, 74,
    84, 100–101, 105–106, 115–116, 137, 139,
    175, 178; neuroimaging and, 12–13, 65, 68,
    72, 100, 106, 115–116, 178; sequencing
    and, 63–65, 116
Cohen, Leonard, 57
Cohn, R., 128
coin game, 137–138
Cole, M., 49
concatenationism, 136, 155–156
Concerto for Horn and Hardart (P.D.Q. Bach), 173
Cone, Edward, 32, 104–106, 130
Conklin, K., 6
Cook, Nicholas, 128–129

Cooke, M., 83
Cooper, S. J., 61
Copland, Aaron, 90
Cortot, Alfred, 121
Covey, Stephen, 13
Crawley, A. M., 70
creativity, social nature of, 152
Creel, S. C., 107
Cross, I., 3
Crystal, D., 126
Csíkszentmihályi, Mikhail, 25, 69, 72, 112, 152
cult of the performer, 153
Cumming, N., 50, 144–145

Dalmatian illusion, 13, 17–18
dance, repetition in, 151–152
Darcy, W., 47–48
DeBellis, M., 66, 169
Debussy, Claude, 52
de capo arias, 134
declarative knowledge, 65–66, 167
Deleuze, Giles, 34–35, 78
Deliège, I., 18, 39, 177
Deloache, J.S., 70
dementia, 149
Dempster, D., 128
DeNora, T., 71
Der Rosenkavalier (Strauss), 7
Desain, P., 65, 166
Deutsch, Diana, 16–17, 30, 162, 169–170
DeVoto, M., 52
Dewey, John, 91
Diaz, F. M., 69
Dido and Aeneas (Purcell), 35
Different Trains (Reich), 73
discursive repetition, 50–51, 144–146, 148–149
Dissanayake, E., 60
DJ Kool Akiem, 80
Donne, John, 71
Don Quixote (Cervantes), 26–27
Dowling, W. J., 86–88, 92
Dunsby, Jonathan, 133–134
dynamic attending, 112

earworms: cadence and, 43; causal factors and,
    100; commercial jingles and, 158; defini-
    tion of, 6, 66; melody and, 10–11, 43, 66,
    76, 82–83; musical phrase length and,
    46, 76, 82–83; music scholarship on, 76;
    other names for, 76; "overlearning" and,
    82–83; pervasiveness of, 76, 81–82; recent
    exposure and, 83; recording technology
    and, 76–77, 81, 83; repeated exposure and,
    82–83; repetitive looping and, 76, 82–83,
    141; song choruses and, 82; timbre and, 82;
    time-filler activities and, 82
Ehrlich, S., 163–164
Eilam, D., 60–61

Electronic Dance Music (EDM), 69
Eliot, T.S., 74
E-mu SP-1200 sampler, 79
Endress, A. D., 25
the Enlightenment, 48
entrainment, 106, 111–116
epiphora, 163
ERP, 166, 178
Evans, D. W., 70
expectation: infant-directed speech and, 24; musical repetition and, 9, 23–25, 72, 92, 101–102, 108–110, 112, 115–116, 138, 153; music and, 10, 91, 93–94, 112

Feld, M., 44, 112, 152
Fernald, A., 20–21
*The Fine Art of Musical Repetition* (Kivy), 32
Fink, Robert, 77–78, 84
Finney, S. A., 63
First Reading (Cone), 104–106
Fitch, William Tecumseh, 5
flow, state of, 25, 69, 112
Formenlehre tradition, 39
*Four Quartets* (Eliot), 74
Freeman, W. J., 57
Friedland, L., 151
Friedson, S. M., 67
*Frohlicher Landmann* (Schumann), 46
Frost, Robert, 14
Fujii, N., 63
fuzzy-trace theory (Reyna and Brainerd), 85–86

Gabrielsson, A., 12, 18, 63, 66, 68, 72, 74, 119–120
Gallope, M., 2
Garcia, L.-M., 50, 69, 152
Garner, J. P., 61
*Generative Theory of Tonal Music* (Lerdahl and Jackendoff), 36, 41
Gernsbacher, M. A., 22, 73, 85, 87
Gerstein, Kirill, 76
gist memory, 85–87
Gjerdingen, R. O., 6, 11, 129
globus pallidus, 61–62
Goehr, Lydia, 19, 34
*Goldberg Variations* (Bach), 32, 93, 154
Gould, Glenn, 90, 93, 154–155
Grahn, J. A., 65, 72
Graybiel, A. M., 61–64
Green, A.D., 12
Green, D.M., 48
Green, L., 136
Greenberg, S., 30
Grétry, Andre-Ernest Modeste, 48–49, 134–135
Grice, P., 84, 164
Griffiths, T. D., 175

groove, 112, 146–147
Guck, M., 41
Guinee, L. N., 19

Halpern, Andrea, 10, 12, 76
Hamilton, A., 155
Handel, George Frideric, 28
Hanninen, Dora, 32, 39
Hansen, J., 113
*Happy Birthday*, 30–31, 34, 107
Hargreaves, D. J., 57, 99, 173
Harnad, S., 37
Harrison, A., 132, 140–142
Hasty, C. F., 35
Haueisen, J., 60
Haydn, Joseph: *Piano Sonata No. 51 in A Major*, 156–157; *Sonata No. 41*, 42–43
Hayes, D. S., 86
Heath, C., 57
Heifitz, Jascha, 138
Henry, Pierre, 79
Hepokoski, J. A., 47–48
Herbert, R., 67, 69
hip hop, 28, 79–80, 151
Holbrook, M.B., 179
Hombert, J.-M., 19–20
Honing, Henkjan, 65, 166, 168
Horlacher, G., 143
Horowitz, Vladimir, 90, 93, 154
Horst, J. S., 70–71
Hove, M. J., 111
Hugo, Victor, 164
Hume, David, 34
humpback whales. *See* whale songs
Hunter, I.M., 85, 89
Hunter, P.G., 98–99
Huron, David, 3, 10, 23–24, 52, 91, 102, 146–148, 158, 173
Husserl, Edmund, 10
Huxley, Aldous, 164

Ideal Reading (Cone). *See* Third Reading (Cone)
*Iedere Nacht Verlang Ik* (Taizé song), 143
*The Imaginary Museum of Musical Works* (Goehr), 34
implicit learning, 106–111, 165–169
infant-directed speech: cross-cultural similarities in, 21; expectation and, 24; musical quality of, 21, 175–176; repetition in, 20–21, 23–24; segmentation in, 23; soothing rhythm and, 20; vocal learning and, 20, 175
Ingalls, Monique, 67
Internet music services, 102–103
inverted U response. *See* Wundt curve
involuntary musical imagery (INMI), 76
*It's Gonna Rain* (Reich), 79

Jackendoff, R., 20, 36, 41, 88
Jackson, J.D., 151–152, 154
Jackson, Jesse, 163
Jacoby, L. L., 168
Jakobovits, L. A., 95–96
James, R.C., 17
James, William, 27, 68
Janata, Petr, 10, 12–13, 32, 59, 112
Janik, V. M., 19
Jankélévitch, V., 2, 169
Jarvella, R. J., 22
jazz, 123, 152
Jem, 29–30, 32
jockeying, 151
John, O.P., 98
Johnson, J. L., 86
Johnstone, Barbara, 41, 160–161, 170, 173–175, 177
Jolicoeur, P., 99
Jones, James Earl, 158
Jones, Mary Reiss, 112
Juslin, P. N., 12

Kalanithi, P. S. A., 62
Kao, M. H., 116
Katz, Mark, 79, 90–91, 126, 138
Keenan, J. M., 22
Keil, Charles, 11–12, 111–112, 152
Kellaris, J. J.., 76
Keren, H., 61
Kessler, E. J., 38
kinesthetic listening, 111–112
King, A.J., 12
King Jr., Martin Luther, 158
Kivy, Peter, 5, 22, 32
Klavierschule (Türk), 134
Knox, L., 14, 164
Koelsch, S., 57, 166
Kotilahti, K, 175
Kraemer, D. J. M., 12
Kramer, Jonathon, 84
Kramer, Joseph, 78–79
Kramer, L., 133
Krumhansl, C. L., 31, 38–39, 87, 169
Kunst-Wilson, W. R., 113

Lady Gaga, 158
Lamont, A., 69
language: allusion in, 170, 173; cognitive science and, 1–3, 19; compared to music, 2–3, 6, 15–18, 22, 41, 43, 49, 55, 72–73, 83–88, 115, 126, 134, 137, 142, 155, 158, 160, 164, 175, 178–180; evolutionary psychology and, 3; formulaic expressions in, 6, 63, 160; information conveyance and, 43; memory and, 87; metalinguistic information and, 162; mimicry and, 160; musical processing

of, 6, 160, 162, 175; repetition in, 14–18, 41, 49, 70, 73, 84–85, 88, 142, 158, 159–165, 170, 173–175; rhythm and, 41; semantics and, 72–73, 88, 178; silence and, 41; syntax and, 178; writing and, 3, 89
Lauter, J. L., 30
Law, Jude, 158
The Leader (McGough), 161–162
Leaver, A. M., 116
LeDrew, S., 174
Lehéricy, S., 64
Lehmann, A., 34, 120
Leman, M., 178
Leonard, H. L, 70
Lerdahl, Fred, 20, 36, 41, 88
Levinson, J., 136, 155–156
Levitin, D. J., 30, 76, 107, 168
Lewin, David, 9–10
Leydon, Rebecca, 50–51, 144–146
Li, C. N., 19–20, 38, 43
The Library of Babel (Borges), 26
Lidov, D., 20, 24, 34, 46, 51–52
Liénard, P., 56, 59
Ligeti, György, 37
Liikkanen, L. A., 76, 81
Lindy Hop, 151
Lippman, E. A., 89
A Literary Nightmare (Twain), 76
literature, repetition in, 163–164
Livingstone, S. R, 128
Lomax, A., 84
looping, 50, 69, 76, 79–80, 82–83, 141
Lorenz, Konrad, 70
Lux Aeterna (Ligeti), 37

Macbeth (Shakespeare), 155
MacDonald, R. R., 33, 173
Mandler, G., 96
Margulis, Elizabeth, 7–9, 15–16, 20, 22, 24, 33, 38, 40–42, 59, 69, 82, 91, 98, 100, 105, 108–110, 148, 156–157, 165, 169, 171, 178
Marvin, E. W., 129, 167–168
McAdams, S., 37
McCartney, Paul, 120
McDermott, J.H., 54
McDonald's, 158
McGarva, A. R., 41
McGough, Roger, 161–162
McGurk, H., 33
McNeill, W. H., 57
McRoberts, G. W., 21
Meisner, S., 164
melody, 43, 47, 58, 82–83
memory: attentional allocation and, 22; delay's impact on, 87; direct social interaction and, 22; gist memory and, 85–87; interactional content and, 88; for jokes and insults,

88–89; motor skills and, 138–139; musical repetition and, 10–11, 22, 25, 32, 115; music and, 22–23, 73, 75, 86–88; repetition and, 177–178; verbatim memory and, 22, 73, 85–86

Mendelssohn, Felix, 153

Merritt, M., 177–179

metric hierarchy, 20

Meyer, Leonard, 9, 11, 24, 44, 51, 69, 91–92

M.I.A., 58

Middleton, Richard, 50, 144–146, 148–149

Miller, E.K., 64

Miller, G., 3

Mirka, D., 27, 145

Miró, Joan, 71–72

Mithen, S., 3, 137

Monaghan, J. L., 25

*Money* (Pink Floyd), 58

*More About the Musical Expertise of Musically Untrained Listeners* (Bigand), 166

Morgan, R. P., 128

*Morgengruss* (Schubert), 10

Morris, D., 60

*Motormouth*, 136

*Moved by Nothing* (Margulis), 22

Mozart, Wolfgang Amadeus: *Don Giovanni*, 170; *Fantasy in C Minor*, 37–38; *The Magic Flute*, 92; *The Marriage of Figaro*, 170; *Piano Concerto in C Major, K. 467*, 90; *Piano Sonata in A Major K. 331*, 118–119; *Piano Sonata in C*, 40–41; *Symphony No. 40*, 71

*Much Ado About Nothing* (Shakespeare), 32

*The Muppets*, 10

Murphy, G. L., 22

Murray, A., 151

musematic repetition, 50–51, 144–146, 148

music. *See also* musical repetition: adolescence and, 179; aesthetic attending and, 71; cognitive science and, 1–4, 12–13, 19, 30, 53, 61, 65–66, 68, 74, 84, 100–101, 105–106, 115–116, 137, 139, 175, 178; compared to language, 2–3, 6, 15–18, 22, 41, 43, 49, 55, 72–73, 83–88, 115, 126, 134, 137, 142, 155, 158, 160, 164, 175, 178–180; complexity measures of, 99–100; copyright law and, 30; as discourse, 19; as domain for play, 71, 173; as embodiment, 12, 19, 25; entrainment and, 111–112; expectation and, 10, 91, 93–94, 112; functional harmony and, 30; implicit learning and, 165–169; information conveyance and, 13–14; live performances *versus* recordings of, 90–91, 123, 126–127, 154–155; memory and, 22–23, 73, 75, 86–88; nuance in, 23, 25; physical responses to, 67–69, 143, 149–150; productive *versus* perceptive capacity in, 166; recording technology and, 89–91, 93,

113, 123, 126; repeated exposure effects and, 96–97, 100–104, 108; ritual and, 57; semantics and, 73; state of flow and, 69; statistical learning studies of, 107–108, 167; subjective experience of, 2–3, 12, 50–51, 74, 141, 144–145, 148, 152, 164; unity and balance debates in, 128–129

musical repetition: advocacy for, 49, 133–134, 147–148; aesthetic function of, 14–16, 84; allusion in, 170–171, 173; animal vocalization and, 19–20; audience response and, 152–153, 170, 173; balance and unity goals and, 129, 133; Baroque Era and, 122–123, 134–135; between-piece forms of, 132–133; cadence and, 23, 46; categorical perception and, 37; coin game and, 137–138; commercial jingles and, 158; communicative function of, 19–20; compared to musical silence, 41; compared to other similarity relations in music, 24–25; compared to rhetorical persuasion, 123; concealment of, 129–130; conceptualization and, 169; context's role in, 27–32, 34–36, 39, 74, 78, 98–99; criticisms of, 3–4, 48–49, 52, 58, 81, 129, 134–135, 147; cultural universality of, 5, 19; culture of mass consumption and, 77–78, 84, 123; delayed forms of, 15–16, 44, 46–47, 49–50, 114, 120, 129, 149, 171; discursive forms of, 50–51, 144–146, 148–149; embellishment and, 122–123, 127; enjoyment and, 4, 14–16, 18, 41, 47, 50–52, 66–67, 72, 74, 77, 81, 92, 95–99, 105, 109, 114, 133, 140–141, 144, 156–157, 173, 180; entrainment and, 106, 112–116; expectation and, 9, 23–25, 72, 92, 101–102, 108–110, 112, 115–116, 138, 153; expressive variation and, 118–123, 126–127, 129–133; feelings of inevitability and, 113; flow state and, 69; focal repetition and, 51; form and, 128; formative repetition and, 51; goal demotion and, 58; groove and, 112, 146; hypermeter and, 41; hypnotic continuity and, 51; immediate forms of, 15–16, 42, 44, 46–47, 49–50, 114, 129–131, 134; implicit learning and, 106–111, 168–169; intentionality and, 59; interest response and, 18, 157; laboratory experiments on, 7–9, 15–16, 38, 40, 42, 59, 84, 87, 97–98, 100–101, 103, 105, 127–128; language training and, 159; learning function of, 22–23, 25, 54, 178; liminality and, 148; listener personality and, 98–99; listeners' life histories and, 31, 108; listening behaviors and, 4, 95, 102, 123; looping processes and, 50, 69, 79–80, 141; melody and, 47, 58; memorization and, 14; memory and, 10–11, 22, 25, 32, 115;

music. (*Cont.*)
   mere exposure effect and, 35–36, 113–114;
   microtiming and, 118–122, 127; minimal
   music and, 77, 79, 81; motor memory and,
   138–139; musematic forms of, 50–51,
   144–146, 148; musical hierarchy and, 51;
   musical notation and, 5, 34, 46, 117–118,
   121–122, 127, 133–134, 143; musical notes
   and, 37–39, 40–41; musical nuance and,
   23, 25; musical phrases and, 46–47, 66, 72;
   musical presentation's impact on, 31–32;
   musical scholarship on, 1–2, 21, 25, 50–51,
   179–180; musical stem completion tests
   and, 10–11; musical syntax and, 12, 50, 52;
   musical training and, 136–139; musical unit
   formation and, 65, 178; nonparticipatory
   music and, 152–153; parallelism and, 41,
   43–44; participatory music performance
   and, 11, 55, 140–144, 148–150, 152;
   participatory subjectivity and, 12, 144, 147;
   passive listening and, 66, 106; perception
   and, 35–36, 38–39; perceptual fluency
   hypothesis and, 72, 96–97, 114, 168;
   performance and, 11, 34, 55, 117–123,
   126–127, 129–134, 140–144, 148–150,
   152; prolongational anticipation
   *versus* prolongational repetition, 36;
   psychoaesthetics research and, 114;
   psychological mechanisms driving, 55,
   77–78, 98; real-world sound and, 58, 80;
   recontextualization and, 32; recording
   technology and, 19, 78–81, 84, 89–90,
   93–94, 121, 123, 126, 153–154; rehearsal
   and, 113, 117, 137–138; reification and,
   43; rondos and, 47, 49–50, 69, 120, 127,
   146–147, 149; sampling and, 28, 32, 58, 79;
   satiation effect and, 97, 101; segmentation
   function of, 23–24, 39–40, 51, 66, 72; as
   sign of musical communication, 136–137;
   similarity and, 176–177; social community
   and, 6, 59, 74, 140–142, 150–151; sonatas
   and, 47–48, 133, 135; source segregation
   and, 53–54; temporal ordering and, 71–72,
   74; therapeutic uses of, 149–150; timbre
   and, 37, 177; Top-40 radio cycles and, 95–96,
   103–104; trance sensations and, 67–69,
   150; transition probabilities and, 107–110;
   tropes and, 144–145; unit length and, 7–9,
   37, 44, 144, 146–149; vamping and,
   142–143; variation and, 176–177; video
   games and, 150; virtual participation and,
   144, 149, 173; within-piece forms of, 132–133
musical silence: acoustic *versus* perceived
   phenomena in, 33–34; after musical
   repetition, 140–142; expectation and,
   116; experiments on, 33, 116; virtual
   participation and, 142

*Music Theory, Phenomenology, and Modes of
   Perception* (Lewin), 9
*musique concrète,* 80

Nakahara, H., 64
Nakamura, J., 69, 96
Narmour, E., 24, 79, 108–109
Nattiez, Jean-Jacques, 23, 52
Nettl, Bruno, 19
Neuhaus, C., 105, 178
neuroscience. *See* cognitive science
Nilsson, U., 57
Norrington, Roger, 129
North, A. C., 30, 57, 99, 143
Norton, A., 63
Novis, S., 79
nursery rhymes, 6, 86
Nyman, Michael, 145

Obama, Barack, 163
obsessive-compulsive disorder, 56, 60
Ockleford, A., 24
Oechslin, M. S., 167
Ohlsson, S., 99–100
Ollen, J., 52
opera, 73, 134, 153
Orr, M. G., 99–100

Palmer, C., 63, 86, 117, 128
Pandora, 102–103
*Paper Planes* (M.I.A.), 58
Pardo, B., 53
Pärt, Arvo, 145
Patel, A. D., 19
Pawley, A., 6
Payne, K.B., 19
Pentecostal trancing, 67
perceptual fluency hypothesis, 72, 96–97, 114, 168
Pereira, C. S., 13, 67–68, 115
"perpetual music track" (Brown), 76, 83
Philip, R., 90, 126
Picker, J. M., 89
*Pierre Menard, Author of Quixote* (Borges), 26–27
Pilotti, M., 24–25
Pinker, Steven, 3
Pink Floyd, 58
pitch perception: absolute pitch and, 30–31,
   107–108, 167–168; among babies,
   107–108; categorical forms of, 37;
   context-dependence of, 31; enhanced pitch
   memory and, 107, 167–168; experiments
   measuring, 31, 167–168; intervals and,
   30–31, 107, 167–168; relationality of, 38;
   relative pitch and, 30–31, 108, 168; rhythm
   and, 112; tonal context and, 31
Pitman, R. K., 61
Pitts, S.E., 2

*Playing Bach on the Keyboard* (Troeger), 122–123
poetry: compared to music, 14–15, 18, 55, 88;
    repetition in, 14, 18, 161–162
*Poker Face* (Lady Gaga), 14, 158
*Polonaise in A Major* (Chopin), 130–132
Poulin-Charronnat, B., 166
Praeger, Ferdinand, 3–4, 25, 48–49, 52, 115
prefrontal cortex, 64
Pressing, J., 112
process pleasure, 50, 69
production competence, 2
Prokofiev, Sergei, 90
Prout, Ebenezer, 49
Purcell, Henry, 35
putamen, 61–62

Raffman, D., 23, 169
Rafii, Z., 53
Rahn, John, 39, 43, 77–78
Rallon, G., 6
Rameau, Jean-Philippe, 7–8, 44–45
Rappaport, Roy, 56
Rauschecker, J. P., 115
Ravel, Maurice, 177
receptive competence, 2
recording technology: earworms and, 76–77,
    81, 83; musical repetition and, 19, 78–81,
    84, 89–90, 93–94, 121, 123, 126, 153–154;
    music and, 89–91, 93, 113, 123, 126
Reich, Steve, 52, 73, 79
Reichardt, Johann Friedrich, 134
relevance theory, 164
Rentfrow, P. J., 99
Repeating Pattern Extraction Technique
    (REPET), 53
repetition. *See also* musical repetition; repetitive
    behaviors: Deleuze on, 34–35; in discourse,
    174–175; functions of, 160–161, 174–175,
    177–178; in language, 14–18, 41, 49, 70, 73,
    84–85, 88, 142, 158, 159–165, 170, 173–175;
    memory and, 177–178; perception and, 35
*Repetition in Discourse* (Johnstone), 170
repetitive behaviors: during childhood, 5, 70–71,
    86, 160; learning function of, 71; normal
    routinization processes and, 60–61, 63, 70,
    85; pathologies and, 56, 60–63; ritual and,
    56–60; social community and, 151–152
Repp, B., 121–122, 126
Reyna, V. F., 85–86
Richman, B., 6, 159–160, 162
Riemann, Hugo, 178
riffing, 151
*Ring Around the Rosie*, 6
*The Ring* cycle (Wagner), 32, 153
*Rite of Spring* (Stravinsky), 143–144
ritual: among animals, 59–60; definition of, 56;
    gestures and, 59–60; purposes of, 57; repetition
    in, 57; social community and, 57–59

Rohrmeier, M., 165
rondos, 47, 49–50, 69, 120, 127, 146–147, 149
Rosen, Charles, 90, 133
Rossano, Matt, 57
Rouget, Gilbert, 67
Rowson, C., 25
Royle, N., 174
Ruwet, Nicolas, 23, 52–53
Rzewski, Frederic, 145

Sachs, J. S., 22, 86–87
Sacks, Oliver, 76, 149
sampling, 28–29, 32, 58, 79
satiation pleasure, 69
Satie, Erik, 145
*Satisfaction* (The Rolling Stones), 12
Scarlatti, Domenico, 93, 154
Schaeffer, Pierre, 79–80
Schellenberg, E. G., 20, 96–99, 107, 168
schematic expectations, 92
Schenker, Heinrich, 36, 48, 128, 133
Schmitt, N., 6
Schnabel, Artur, 90, 121
*Schnitterliedchen* (*The Reaper's Song*, Schumann),
    46–47
Schoenberg, Arnold, 5, 78–79
Schön, D., 175
*School House Rock*, 86
Schubert, Franz: *Moment Musical Op. 94 No. 3*,
    129; *Moment Musical Op. 94 No. 4*, 109–
    111; *Morgengruss*, 10; musical repetition
    and, 147–148; piano sonatas of, 135; *String
    Quartet in G Major, Opus 161*, 58
Schuftan, C., 80
Schulkind, M. D., 32
Schumann, Robert: Horowitz and, 154; musi-
    cal lab experiments and, 108; *Opus 68*,
    46; *Schnitterliedchen* (*The Reaper's Song*),
    46–47; *Träumerei*, 121–122
Scott, Raymond, 145
Scott, S.K., 115
Searcy, W. A., 20
Sears, L. L., 62
Seashore, Carl, 117
Sebald, W. G., 84
Second Reading (Cone), 104–106
semantic satiation, 17–18, 88
semiotics, 23–24, 25
SEM (Strong Experiences of Music) Project,
    66–67
Serkin, Rudolf, 90
*Seven Habits of Highly Effective People* (Covey), 13
Severance, E., 17
Shaffer, L.H., 117, 120, 127
Shakespeare, William, 32, 153, 155
Shakuhachi (Japanese wind instrument), 34
Shatner, William, 158
Sherzer, J., 163–164

Shickele, Peter (P.D.Q. Bach), 173
Shockley, K., 111
Shore, B., 78
*sillon fermé* (closed groove), 80
Silvia, Paul, 18
Simcock, G., 70
Sisman, E.R., 24, 49
Sloboda, J. A., 120, 166
Smith, Adam, 55
Smith, J.D., 13, 166
Smith, N.A., 107
Smyth, D. H., 128, 133
Sokolov, Grigory, 130–132
songbirds, 19–20, 61, 116
sound waves, physics of, 53
speech. *See* language
speech-to-song illusion (Deutch), 16–18, 162, 169–170, 175
Sperber, D., 164
Spotify, 102
Spring Heel Jack, 145
Stahl, B., 63
*The Star-Spangled Banner,* 66
statistical learning studies, 23, 106–108, 167
Stein, D. J., 56
stereotypy, 61
Stern, D. N., 21
Stickgold, R., 150
Strauss, Richard von, 7–8
Stravinsky, Igor, 143–144
subjectivity. *See under* music
subvocalization, 13, 162
superexpressive voice, 12
*Superstition* (Stevie Wonder), 142–143, 149
Suzuki, R., 19, 136
Swain, J. P., 178
*Sweet Anticipation* (Huron), 10, 102
Swingle Singers, 29, 32
*Symphony for 12 Radios* (Cage), 5
Szpunar, K. K., 96–97

Taizé, 140–144, 148–149
*Talking It Over* (Barnes), 164
*Tambourin* (Rameau), 44–45
Tan, S.-L., 83, 97
Tannen, D., 6
Tart, M., 86
Taruskin, Richard, 129
tension peaks 101
Tetris, 150
*They* (Jem), 29–30
"they're playing our song" phenomenon, 32
Third Reading (Cone), 104–106, 111
Tillmann, B., 86–88
timbre, 37, 82, 109, 144–145, 177
Todd, N. P. M., 13, 120
Tone Matrix, 5
top-rocking, 151

Torres, J., 33
Toscanini, Arturo, 153–154
Tovey, Donald, 58
Trainor, L.J., 20
trance sensations, 67–69, 150
transition probabilities, 107–110
Trehub, S., 20, 107, 168
*Tristan and Isolde* (Wagner), 129
*Trois Nouvelles Études* (Chopin), 120
Tumlin, M. A., 107
Turino, T. R., 11
Türk, Daniel, 134
Twain, Mark, 76
*Twinkle Twinkle Little Star,* 38, 43–44
Tyack, P. L., 19

*Umbrella* (Rhianna), 158
*An Uncommon Reader* (Bennett), 155
Unyk, A. M., 20
Ussachevksy, Vladimir, 79
*The Usual Suspects,* 32

Vakil, E., 64
vamping, 142–143, 151
van Kranenburg, P., 53
Van Lancker-Sidtis, D., 6
Van Zandt, B.J., 96
verbatim memory, 22, 73, 85–88
veridical expectations, 92
Vitz, P. C., 99
Volk, A., 53

Wagner, Cosima, 18
Wagner, Richard: Israel and, 31; Nazi appropriation of, 31; Praeger on, 3; on repetition, 18–19; *Ride of the Valkyries* and, 153; *Ring cycle* and, 32, 153; *Tristan and Isolde,* 129
Wallace, W. T., 86
Warker, J. A., 10
Washburn, M.F. 17
Weber, M., 12
Wessinger, C. M., 30
whale songs, 19–20
*When Program Notes Don't Help* (Margulis), 15
*Wilder Reiter* (Schumann), 46
Williams, T. I., 76, 82
Williamson, V. J., 83
Wiltermuth, S.S., 57
"Wittgenstein's puzzle," 92, 108–109
*Women, Bird by Moonlight* (Miró), 71–72
Wonder, Stevie, 142–144, 149
Wong, Patrick, 100, 105, 108
Wundt curve (inverted U), 95–100, 104

Zacks, Jeffrey, 59
Zajonc, R.B., 35, 96, 113
Zaslaw, Neal, 135
Zuckerkandl, V., 1, 4